DATE DUE

DEMCO 38-297

The Tax Decade

C. EUGENE STEUERLE

The Tax Decade

How Taxes Came to Dominate the Public Agenda

THE URBAN INSTITUTE PRESS
Washington, D.C.

THE URBAN INSTITUTE PRESS
2100 M Street, N.W.
Washington, D.C. 20037

Library of Congress Cataloging in Publication Data

The Tax Decade: How Taxes Came to Dominate the Public Agenda/C. Eugene Steuerle.

1. Taxation—United States   I. Title.

| HJ2381.S74 | 1991 | 91-31917 |
| 336.2'00973--dc20 | | CIP |

ISBN 0-87766-523-0 (alk. paper)
ISBN 0-87766-522-2 (alk. paper; casebound)

Urban Institute books are printed on acid-free paper whenever possible.

Printed in the United States of America.

Distributed by:
National Book Network

4720 Boston Way
Lanham, MD 20706

3 Henrietta Street
London   WC2E 8LU   ENGLAND

To Geraldine Gerardi, Thomas Neubig, Susan Nelson, and Victor Thuronyi, who were present at the creation; to former and current public servants at the Office of Tax Policy and the Joint Committee on Taxation, who miraculously manage to restore and keep running a tax machine even when needed repair parts are denied them; and to Norma, Kristin, and Lynne, who have borne far more than a decade of my own idiosyncratic changes.

ACKNOWLEDGMENTS

For helpful comments and keen insights, the author is grateful to Charles Davenport, James Tobin, and John Witte. Elliot Brownlee, Timothy Conlan, Joseph Cordes, Richard Goode, Arjo Klamer, Thomas Neubig, and Emil Sunley offered many useful suggestions, corrected a number of oversights and errors, and provided much needed personal support for this endeavor. Kyna Rubin edited the manuscript and remarkably made clear what would otherwise have been left obtuse; Jon Bakija undertook invaluable research assistance, graphics work, and myriad other analyses. Ann Guillot not only typed and corrected many drafts, but almost performed the impossible in keeping this endeavor operating in smooth order while undertaking other vital projects at the Institute and at home. Isabel Sawhill, a colleague in the very best sense of the word, made it all possible in the first place. Indispensable support was provided by the Ford Foundation and the John D. and Catherine T. MacArthur Foundation, both of which also financed almost a decade of essential research on changing domestic priorities.

CONTENTS

Tables

Figures

FOREWORD

For 23 years the Institute has worked to improve the quality of American life by examining our nation's social and economic problems and the government policies and programs designed to alleviate them. During our early period, most Institute work was devoted to specific issues such as housing, transportation, drugs, and crime—problems whose solutions would benefit our society's most disadvantaged groups. In 1980, our agenda expanded to address the finance and budget sides of these problems, as well as larger issues that directly affect all Americans. Few aspects of broad national policy have more ubiquitous impact on the well-being of all Americans than federal tax and spending policy.

This book represents the Institute's most recent contribution to broad tax and budgeting issues. It follows studies such as Joseph J. Minarik's *Making Tax Choices* (1985), Rudolph Penner's and Alan Abramson's *Broken Purse Strings* (1988), and Isabel Sawhill's edited volume, *Challenge to Leadership: Economic and Social Issues for the Next Decade* (1988).

Government expenditure decisions are often devoted to the particular problems of time and place. Tax policy, in contrast, represents the means by which we finance those government expenditures, whatever they happen to be. The tax policy debate, therefore, will necessarily be with us as long as we have government. As Oliver Wendell Holmes, Jr. so aptly stated, "taxes are what we pay for civilized society." Government cannot spend for social purposes unless tax policy raises the needed revenues. The dilemma is that taxes impose costs upon the very civilization that the expenditures are designed to promote.

Attaining a balance between the benefits and costs of taxes is a delicate and often acrimonious affair. This book represents a finely crafted attempt to examine how that balance was achieved from 1981 to 1990. But it is more than that. The author ties the tax policy debate into the broader expenditure and budget debates of the time. More importantly, he shows how the reform of taxes and of expenditures hidden within the tax system provide important lessions for future reform of all types of federal government policy.

In policy discussions, the perspective of an analyst or author is often central to the nature of the presentation. This author's participation in, and sometimes design of, many of the decade's policy changes also give him firsthand knowledge of many of the events that he discusses. While the author presents explicitly and forcefully his own viewpoint, he also presents information with balance and objectivity—thus throwing significant light on a particularly interesting period of fiscal policymaking.

William Gorham
President

PREFACE

The years 1981 to 1990 constituted a decade during which there was a tremendous outpouring of tax legislation and a corresponding shift among individuals and businesses of hundreds of billions of dollars of tax liability. This book is motivated by my sense of the need for a comprehensive examination of how the tax and related budget events of this decade wove together. One of my goals is to lay out the story in a way that is complete, that dispels some common myths about how tax policy was changed, and that relates the enactment of different tax bills to one another.

In truth, I have a second goal. The events of the tax decade have significant implications for the future direction of budget, tax, and expenditure policymaking. For instance, tax reduction in 1981, tax reform in 1986, and deficit reduction in 1990 were determined partly in response to changing economic conditions and partly by the ways that these "reforms" were organized and put forward. These events provide telling examples of the ways in which tax and expenditure policies can and must continually be changed to meet the evolving demands of our society.

Eliminating the old to make room for the new is one of the basic requirements of government, one that leaders can attempt to tackle in an efficient and planned way or one that they only deal with when crises force them to do so. Making broad and often comprehensive trade-offs among both expenditure and tax programs is necessary and probably inevitable if progressive government is to succeed as we move into the 21st century. In sum, while I hope to shed light on the economic history surrounding the tax decade itself, my second hope is that readers will glean from this brief book some ideas about how future governmental reform efforts might be organized efficiently, fairly, and comprehensively.

My perspective is that of both an economist and a participant in the tax policy process. I will not attempt to separate the perspectives

I obtained from the two roles. I am not sure that I could achieve that separation if I desired; even if achieved, it would probably reduce the value of this book by leaving out much of what I know. During the tax decade I spent three years studying tax, budget, and other economic issues at three different research institutes in Washington, D.C.: The Brookings Institution, the American Enterprise Institute, and The Urban Institute. I served most of the years of the decade at the U.S. Treasury Department in a variety of roles, including head of the economic staff analyzing domestic tax issues, Economic Tax Coordinator of the Treasury Department's 1984–86 Project for Fundamental Tax Reform, and Deputy Assistant Secretary of the Treasury for Tax Analysis.[1]

In my role as economic coordinator, I had the privilege of setting forth the original organization and design of the Treasury's tax reform proposals, an outline that was never totally abandoned as these proposals proceeded from the Treasury's original program to final enactment in 1986, with adjustments along the way by the Reagan administration, the House of Representatives, and the Senate. In my other roles at the Treasury, I gained perspective on the economic events of the decade and—through participation in a wide range of tax, health, welfare, Social Security, and other expenditure and budget initiatives—on the nature of the reform process itself.

There already exist books that cover several of the events of the decade—in particular, the political debates that took place during the 1981 enactment of tax reduction and the 1984–1986 tax reform process.[2] These works tend to complement one another, and readers interested in the sequence of events and the personal actions and expressed motivations of various policymakers are encouraged to refer to these sources. This book does not attempt to re-catalogue these events, nor to discuss personalities, who said what, where, and when. Instead, I emphasize how the events of the decade fit together, the role of economic factors on subsequent shifts in the fiscal and tax structure of the nation, the very real effect of initial organization on enactments of economic policy, and the implications for both past and future policymaking of the movement to a new era of trade-offs. I have also chosen to present more data than has typically been made available because I believe readers are entitled to come to their own conclusions, even when different from my own, about what transpired.

Parts of this book were first published or presented before the American Enterprise Institute, the American Tax Policy Institute, the American Law Institute—American Bar Association Committee on

Continuing Education, The Brookings Institution, the Internal Revenue Service, the National Tax Journal, and Tax Notes, and are reprinted with permission.[3]

Notes

1. The Office of Tax Analysis is the government's principal office for analyzing the economics of tax issues. It works closely with tax lawyers in the Offices of Tax Legislative Counsel, International Tax Counsel, and Benefits Tax Counsel. Together, they form the Office of Tax Policy within the Treasury Department.

2. For the politician's perspective on some of the events of the tax decade, see Regan (1988a) and Stockman (1986). Two important books emphasizing the political process behind tax reform were Birnbaum and Murray (1987) and Conlan, Wrightson, and Beam (1990). The number of articles on tax reform is even more extensive. Only a partial list can be provided here. See, for instance, Haskel (1987); Verdier (1988); McLure (1988); Minarik (1987); and Witte (1989).

3. See Steuerle 1991, 1990a, 1988, 1987a, 1987b, 1986a, 1986b, 1985a, 1985b, 1983a, various years; and Steuerle and Hartzmark 1981.

Chapter One

INTRODUCTION

Between 1981 and 1990, the United States witnessed more frequent and detailed changes in federal tax law than ever before in its history. Barely had one new act passed Congress than another was being debated. A dramatic cut in income taxes in 1981 was followed by large tax increases in 1982, 1983, and 1984—both to reduce the deficit and to deal with the long-term insolvency of the Social Security program. By mid-1984, analysis and debate on major tax reform was underway, culminating in the Tax Reform Act of 1986— the most comprehensive reform of U.S. tax laws ever undertaken. Following the stock market's one-day nosedive in 1987, still another set of tax increases was to be enacted. Even 1988 and 1989, relatively calm years on the tax front, were to witness the passing, and then retraction, of a surtax on the elderly to pay for an expansion of Medicare to cover catastrophic health needs. In 1990, substantial increases in taxes and fees were to become the dominant source of funds for the largest deficit reduction package in the nation's history, excluding years following the end of wars.

Although tax policy dominated the public agenda from the years 1981 to 1990, the nature of these changes is often misunderstood. Conventional liberal wisdom holds that most of the tax bills of the decade were caused by deficits created through Ronald Reagan's miscalculations of 1981. Conventional conservative wisdom holds that congressional pressures for ever-expanding expenditure programs forced substantial tax increases on the nation.

Among students of politics an alternative set of explanations attempts to trace legislative activity mainly to the self-interest of actors. Thus, a common reason offered for government failure is the ability of special interests to unite against an unorganized public. Self-interest, it is argued, also drives politicians to be more motivated by the desire to be reelected than to serve the country.[1] A similar complaint is that government operates like a "Leviathan" that gobbles up all resources possible in order to support politicians and bureaucrats aggrandizing their power. These theories typically attempt to explain events in what is believed to be a "scientific" or deterministic fashion. Knowing fact A, one can predict event B.

Unfortunately, while such simple theories and explanations often contain an element of truth, they do not take us very far in trying to understand the tax decade. They ignore the relationship of the events of the decade to what had transpired in the period before. They provide little guidance on how Ronald Reagan, arguably one of the most conservative presidents of the 20th century, became an advocate of tax reform. They hardly explain why the many deficit reduction bills that were signed by two Republican presidents were dominated by tax rather than expenditure changes.

A related difficulty with many of the simpler explanations of government behavior is that they focus on the size of the overall government pie, which in many ways was never changed more than modestly, rather than on the ingredients of the pie, which were to change substantially. Whatever the extent of any particular tax provision, it was usually exaggerated both by those who wanted to extol its virtues and those who wished to claim its evil consequences.

In weaving together the story of the tax decade, this book emphasizes four factors. First, the nation was clearly moving into a new fiscal era by the mid- to late-1970s, and much of the political anguish over making policy changes since that time simply reflected the search for how to make trade-offs in this new era. Second, most of the government legislation enacted during the 1981 to 1990 period was a response—even if inappropriate or inadequate—to economic and social stresses placed on the nation. Third, the effectiveness of the response depended greatly upon how policy proposals were organized, how information was gathered, and whether principles were used as guides or constraints on action. Finally, consensus for action was often achieved by appealing simultaneously to traditional liberal and conservative principles. Many of the reforms of the tax decade were achieved only because a progressive, broad-based tax system could be argued to be consistent with *both* traditions.

A NEW ERA OF FISCAL POLICY

From the late 1970s onward, our country was moving into a new era of policymaking—one that was inevitable no matter who had been elected to the Presidency or the Congress. In this new era, reforming old expenditure or tax rules or meeting new priorities required that trade-offs be made explicitly among many existing programs. Tax reform, for instance, provided for lower rates and tax relief for the poor by reducing expenditures hidden in the tax code.

Such trade-offs were more easily avoided in the period between World War II and the mid-1970s because increased funding for both expansion of domestic expenditures and tax reductions was made available almost automatically, and often without explicit legislation. New programs, therefore, could be initiated and financed without serious attention to old programs. Even mistakes in fiscal policy would be unlikely to place much pressure on the budget or increase deficits more than temporarily. With the end of this "Easy Financing Era" in the mid-1970s, government policy could no longer be made in the old way. The agony of moving to the new era came not from demands that were extraordinary by historical standards, but from the simple requirement that meeting new demands required politicians to identify losers—individuals and businesses that would face increased taxes or reduced expenditures.

Does this movement to a new era imply that it didn't matter who held political office? That such events as tax reform were foreordained? Hardly. It does imply that personalities and proposals interacted with historical developments that themselves were forcing change. Contrary to conventional wisdom, it also implies that the requirement to make significant budgetary trade-offs was a historical development that was accelerated, but not *caused*, by the deficit-increasing policies of the early Reagan administration. There are still many who believe that the stalemate in government policymaking is solely due to the early 1981 decisions, to naive supply-siders, and to Ronald Reagan's inability to understand numbers.

GOVERNMENT RESPONSE TO CHANGING ECONOMIC AND SOCIAL CONDITIONS

As noted, unmitigated focus on any one explanation for events can sometimes lead to a rather myopic and distorted view of history as a whole. While personalities and motivations for individual behavior are important, legislative action is almost inevitably a reaction to some felt need or demand in society. Government typically does respond, even if belatedly, to significant economic and social pressures.

Some of these pressures are emphasized in this book. The dramatic tax cuts of 1981, for instance, must be related to the distortions and rapidly rising tax rates caused by accelerating inflation in the late 1970s. Tax reform in 1986 came about in part because of rapid increases in taxes on families and on the poor and because of the extensive use of tax shelters throughout the economy. Various deficit reduction acts from 1982 to 1990 were a response to a large and growing deficit. The historic switch after 1981 away from the deficit-increasing bills of the earlier postwar period certainly came about in response to the fiscal pressures of the new era.

THE ORGANIZATION OF POLICY INITIATIVES

Although economic events influence the passage of legislation and shifts in fiscal policy, they do not determine the exact nature of the response. One important lesson from the tax decade is the extraordinary importance for policymaking of the way in which a staff and a project are organized. The 1981 tax bill, for instance, was organized mainly as part of a political campaign. Its lack of underlying principles eventually was to lead to a "Christmas tree" bill in which every ornament could be added with little or no justification required. Tax reform in 1986, on the other hand, demonstrated the value of organizing individuals to undertake the mission of reporting to the public on the ways in which the laws can be reformed so as to meet with various accepted criteria and principles and, equally important, to note which aspects of the law meet no standards at all.

I cannot emphasize enough how often breakdowns in governmental functioning, for instance, the failure to provide further reform of tax, welfare, health, or other systems, can be traced in part to related organizational failures. Both policy and administration can be developed around principles, goals, and measures of well-being and the impact of programs on that well-being. As will be seen, the near collapse of a deficit reduction effort in 1990, as well as its failure to pare or make more efficient a variety of expenditure programs, can be traced to lack of organization around more explicit principles and measures of the effectiveness of programs at meeting designated needs of society. In fact, most proposals and studies released by the executive branch today—despite the large investment made by the public in the information-gathering institutions of that branch—are so carefully nuanced to avoid offending particular interests that the problems at hand are seldom revealed. The public is denied the information for which it has paid. Should it then be any surprise when there are breakdowns in the functioning of governmental agencies that regulate housing, savings and loan, and other policies?

The advantage of organizing in a principled fashion is hardly that doing so will always provide clearcut guides to action on controversial political issues. Far from it. The advantage is in offering one of the few viable alternatives to organizing only around the needs of special interests or only in response to emergencies. Principles can guide a process and, even when in conflict, can constrain the amount of attention that will be given to alternatives that meet no standard at all. Finally, organizing on the basis of principles recognizes that there are many in society whose vote or analysis of issues is motivated by concern for the well-being of others. These voters and officials can be empowered through knowledge and, even when in a minority, can be crucial to the final outcome of a democratic process.

TOWARD LIBERAL AND CONSERVATIVE CONSENSUS

Passage of legislation often requires a consensus that cuts across party lines. The story of this book can only be understood if it is recognized that a progressive and broad-based tax structure is in many ways *both* a liberal and a conservative policy. Maintenance of this structure—especially when compared to other financing alternatives—can appeal to many of the principles of both liberals and conservatives. Of course, labels themselves are arbitrary. Effective government is no more the domain of liberals or conservatives than are effective business practices. For the moment, however, let's accept the labels and see why a progressive and fair tax structure can be argued to meet both liberal and conservative goals.[2]

The Liberal Case

The liberal or progressive case, while usually well understood, needs to be related to the historical development of the income tax. Since taxes or fees must be collected to pay for government goods and services, the debate over income taxation cannot be—and never was—separated from the relative merits of alternative sources of taxation. It is not surprising, for instance, that the development of the income tax followed closely upon the heels of significant popular opposition to tariffs, this country's principal source of revenues until the 20th century.[3]

From its inception, the income tax has always been a progressive tax. Of all major taxes in developed countries, only income taxes significantly promote progressivity by taxing those with higher incomes at higher rates. Therefore, in favoring the income tax over other forms of taxation, advocates of an income tax were usually carrying the banner for substantial progression in the overall tax system.[4]

A debate over size of government has also accompanied the income tax from its inception. Those who favored larger income taxes often favored more government expenditures, and vice-versa. This again must be put into context. In the history of taxation, the broad implementation of the income tax is still not even a century old; hence, its "reforms" were likely to be correlated with its early growth. To add to this tendency, many tax reformers decry special preferences in the tax code, but, in so doing, argue effectively for expansion of the tax base. Absent other changes or offsets such as the rate reduction offered in the 1986 tax reform, base broadening leads to increased levels of taxation and increased revenues for the government to spend.

The Conservative Case

As already noted, the popular definitions of "conservative" and "liberal" are arbitrary and change over time. To the extent that a conservative policy tends to be one that constrains the amount of governmental interference in the economy, there are two pragmatic reasons why the progressive income tax system may support this policy goal.

First, the popular notion of progressivity often requires that taxes on middle- and low-income classes—*and the expenditures that those taxes would support*—be limited in size. Suppose that a country decides that it wants its overall tax system to be progressive, as defined by taxing higher income individuals at significantly higher tax rates.[5] If a government then seeks to increase its expenditures, it often finds that it must expand taxes to cover more middle- and low-income individuals. Tax rates must be increased not just for upper-income individuals, but throughout the income distribution. Income tax systems, for instance, have generally applied a zero rate of tax to the first dollars of income by providing exemptions, credits, and similar forms of tax relief. These income exemptions or credits, which add to the progressivity of the income tax when considered in isolation, generally are not available for other taxes such as sales taxes, because they reduce substantially the overall amount of revenue that can be collected.[6]

Second, the most progressive taxes are usually more transparent or less hidden than other taxes. The annual exercise of reporting by taxpayers allows them to see exactly how much they are paying to support government. Unlike other types of taxes, the individual income tax is not hidden in the purchase price of a product or taken out of a flow of payments without the knowledge of the participants.

Table 1.1 shows overall levels of taxation in a number of developed countries, as well as the reliance of each upon different types of taxes. Compared to the European Economic Community (EEC), the United States collects about the same percentage of gross domestic product through the progressive personal income tax. On the other hand, the average EEC country collects almost 8 percentage points more of gross domestic product in the form of taxes on goods and services than the U.S. (13.2 percent versus 5.0 percent). Although there are a number of exceptions such as Sweden, Australia, and Canada, the stricter reliance of the United States upon income taxation, and its corresponding failure to adopt a more regressive national tax on goods and services, is correlated with its smaller size government.

Figure 1.1 presents the results of surveys on the popularity of various types of taxes in the United States. The federal income tax and the property tax have generally been the two most unpopular taxes. It should not be surprising that when there is disenchantment with government, it is directed toward those taxes for which costs are most visible.

Expenditures in the Tax Code

Another area on which liberals and conservatives sometimes unite is on reducing government expenditures hidden in the tax code. Each may be driven by the notion that fairness in income taxation means that taxpayers will be treated equally if their income or well-being is the same. Tax preferences or expenditures hidden in the tax code, therefore, tend to violate the principle of fairness. Each year the Department of the Treasury publishes estimates of the hundreds of billions of dollars in expenditures that are provided through special

Table 1.1 TAX RECEIPTS IN VARIOUS COUNTRIES AS A PERCENTAGE OF GDP, 1987

	Total tax receipts % of GDP	Personal income tax	Corporate income tax	Tax structures as % of GDP		Taxes on goods and services	Other taxes
				Social Security contributions			
				Employees	Employers		
United States	30.0	10.9	2.4	3.3	5.0	5.0	3.4
Japan	30.2	7.2	6.9	3.1	4.5	3.9	4.6
Australia	31.3	14.2	3.2	0.0	0.0	9.3	4.6
Switzerland	32.0	10.9	2.0	3.3	3.2	6.1	6.5
Canada	34.4	13.3	2.8	1.6	2.9	9.9	3.9
United Kingdom	37.5	10.0	4.0	3.1	3.5	11.8	5.2
Germany	37.6	10.9	1.9	6.1	7.2	9.6	2.0
Ireland	39.9	13.8	1.3	2.0	3.5	17.0	2.3
France	44.8	5.7	2.3	5.5	12.2	13.1	6.0
Netherlands	48.0	9.5	3.7	9.0	8.2	12.5	5.2
Sweden	56.7	21.1	2.3	0.0	13.2	13.7	6.4
EEC average[1]	40.6	10.7	3.0	4.1	6.8	13.2	3.9
OECD average[1]	38.8	11.9	3.1	3.1	5.5	11.8	4.2

Source: OECD (1990).
1. Unweighted. EEC = European Economic Community; OECD = Organisation for Economic Co-operation and Development.

Figure 1.1 COMPARISON OF OPINIONS ABOUT WORST TAX—THAT IS, THE
LEAST FAIR, 1972–1989

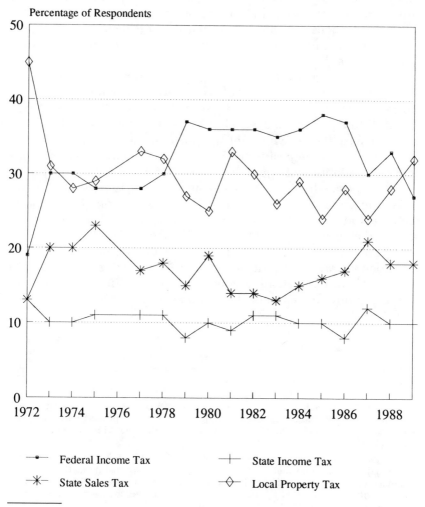

Source: ACIR (1989, p. 7).

tax exclusions, deductions, and credits.[7] These preferences are sometimes put in the tax code to hide their cost.[8]

When advocates of a fair tax system—that is, one that taxes equally
those with equal incomes—oppose many or most of the expenditures
in the tax system, they may also push forward the conservative agenda
of less governmental interference in the economy.[9] In contrast, those

favoring tax expenditures indirectly support the higher tax rates that are then necessary to raise the same amount of net revenue. Reduction of tax expenditures by itself usually has the same effect on the economy as does reduction of similar direct expenditures. The two approaches mainly differ in the way they are accounted for in the governmental budget.

In summary, a fair and progressive tax system—defined as one that imposes low or zero rates of tax on low-income individuals, that increases tax rates significantly as income rises, and that taxes equally those with equal income—is also one that encourages lean government. Those liberals who want significant expansion of government often are put in the position of favoring a less steep gradation of tax rates, the adoption of regressive tax systems, and the unequal treatment of those who are equally situated. In turn, those conservatives who oppose progressive and fair income taxation on grounds of incentives often find themselves supporting the higher expenditure levels that become possible only with more regressive taxes, the hiding of tax burdens in less transparent taxes, and the multiplication of expenditures within the tax code itself. With this background, it is possible to understand how both political parties could at times unite behind the major tax changes that we are about to examine.[10]

Notes

1. John Witte notes that a newer wave of congressional scholars views Congress primarily as a collection of independent individuals, driven primarily by the reelection motive. He refers to this strain of research as the "individualist model." See Witte (1991a).

2. For a detailed discussion of the development of the American income tax and the role of equity principles therein, see Witte 1985. Witte also maintains that wars and financial crises have played a decisive role in the development of the income tax. I would agree that catalysts are needed for change, as will be seen in forthcoming chapters.

3. Early supporters of the income tax "argued that their tax would not touch the wages and salaries of ordinary people but would, instead, attack the unearned profits and rents of monopolists. Thus, they firmly believed that the income tax could itself contribute to an assault on monopoly power . . . Democratic party leaders such as (William Jennings) Bryan . . . added income taxation to tariff reform as a central party cause" (Brownlee 1989, p. 1616).

4. An income tax can also be designed to be proportional or regressive. All income taxes, however, have been progressive, partly because of the exemption of lower income individuals from taxation. See, however, the discussion of flat-rate taxes in chapter 3.

5. As noted, the definition of progressivity is itself arbitrary. Many economists define a progressive system as one that makes more equal the distribution of after-tax income. In the popular conception, however, a progressive tax system is one with tax rates that rise with income. In a number of cases, proportional and even declining tax rates can support a more equal distribution of after-tax income.

6. Whether tax rates or government expenditures should increase is another issue that depends at each point in time on a comparison of the overall benefits and costs of the changes being considered.

7. See OMB, various years.

8. Many tax expenditures do not result from cynical attempts to mislead the public. Instead, members of taxwriting committees in Congress add special preferences into the tax code because it is the one instrument over which they exercise control. In a few cases, one might even argue that the IRS is a more efficient administrator of certain programs than the departments that administer direct expenditures.

9. In many cases, advocates of tax reform actually favor increases in direct expenditures. Some may reconcile these two views by arguing that tax expenditures are simply inappropriate vehicles for policy. Such would be the likely position taken by Surrey and McDaniel (1985).

10. Here are a few of the many works offering perspectives on tax equity principles. Richard A. Musgrave provides an overview of classical economic justifications for horizontal and vertical equity in Musgrave (1959, 1990). Arthur Okun presents a seminal exposition of the liberal case for progressive income redistribution in Okun (1975). Three books present in different ways what might be considered a conservative perspective. Henry C. Simons (1938) presents an extensive case for horizontal equity and accepts the "aesthetic judgment" that taxes might be used to alleviate an "unlovely" degree of inequality. Walter J. Blum and Harry Kalven (1953) draw some similar conclusions. Milton Friedman (1962) makes a case for the use of tax policy as a tool for alleviating poverty.

Chapter Two

POSTWAR CHANGES IN THE OVERALL TAX SYSTEM

The post-World War II era was to witness many changes in taxation due to new tax laws and an evolving economy. The multiple changes of the 1981–1990 tax decade can only be understood by first examining the economic events and tax changes that led up to this period.

LEVELS OF TAXATION

The vast expansion of income taxation in the United States can be directly associated with the financing of this nation's participation in World War II. Prior to the war, the individual income tax applied only to a small portion of the population. In the 1930s, individual income taxes were never more than 1.4 percent of GNP and corporate income taxes were never more than 1.6 percent of GNP (see figure 2.1 or, for more complete data, appendix table A.1). By 1943 these had risen, respectively, to 8.3 percent of GNP and 7.1 percent of GNP. "From a class tax to a mass tax" was a common expression used to describe the World War II explosion in coverage and collections.

As the United States prepared for peacetime, income taxes were reduced, but only modestly. For the individual income tax, a postwar low of 5.9 percent of GNP reached in 1949 was still over four times greater than the highest percentage that had ever applied before World War II. Withholding on wages—the principal administrative mechanism adopted to implement new, higher levels of taxation during the war—was maintained. By the 1950s, even the small tax reductions of the late 1940s were largely offset by tax increases used to finance the Korean War. From that point on, federal individual income taxes remained a fairly constant percentage of total GNP. They

Figure 2.1 TAX RECEIPTS AS A PERCENTAGE OF GNP

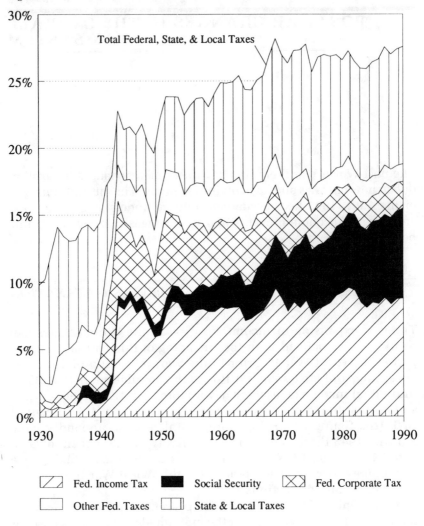

Sources: U.S. Department of Commerce (1986); and U.S. Department of Commerce, *Survey of Current Business* various years (Tables 1.1, 3.2, 3.3, 3.6).
Note: See appendix table A.1.

hit a low of 7.1 percent of GNP in 1964, climbed quickly to a high of 9.5 percent of GNP in 1969, fell again, and then hit another high of 9.6 percent in 1981.

After Korea, total federal, state and local tax receipts increased gradually over time. In 1954 these receipts stood at 22.5 percent of GNP, but then rose gradually to a high of 28.2 percent of GNP in 1969, when there was a surtax to help pay for the Vietnam War. From 1969 on, total tax receipts declined slightly on occasion, but for the most part there was little change. Total taxes as a percentage of GNP dipped below 26 percent only in 1974 and, as we shall see, in 1983 and 1984.[1]

State and Local Taxes: The Main Source of Growth

Actually, federal tax receipts were even more constant than total tax receipts. State and local taxes were the main source of growth in the postwar era. These taxes rose from 6 percent of GNP in 1954 to a postwar high of 9.6 percent in 1972.[2] This increase of 3.6 percentage points compared to a total increase in all taxes, including federal taxes, of 4.8 percentage points over the same period. From 1947 to 1972, state and local taxes almost doubled as a percentage of GNP. From a longer-term perspective, state and local taxes might be viewed as simply recovering from their dramatic drop in importance as the federal government role expanded throughout the 1930s and 1940s. The mid- to late-1970s, however, were to witness a tax revolt that was reflected in a modest decline in state and local tax collections relative to GNP. Much of this revolt at the state and local level centered on the property tax.

The post-World War II increase in state and local tax collections came partly through higher tax rates on sales and income and partly through the adoption of new taxes in many states. State and local individual income taxes, for instance, grew steadily in importance over the entire postwar period, rising from 0.19 percent of GNP in 1946 to over 1 percent by 1969 and over 1.5 percent by the late 1970s. Not only did many more states adopt an individual income tax, but growth in the economy forced taxpayers into higher tax rate brackets over time. By the end of the 1970s, the combination of federal, state and local income taxes had risen to an all-time high as a percentage of income because of state and local rather than federal tax increases.

The Rise of Social Security Taxes and the Fall of Corporate and Excise Taxes

The most dramatic changes over the postwar period, however, were neither in the level of individual income tax collections nor in the overall levels of taxation. Instead, they were in the composition of tax receipts. Here Social Security taxes stand out for their large and consistent growth without regard to economic or political cycles. In fact, the pattern of Social Security taxation was so consistent that it can be traced by a rule of thumb: Social Security tax rates were to rise by roughly 3 percentage points per decade. The combined employer and employee tax rates equaled 3.0 percent in 1950; 6.0 percent in 1960; 9.6 percent in 1970; 12.26 percent in 1980; and, even before the decade of the 1970s was over, already had been scheduled to rise to 15.3 percent by 1990. These rate increases, as well as expansions of the Social Security tax base, resulted in Social Security taxes rising from less than 1 percent of GNP before 1950 to over 5 percent of GNP by 1979.

Since Social Security and state and local taxes went up far more than total taxes, something must have gone down. Two main sources of taxation were to decline in importance. First, other federal taxes (mainly excise taxes) became an increasingly smaller portion of total receipts of the federal government. These declines were due to conscious decisions to rely less upon excise taxes, as witnessed in a tax act passed in 1965, and to the erosion of excise tax bases because of inflation and the rising importance of other, untaxed services and goods. Because most federal excises were stated in terms of cents per carton or per gallon, excise tax payments mainly rose with quantities of purchase, not with the much faster increases in prices and incomes in the economy.

Corporate income taxes were the second major source of decline. Corporate profits gradually became a smaller portion of national income, and the corporate tax base fell correspondingly. One reason for the decline, however, was the large increase in interest rates that took place between the end of World War II and the late 1970s. Higher interest rates meant that a smaller portion of the returns to capital— that is, a smaller proportion of the total income to both bondholders and stockholders in a firm—were subject to corporate income taxation. In addition, corporate taxes fell along with the expansion of tax preferences for business investment and with the relative growth in foreign income sources, which were more lightly taxed in the United States.

Total Taxes: An Inadequate Explanation for a Revolt

At this point, the overall trends in levels of taxation reveal little as to why major tax changes were to take place in the 1980s. The slight increase in combined federal, state, and local individual income taxes—reflected mainly in state and local income taxes—may have helped add to a backlash against the individual income tax. All in all, however, individual taxes and total tax collections were not much higher at the beginning of the 1980s than in many prior postwar years.

Yet it should not be surprising that if there was to be a backlash against taxes, as occurred especially in the mid-to-late 1970s and the early 1980s, it would be directed most at the two taxes that historically had been the most unpopular: the property tax and the income tax. The state and local property tax revolt was already in full swing by the late 1970s. As for the income tax itself, one would also expect that most attention would be directed toward the larger federal income tax rather than the smaller state income tax. There was one major consequence to focusing attention only on certain sources of taxation, while ignoring the major sources of growth in overall levels of taxation such as Social Security taxes: the tax revolt would fail to lessen overall levels of taxation more than slightly and temporarily.[3]

To understand the many tax changes of the tax decade requires moving beyond examination of the levels of taxation to important changes taking place within the federal income taxes themselves. The most important of these were increases in marginal tax rates on the marginal or last dollar earned (defined on pp. 22) and the growth in the tax shelter market, both of which were closely related to a rising rate of inflation. These were to provide important catalysts for future tax revisions, especially tax cuts in 1981 and tax reform in 1986.

THE INDIVIDUAL INCOME TAX BASE

Levels of taxation are often bandied about in political campaigns ("no new taxes"), but they give a misleading picture of the effect of governmental activity on the use of resources in the economy. Even if levels of taxation or average tax rates stay constant, changes in exclusions, deductions, and credits can affect the size of the tax base. These sources of tax reduction are often referred to as tax preferences.

Exclusions are the least recognized source of preference, but over recent decades have become the most important. Exclusions are not even counted in income subject to tax nor are they reported on tax returns. Instead, total income, adjusted gross income, and taxable income—those income measures reported on individual income tax returns—"exclude" income when it comes from certain sources or is used in certain ways.

Many of these exclusions apply to a large percentage of the population, including much of the middle class. Among the largest sources of exclusion, for instance, have been employer contributions to (and earnings from) health, pension, and profit-sharing plans.[4] From 1947 to 1979, the net exclusion applying to health and pension plans alone increased from 0.7 percent to 4.2 percent of personal income.[5]

Nontaxable public transfer payments such as Social Security also grew considerably over the same period, as did other nontaxable labor compensation such as employer-provided life insurance. The expansion and growth in the value of home ownership, which is favored by the tax system, was another source of growth in exclusions.[6]

Although not all exclusions grew at equivalent rates, total exclusions grew from about 11 percent to 19 percent of personal income from 1947 to the end of the 1970s.

Deductions reported on tax returns also increased over this same period. Itemized deductions are allowed for state and local taxes, interest, contributions to charity, extraordinary health expenses, and other miscellaneous items. As a percentage of personal income, these grew from 3.7 percent in 1947 to 10.1 percent in 1969, and then leveled off slightly to 9 percent by 1979. This slight reduction, however, was mainly due to the growth of the standard deduction—an allowance for a minimum amount of deductions that may be taken in lieu of itemizing or detailing deductions on a tax return. All in all, the standard deduction grew from a postwar low of 2.4 percent of income in 1969 to 6.5 percent by 1979. Tax credits were also to expand slightly in number and value over this period, leading to another source of tax base erosion.

The most dramatic change in the individual tax base over the postwar era, however, was not in the expanded use of exclusions, deductions, and credits, but in the declining value of the personal exemption allowed to each taxpayer and dependent regardless of how income is spent. On taxable returns, that exemption had eroded from over 24 percent to 9.3 percent of personal income between 1947 and 1979. This decline was also an important factor in decreasing the amount of income attributable to nontaxable individuals. As these individuals moved into the tax system, the tax base expanded further.

Summary of Changes in the Tax Base

Table 2.1 summarizes how the tax base had changed over the postwar era as the country approached the 1980s. Keep in mind the important distinction between the sources of base erosion and base expansion. The increased use of exclusions, deductions, and credits all implied increasing sources of differentiation in tax burdens according to sources or types of income and uses of that income. These preferences were generally conditional upon *behavioral* actions. On the other hand, the decline in the value of the personal exemption on taxable returns and the increased taxation of formerly nontaxable individuals represented an elimination of the nontaxability of the first dollars earned by taxpayers.[7] These sources were sufficient to more than pay for the entire erosion of the tax base from all of the additional uses of exclusions, deductions, and credits. For a typical taxpayer, this meant that a larger portion of income would be subject to tax unless the taxpayer engaged in preferred activities.

Table 2.1 AGGREGATE CHANGE IN THE INDIVIDUAL INCOME TAX BASE,
1947–1979
(As a Percentage of Per Capita Personal Income)

Increases in Tax Base Due to Declining Importance of:	
Personal Exemptions	14.0
AGI of Nontaxable Individuals, Nonreported AGI & Reconciliation	10.3
Total Increase	24.3
Decreases in Tax Base Due to Further Use of:	
Net Exclusions from AGI	9.5
Itemizations	5.3
Standard Deductions	2.1
Income Offset by Credits	1.2
Total Decrease	18.0
Net Increase in Tax Base	6.3

Source: Steuerle and Hartzmark (1981, p. 153). Originally derived from the Bureau of Economic Analysis (*National Income and Product Accounts, Survey of Current Business*, and unpublished data) and the Internal Revenue Service Statistics of Income Division (*Individual Income Tax Returns*).

TAX-EXEMPT LEVELS OF INCOME

Minimum tax-exempt levels of income—those levels below which no income tax is due—are mainly determined by the personal exemption and the standard deduction.[8] Figure 2.2 presents data on tax-exempt levels of income and compares these figures to per capita personal income for the same years (details are contained in appendix A.2). As can be seen, tax-exempt levels of income in 1948 were close to one-half of per capita personal income, but by 1981 had declined to a much smaller percentage. In effect, more and more people were pulled into the tax system throughout the post-World War II era.

Beginning with the *Economic Report of the President* in 1964, the government began publishing statistics as to the number of persons

Figure 2.2 TAX-EXEMPT THRESHOLD PER FAMILY MEMBER, EXPRESSED AS A PERCENTAGE OF PER CAPITA PERSONAL INCOME, BY FILING STATUS, 1948 AND 1981

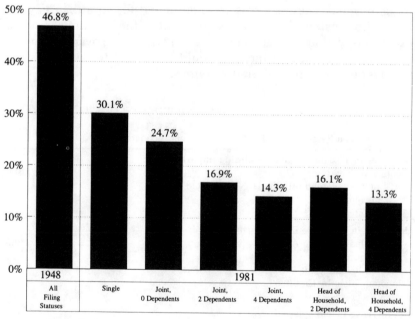

Sources: U.S. Department of Commerce, Bureau of Economic Analysis (1986, and various years); and the Internal Revenue Service Statistics of Income Division (*Individual Income Tax Returns*).

measured as being in "poverty." Since then, poverty levels have only been adjusted each year for changes in the inflation rate. Since the inflation rate is less than the rate of growth in income, over time the poverty level falls relative to such measures as per capita personal income.[9]

The publication of these poverty statistics had a dramatic impact on the development of the tax law in the late 1960s and early 1970s. Various tax acts attempted to adjust upward the tax-exempt levels of income to reflect changes in these published poverty levels. A joint return with two children—the prototypical example presented in congressional tax debates at the time—would be granted a tax-exempt level of income not deviating too far from the poverty level. Because tax brackets were not adjusted automatically for inflation before 1985, the adjustments upward in tax-exempt levels were dependent upon the passage of new tax acts, each of which claimed to reduce the tax burden on low-income individuals. Of course, what was really happening was that inflation and real growth in the economy were decreasing the relative value of these tax exemptions even more than the tax acts were readjusting them for inflation.

At the end of the 1970s, concern over the size of the deficit led policymakers to defer any additional tax reductions just at a time when inflation rates were increasing dramatically. As a result, the tax-exempt level of income eroded quickly within a few years, and the average income tax rate for a family of four in poverty began rising quickly from 0 percent in 1978 to 2.85 percent in 1981.[10] Over these same three years, tax-exempt levels of income rose hardly at all, while per capita personal income increased from less than $7,900 to over $10,900 (or by over 39 percent), mainly due to inflation.

Not all low-income individuals suffered equally. The tax-exempt level discussed above is the minimum level set by the personal exemption and standard deduction independently of other exclusions and deductions. For groups with sizable exclusions, including those receiving significant amounts of Social Security or other nontaxable transfer income, the tax-exempt level was much higher. Hence the tax increase on low-income individuals was not uniform, but applied mainly to workers whose income was paid in cash other than in some excluded or preferred form.

Raising the Tax Burden on Households with Dependents

One part of this story was later to become crucial to the development of tax reform, although it was barely noticed at the end of the 1970s. Figure 2.2 shows that the percentage change in tax-exempt levels of income varied dramatically among households of different sizes. In 1948, tax-exempt levels of income per family member were equal to 46.8 percent of per capita personal income in the economy. In effect, the tax-exempt level per person was roughly half of the average per-person income in the United States. This was true for all types of households. By 1981, the percentage had fallen to 30.1 percent for single returns, 24.7 percent for joint returns with no dependents, and a mere 13.3 percent for a head of household with four dependents.

What was the cause of these differences among households of different sizes? One small differential was created in 1964 when single individuals were given an additional tax break that raised their minimum standard deduction above that of a married person filing as part of a joint return. More importantly, Congress continued to ignore the erosion of the personal exemption while making increasing use of the standard deduction as the tool by which it would adjust upward tax-exempt levels of income. The standard deduction, however, is the same for households with and without dependents. The only real difference allowed for household size, therefore, was for the presence of a spouse. Increases in the personal exemption, had they been used instead, would have adjusted for household size. By failing to increase the personal exemption in line with income growth, Congress effectively raised the relative tax burden on households with dependents.

CHANGES IN TAX RATES

Increases in taxes on the poor and on low-income workers were only one reflection of a broader phenomenon: real income growth and inflation moved individuals into higher income tax brackets. This phenomenon became commonly known as "bracket creep."

Economists place special emphasis on the tax bracket into which the taxpayer's last dollar of income falls. This tax bracket reflects the marginal tax rate, or the rate paid on any additional dollar of income. To the extent that taxes affect behavior—decisions to work more or to save and invest additional dollars of income—it is this marginal or last tax rate that is often considered the most important in making substitutions of work for leisure or saving for consumption.[11]

The distribution of returns by marginal rate of tax in 1961 and 1979 is presented in figure 2.3. Although most discussions of the progressivity of the tax system focus on the very top rate paid only by the highest income taxpayers—such a myopic view was to dominate the debates over the 1981 and the 1986 tax acts—in fact, few taxpayers pay the top rate. Take the year 1961, remembered by some as the heyday of the era of progressive taxation because of a top rate of 90 percent. In truth, the tax rate structure was mainly a flat rate for the vast majority of taxable returns. Only 10 percent of tax returns had any positive marginal tax rate other than 20 to 22 percent. By 1979, however, the effective structure of rates had become much more progressive, with roughly half of all returns paying higher marginal tax rates than in 1961, and three-tenths paying lower rates (two-tenths remained nontaxable). Some of the greatest differences

Figure 2.3 CUMULATIVE PERCENT OF FEDERAL INCOME TAX RETURNS TAXED AT OR BELOW EACH SUCCESSIVE MARGINAL RATE

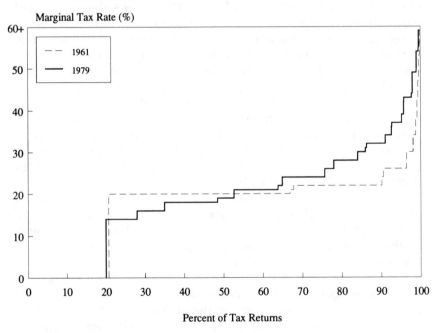

Source: Steuerle and Hartzmark (1981, p. 153). Originally derived from the Bureau of Economic Analysis (*National Income and Product Accounts, Survey of Current Business*, and unpublished data) and the Internal Revenue Service Statistics of Income Division (*Individual Income Tax Returns*).

occurred for tax returns with the highest marginal rate of tax. For instance, for returns at the 95th percentile (those returns just falling into the richest 5 percent of all returns), the marginal tax rate increased from 26 percent in 1961 to 38 percent in 1979.

Tax Rates at Half the Median, the Median, and Twice the Median Income

Figure 2.3 reflects the distribution of returns and takes into account all changes in deductions, credits and other tax provisions. An alternative but closely related calculation is presented in figure 2.4 (with detailed data in appendix A.3). In the latter figure, average and marginal tax rates are compared for families at one-half of median income, median income, and twice median income.

For lower income individuals at one-half median income, the average tax rate tended to rise fairly steadily, with some offset in a year like 1977, right after a tax bill temporarily reduced rates. Marginal rates increased more dramatically. By 1960, these households had moved from being nontaxable to being taxable on additional dollars of income at a marginal rate of 20 percent. While that marginal rate then became more steady or declined, more and more income became subject to the first rates of tax. Hence, for a period of time these households saw higher average rates and lower marginal rates.

Median-income households also found that their average rates rose for much the same reason. Personal exemptions or standard deductions became less and less valuable, so that a higher percentage of income became subject to tax. Marginal rates, on the other hand, both rose and fell, although they did reach a peak of about 24 to 25 percent between 1978 and 1980.

For households at twice median income, it was the change in marginal tax rates that was most dramatic. In the 13-year period from 1967 to 1980, the marginal tax rate for these households almost doubled from about 22 percent to 43 percent. Their average rate of tax also peaked in 1981 at 19.11 percent

The overall change to the schedule of marginal rates is again demonstrated in figure 2.3. The individual tax system was becoming more progressive because some cuts at the bottom were being offset by increases in taxes at the top. What made marginal rates increase so much more than average rates, however, was the progressive tax structure: the first rates of tax apply to everyone, whereas the highest rates of tax apply only to a minority of returns. Thus, a lowering of the first rate of tax from 20 to 14 percent in the early 1960s applied

Figure 2.4 FEDERAL INCOME TAX RATES FOR A FAMILY OF FOUR AT
VARIOUS INCOME LEVELS, 1955–1980

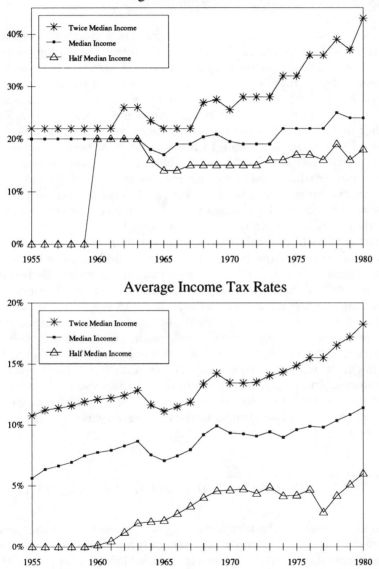

Sources: U.S. Department of the Treasury, Office of Tax Analysis (Allen Lerman);
U.S. Bureau of the Census, various years.

to all taxable taxpayers, who then paid less tax on those first dollars of income. Offsetting this reduction in bottom rates for all taxpayers while maintaining revenues required a significant increase in the marginal rates paid by a smaller number of taxpayers over what was often a smaller tax base.

Keep in mind that most of the tax rate increases were brought about by inflation. Except in wartime, Congress has seldom passed legislation directly increasing tax rates, and never by very much. These inflation-induced tax increases were offset in two principal ways. First, Congress would occasionally pass tax decreases—usually under the pretext that such decreases were encouraging growth, rather than simply making up for tax increases of the past. Second, many individuals were able to lower their total tax burden (even when their marginal rate stayed high) by increasing their use of exclusions, deductions, and other preferences. The higher rates, of course, encouraged switches of income and consumption toward tax-favored categories. The beneficiaries of these congressional enactments and further sheltering of income were frequently not the same as the victims of the inflation-induced tax increases.

The tax revolt of the late 1970s is closely tied to these increases in marginal tax rates, particularly those on the upper-middle income classes. As inflation rates increased, bracket creep accelerated. The doubling of marginal tax rates within a mere 13 years for a household at twice median income inevitably brought about a reaction. The increase in the number of two-earner families was one factor behind this rise in the number of taxpayers facing high rates; for them, the higher rates were not necessarily due to high individual earnings, but to combining their income with that of their spouses. Note also that state income tax rates were increasing rapidly too, though the overall revolt of taxpayers against the income tax was directed almost solely against the federal income tax.

CORPORATE AND CAPITAL INCOME TAXATION

Postwar changes in the taxation of capital income was another, even more complex matter. One of the main culprits, again, was inflation, which interacts in strange ways with a wide variety of tax provisions. Inflation so distorts the measure of capital and corporate income that it is often impossible to tell whether taxes have gone up or down on any particular item of capital income or any particular taxpayer simply by looking at information reported on financial statements or tax returns. One analyst or newspaper columnist could easily publish notes on capital owners paying zero or negative tax, while another could find examples where capital owners paid multiple layers of tax adding up to an exorbitant tax bite.

Together, inflation and taxation can combine to create the type of stagnation witnessed in the United States during the late 1970s and early 1980s. The issues are fairly technical in nature, but because they form such an important prelude to the tax changes of the 1981–1990 decade, they will be covered briefly in the remainder of this chapter.[12]

Taxation of Different Sources of Capital Income

Individuals who receive capital income in the form of interest payments can face a tax system that is especially onerous. In a world with 5 percent inflation and a 5 percent real rate of return, the total interest rate would be 10 percent. If an individual is in a 50 percent bracket, 5 percentage points of the 10 percent return would be paid to the government, leaving the individual with a zero after-tax rate of return. The tax rate would be 100 percent.

In fact, while the taxation of interest income may be easily perceived by the public, it is not really a representative example. Little income from capital is subject to individual income taxation. Over 80 percent of the assets of individuals, for instance, receives some tax preference that excludes part of the income from taxation. These preferences apply to capital gains, pension funds, individual retirement accounts, consumer durables, owner-occupied housing, second homes, land, and commercial real estate. In the case of most assets, an individual can exclude any increase in value from taxation simply by not selling the asset.

Interest deductions reported on tax returns, moreover, are much larger than interest receipts declared even though, for society as a whole, all interest is paid from someone to someone else. The excess inflationary tax on interest received, therefore, is more than offset by an excess subsidy on borrowing or on interest paid. For instance, of a total of $446.1 billion of estimated income from capital received by individuals in 1982—interest, dividends, and other returns to businesses—only $143.5 billion, or less than one-third, was reported on individual income tax returns as income subject to tax.[13]

Capital gains presents another example of an item of income for which it is hard to draw a simple picture. On the one hand, most capital gains are not realized immediately, as assets are often held for years or until death. Each year hundreds of billions of dollars of gains forego any taxation. On the other hand, in aggregate, total gains in the economy are about equal to inflationary gains on existing assets, plus income that has already been taxed once as retained earnings of corporations (Halperin and Steuerle 1988). In effect, our tax system allows many people with substantial income to pay no tax on income earned as capital gains, while others are taxed when there are no real capital gains.

This does not imply that capital income is not subject to taxation. In fact, corporation income taxes in most years are well in excess of individual taxes estimated for all capital income.

Total Returns to Corporate Capital

Figure 2.5 presents one perspective on corporate capital income and its taxation over the postwar period. Corporations, by producing a greater proportion of output of the entire economy, simultaneously increase their share of domestic income earned by selling that output. Still, corporate profits drop fairly significantly over much of this

Figure 2.5 PROFITS, RETURNS TO CAPITAL OWNERS, TAXES, AND INTEREST
INCOME OF NON-FINANCIAL CORPORATIONS, 1940–1990

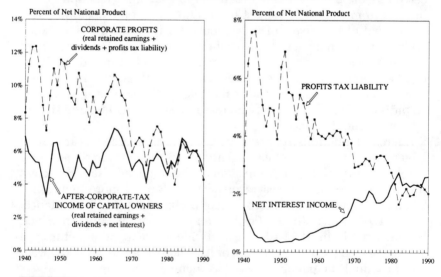

Sources: U.S. Department of Commerce (1986); and U.S. Department of Commerce, *Survey of Current Business*, various years (Tables 1.9 and 1.19).

period, as do items that depend upon profits: corporate tax collections and the real (adjusted for inflation) retained earnings. Yet despite all of these changes, the share of domestic income received by owners of corporate capital does not change dramatically, but remains rather steady at around 5.5 percent of net national product.

How can this happen? How can capital owners as a whole be just as well off, at least relative to other income recipients, as they were before the dramatic drop in corporate profits? The decline in total corporate profits earned by owners of corporate capital is just about matched by a combination of two items: (1) a decrease in corporate taxes and (2) an increase in the net amount of interest payments to bondholders.

Note, again, that in the case of individuals, interest payments are overstated by the rate of inflation. Corporate bondholders perceive a much higher rate of return than they really receive. By the same token, corporate shareholders are given a financial statement that understates the amount of income that the corporation earns. In fact, the two are a wash, as interest deducted by the corporation on behalf of its shareholders is received by the bondholders. For instance, if $1,000 is paid out, $500 of which represents nothing more than a return for inflation, the $500 overstatement of interest paid by the corporation is matched by a $500 overstatement of interest received by the corporate bondholder.

Depreciable Assets

Misstatement of real interest income in a world of inflation is only one problem. Inflation also reduces the value of depreciation allowances that can be taken over time. In this case, however, Congress has acted often to offset these inflationary effects.

Although many were to criticize the Reagan-era reductions in the tax on depreciable assets, as discussed in the next chapter, these tax cuts were only the latest in a long series of related actions that took place throughout the postwar era. Before 1981, there already had been three major reductions in the time period over which the cost of assets could be depreciated or written off.[14] In short, about every 8 to 10 years, Congress or the administration had acted to provide an incentive for the purchase of new depreciable assets.

In addition, investment credits of up to 7 percent were provided for investments in equipment through the Revenue Act of 1962. After two suspensions between 1966 and 1967 and between 1969 and 1971, the investment credit was reinstated in 1971, and liberalized. In 1975 the maximum credit was increased to 10 percent.[15]

Although these business tax changes were partly a reaction to inflation, depreciation allowances have never been adjusted directly for inflation. Hence, additional inflation erodes the value of allowances granted under a fixed schedule. Thus, a corporation allowed to deduct, say, $100 next year would not be allowed to take into account that the $100 had been reduced in value because of inflation.

Statutory changes and inflation, therefore, worked in opposite directions. Nonetheless, the marginal rate of tax on new depreciable capital—that is, the effective tax rate on new purchases—declined more than did average rates of tax on existing assets. Average rates stayed up because higher rates of inflation kept increasing the tax rate on the old capital. For new capital, however, it has been estimated that the tax rate on equipment fell to about 20 percent by the late 1970s, well below the tax rate on structures and the statutory tax rate of 46 percent that applied at the time (Hulten and Robertson 1984, p. 337).

Corporate tax is assessed on all equity returns from the corporate sector, not just returns from depreciable plant and equipment. Corporations profit from ideas, invention, new techniques, good marketing practices, and innovation. A company moving to a new region or country may "invest" a substantial amount into learning about the laws and customs of that area. Some companies have also been able to garner profits as monopolies or as members of small oligopolies. Service industries, which have employed larger and larger portions of the population in the last decades, generate significant profits from their activities even when there is little investment in plant and equipment. These other types of investments often did not benefit, at least directly, from the tax reductions offered to physical capital.

TAX ARBITRAGE AND TAX SHELTERS

The late 1970s and early 1980s were a period of significant tax-induced activity in the financial markets. Much of this activity falls under the technical heading of "tax arbitrage," which mainly involves borrowing to buy tax-preferred assets.

Arbitrage profits can be obtained when there are differential rates of return, as when a stock investor borrows at a 10 percent rate of interest to invest in a stock that he believes is going to produce a return of 12 percent. Tax arbitrage is arbitrage activity that is influenced by the differential tax treatment of different sources of income even when economic arbitrage is not profitable.[16]

How Tax Arbitrage Works

The story of tax arbitrage is the following. Where tax differentials exist, a person is led to purchase the asset with the lower rate of tax. Tax arbitrage exaggerates this effect by allowing taxpayers to borrow (or "sell short" assets) to obtain the money to purchase the preferred assets.

When the taxation of capital income was examined above, almost 80 percent of assets were noted to benefit from some preference or another. Seldom are assets subject to tax on both their cash yield and their change in value. For instance, houses and stocks may provide rental and dividend streams, but the gains in value are not subject to tax until sale, if ever. Even depreciable assets benefit from allowances that accelerate the amount of deductions taken and, hence, that provide an interest-free loan from the government.

Interest income is the one major exception. The entire real income stream, plus the entire return due to inflation, are subject to tax. This inclusion of the entire inflationary component is true for almost no other asset.[17]

The high *positive* rate on interest income, as noted before, is matched exactly by a high *negative* rate on interest paid. By borrowing, the taxpayer converts the penalty on interest income into a subsidy for borrowing.[18] Tax arbitrage typically involves combining the subsidy for borrowing with a subsidy for owning or buying a tax-preferred asset.[19]

When taxpayers engage in tax arbitrage, it shows up in the economy through an increase in the number of financial transactions. Additional borrowing or increased leveraging (increased ratios of debts to assets) often provides additional sources of tax reduction. Because the subsidies for tax arbitrage increase with additional tax breaks and with inflation, tax arbitrage is responsible for much of the increased private demand for borrowing that took place over the postwar era.[20]

A taxpayer may not know that he is engaging in tax arbitrage. For instance, a person may put money into an individual retirement account (IRA) and, as a consequence, have less cash available for other purposes. Later, a mortgage may be paid off more slowly or additional borrowing may be used to finance an addition to a house or to pay educational expenses. Since the additional borrowing is made necessary by the deposit in the IRA, the taxpayer is effectively engaging in tax arbitrage.

Note also that the arbitrager is often playing tax games that add nothing to the total productivity in the economy. Tax-motivated borrowing and investing involve transaction costs that must be paid, and these costs subtract from national well-being. Nor is additional saving necessarily generated when an investment is financed through borrowing, or negative saving.

The Pervasiveness of Tax Arbitrage

Although the previous discussion was a bit technical, one cannot emphasize enough how pervasive tax arbitrage was by the end of the 1970s and, to some extent, remains today. Tax arbitrage affects the lives and habits of almost every individual and business in society. Taxpayers continually engage in tax arbitrage. Examples include borrowing to purchase housing, consumer durables, pension assets and IRAs, state and local bonds, and real estate and corporate stock for which special treatment or exclusions are provided for capital gains. Businesses often engage in tax arbitrage when they borrow to buy stock, create a merger, or engage in a leveraged buyout of another company. Within a business, borrowing to purchase equipment may involve some amount of tax arbitrage, as can borrowing to buy inventory that is favorably treated through the allowance of favorable methods of accounting.[21] Some corporations purchase stock of other companies and are allowed to deduct dividends from income even when interest costs of financing the purchase are also deducted.

This list of examples makes obvious that tax arbitrage can permeate almost every financial transaction in which both individuals and businesses engage. The resulting system of capital income taxation can create serious distortions in the allocation of capital, and can cause taxpayers with equal incomes to pay very different rates of tax.

As one example of the perverse effects of tax arbitrage, farmland purchased with borrowed dollars gradually became more and more of a tax-favored asset as inflation rates increased throughout the late 1960s and 1970s (Davenport et al. 1982). The increased value of the farmland would not be subject to tax unless sold, but the inflationary component of the interest rate would be deducted. For many successful farmers, little or no net income was declared as taxable, while for many others the leveraged purchase of additional farmland became a good way to offset existing taxable income from a job or the successful operation of another farm. Note, however, who was kept from bidding in this type of market: the potential, young farmer, who could not benefit from additional tax deductions because he had no other source of taxable income to offset. Tax arbitrage helped to drive out of the farm sector a significant number of individuals, including the children of existing farmers who may have been the optimal owners of the farmland from a productivity standpoint. When interest rates shot up and commodity prices fell in the early 1980s, many farmers with tax-induced borrowing were also driven to bankruptcy.

Tax Shelters

Perhaps the most visible form of tax arbitrage is the tax shelter. In the 1970s many types of tax shelters came to be highly publicized and marketed on the basis of tax savings offered. Doctors, lawyers, and other professionals could be seen to pay almost no tax on substantial earnings when they owned significant amounts of such shelters.

Along with the growth in tax shelters came a large number of administrative problems. Many shelters were eventually tagged as "abusive," meaning that the deductions and credits often were not legitimate. Investment credits were claimed for items that were really not eligible for a credit. Valuations of property were inflated to gain additional deductions. Nonrecourse debt—debt for which the taxpayer was not liable in case of bankruptcy—allowed an investor to put almost no money at risk, while taking deductions that were a multiple of his investment; sometimes no investment at all was made and the whole set of transactions was a sham.

By the late 1970s, the growth in abusive shelters and incorrect taking of deductions had become serious enough to demand special attention by the government. From the late 1970s to the late 1980s, several successive commissioners of the Internal Revenue Service— Jerome Kurtz, Roscoe L. Egger, Jr., and Lawrence B. Gibbs—responded to this new situation by requiring that a large percentage of the audit staff of the IRS devote itself to tax shelters. Audit rates for ordinary taxpayers began to decline at the same time. While these tax policy and administrative problems were beginning to demand attention, however, the reactions of legislators were initially quite limited, perhaps because of a fear of offending taxpayers who were already revolting against inflation-induced tax increases.

INFLATION RATES AND INTEREST PAYMENTS

We have already noted how inflation led to large increases in tax rates on individuals, a shift in the measured amount of corporate income paid to bondholders rather than shareholders, and growth in the tax shelter industry. It is almost impossible to understand the reaction of the voter to the tax system prevalent by the end of the 1970s without simultaneous reference to inflation. Moreover, inflation's effect on taxes was becoming more pronounced as inflation rates crept gradually upward throughout the 1960s and 1970s. As measured by the consumer price index, the index most observed by the public, inflation reached a high of 13.3 percent in 1979 (see figure 2.6).[22] In contrast, the inflation rate had been less than 2 percent in most years before 1966.

Inflation also played havoc with the financial systems. Inflation made existing financial statements of depreciation, as well as interest paid and received, quite misleading. Inflation caused property and real estate values to rise appreciably, while individuals adjusted their portfolios constantly to new levels of inflation and interest. At a time of accelerating inflation, individuals with prior fixed investments in many pensions and interest-bearing assets faced a significant decline in the value of their assets, while borrowers often achieved a large gain. Sometimes borrowers even found themselves being *paid* to borrow and dissave. As an example, a household borrowing at an 8 percent interest rate in 1976 found that when inflation rose to 10 percent, it was paying negative rates of interest on its old debt.

The effects mentioned in the previous paragraph were independent of the tax system. With the rise in inflation, however, came a rise in interest rates that in turn led to an increase in the tax advantages of borrowing (as well as in the tax penalties for lending). Direct payments of interest by lenders such as households and corporations rose from 4.5 percent of gross national product in 1948 to 10.7 percent in 1973 and 16.7 percent in 1981. With the increase in interest payments came an increase in the tax benefits from deductions associated with those payments.

The tax relief provided for private interest paid was $61 billion or 2 percent of GNP more than the tax payments made on private in-

Figure 2.6 ANNUAL INFLATION RATES, 1950–1990
Percent Change in Seasonally Adjusted
Consumer Price Index for Urban Wage Earners

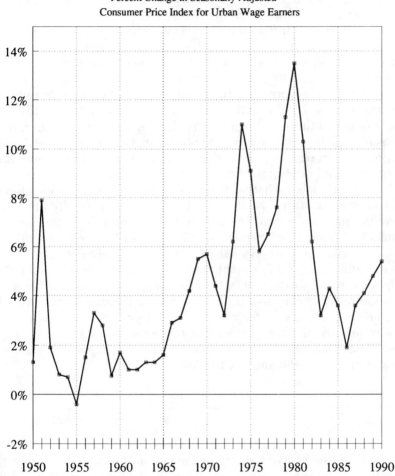

Source: U.S. Department of Labor, Bureau of Labor Statistics (listed in the
Economic Report of the President 1991, p. 351).

terest received in 1981.[23] This huge subsidy for borrowing added
enormously to the tax arbitrage and tax shelter opportunities present
in the economy and helped lead to stagnation by driving saving
toward tax-motivated, not economic, investment.

To summarize how inflation, taxation, and monetary policy in-
teract, start with the premise that to prevent investment in unproductive assets, the after-tax rate of return must be positive. Then, an

investor would be willing to invest in an unproductive asset producing negative income only if tax breaks more than offset the negative economic income from the investment.

With 10 percent inflation and interest deductions allowed at a 50 percent tax rate, note that the after-tax rate of interest is positive only if it is 20 percent or higher.[24] Unless the Federal Reserve Board raises interest rates to 20 percent or more, in real terms the borrower is paid by the government to borrow. When the after-tax rate of interest is effectively negative, the required return from the investment financed through borrowing is also negative. For instance, if a person were to purchase a vacation home that remained unused and depreciated in real value over time, the investor would be better off borrowing and buying the home.

It is questionable whether the Federal Reserve Board understood this connection fully. At the end of the 1970s, it finally allowed interest rates to rise significantly—in fact, the prime rate charged by banks rose from 12.67 percent in 1979 to 15.27 percent in 1980 to 18.87 percent in 1981—as inflation rates themselves stayed in or near double digits (U.S. Department of Commerce 1990, p. 508). By moving toward positive, after-tax interest rates, the Federal Reserve was indirectly forcing investment back toward those assets that would produce a positive economic return to society independently of the tax system. At the same time, this tightened monetary policy has also been associated with the back-to-back recessions that were to follow in 1979–1980 and 1981–1982.

SUMMARY

For most of the postwar era up to the end of the Carter presidency, several tax issues grew in importance. Exclusions, deductions, and credits continued to erode the individual income tax base, although they were offset by the decline in the value of the personal exemption. This decline, in turn, led to increased income taxation of the poor and a shift in relative tax burdens toward households with dependents. Average income tax rates rose mainly for those who worked, but marginal tax rates were almost to double for taxpayers in the upper part of the middle-income class. Capital income taxation could vary anywhere from negative tax rates to rates in excess of 100 percent. With negative rates came a rapid growth in the tax shelter industry and the ability of those with substantial earnings to pay no income tax. Meanwhile, inflation rates had risen almost continually from one cycle to another until the Federal Reserve decided to tighten monetary policy at the end of the 1970s. Into this scene was to step Ronald Reagan.

Notes

1. Of course, the gap between expenditures and taxes—the deficit—was also to rise later. If taxes were to cover expenditures, then tax rates would have been much higher in the 1980s.

2. Note, however, that state and local taxes had actually reached similar levels during 1932 and 1933 and were then eclipsed by federal tax increases throughout the late 1930s and early 1940s.

3. The tax revolt cannot really be separated from dissatisfaction of the public with the spending programs financed by their tax collections. The tax revolts of the mid-1970s and early 1980s followed the failure to achieve quick and easy successes in Vietnam, to eliminate poverty through welfare programs, and to solve the oil and hostage crises. Rising inflation, as discussed later, was also a crucial factor in reducing the public's faith in government.

4. With pension plans, the exclusion from current income actually operates as a deferral of income subject to tax. Employer contributions and the earnings within a pension plan are taxed when withdrawn. The value of the deferral is equivalent to non-taxation of the earnings within the plan if the taxpayer is in the same tax bracket at the time of withdrawal as at the time of deposit.

5. Steuerle and Hartzmark (1981). Subsequent figures in this section can be found in the same source.

6. The value of home ownership is enhanced because of the nontaxability of a homeowner's rental income that is saved by owning rather than investing a similar amount of money in the bank, paying tax on the interest, and then renting a similar home.

7. In table 2.1, the income of nontaxable individuals cannot be separated from nonreported income and certain reconciliation items, including possible improvements in compliance, and error terms. Hence, they are reported as one number.

8. General tax credits were available only briefly from 1975 through 1978. Minimum tax-exempt levels may be exceeded by those who have additional sources of nontaxable income such as Social Security.

9. For a discussion of the many problems associated with adjusting poverty measures for inflation, see Ruggles (1990).

10. This example excludes use of the earned income tax credit. If included, the average tax rate on those just falling into poverty rose from − 2.01 percent in 1978 to 1.89 percent in 1981. See Steuerle and Wilson (1986).

11. Of course, other tax rates may also affect behavior because they change the amount of income available for consumption or saving.

12. These issues can only be treated briefly here. For a more thorough analysis, see Steuerle (1985b).

13. For further details, see Steuerle (1985b, pp. 9–45).

14. These three changes were 1) the adoption of accelerated methods of depreciation such as "double declining balance" or "sum-of-the-years'-digits" in the Internal Revenue Code of 1954; 2) the 1962 "Guidelines for Depreciation," which reduced write-off periods by about 30 to 40 percent; and 3) the introduction of the asset depreciation range (ADR) system in 1971, which allowed taxpayers to use tax lives that were 20 percent shorter than the guidelines defined.

15. The corporate rate had also declined slightly from 52 percent in the years before 1964 to 48 percent by 1965, and to 46 percent by 1979 and thereafter. These numbers exclude a surtax from 1968 to 1970 because of the Vietnam War.

16. For further discussion of tax arbitrage and its many implications, see Steuerle (1985b), especially chapters 5 and 6. The term, "tax arbitrage," is, I believe, due to Professor David Bradford of Princeton University.

17. The major exception is an asset that is "marked to market" or treated as if sold by the end of each year, so that all gains, both inflationary and real, are recognized immediately.

18. In economic terms, normal tax arbitrage requires two conditions: 1) the differential tax treatment of the income from different assets, and 2) different tax rates for different taxpayers. Without the latter, there is no gain from borrowing from another person. If a borrower gets additional tax benefits out of deducting more than the real component of the interest rate, a lender in the same tax bracket pays a penalty of an equal amount. When tax rates differ, however, the borrower will generate tax benefits that will not be offset by a penalty on the lender—as when a nonprofit institution puts money in a bank that is borrowed by someone engaging in tax arbitrage.

19. In some cases, the preferred asset purchased with the borrowed money may itself be interest-bearing. For instance, borrowing to purchase a pension or individual retirement account may allow the taxpayer to pay 10 percent interest, deduct a portion of that interest from taxable income, and yet to defer reporting any of the 10 percent interest that might be received on the retirement asset. This is an example of what I have defined as pure tax arbitrage, since the same asset is both bought and sold. In contrast, normal tax arbitrage typically requires the existence of some real asset that another person or entity sells to the borrower.

20. In many cases, the preferred asset being bought by the taxpayer seeking tax relief will be purchased from another taxpayer who cannot receive the same relief because of the tax bracket into which he falls. For instance, a nonprofit institution might gain little from the special tax relief applied to real estate and might, therefore, try to sell its real estate assets to taxpayers in higher brackets. In the early 1980s, some colleges attempted to sell and lease back their buildings for just that reason. See Galper and Toder 1983.

21. For instance, under the LIFO (last-in-first-out) method of accounting, a firm is allowed to deduct first the cost of items purchased last. This provides a form of adjustment for inflation, but no inflation adjustment is made to reduce the amount of deduction for interest paid.

22. The rate of inflation used for national income accounting was usually lower than the rate of increase in the consumer price index. For instance, the percent change in the implicit price deflator for GNP peaked at 9.7 percent in 1981. See *Economic Report of the President, 1990*, Table C-3, p. 299.

23. Technically, interest paid equals interest received on a worldwide, not domestic basis. See Steuerle (1985b, pp. 52 and 56), for details of these calculations.

24. The tax code at this time contained almost no limit on the deduction of personal interest and mortgage interest, while an investment interest limitation was mainly ineffective.

Chapter Three

THE EARLY REAGAN ERA

In the 1980 campaign, Ronald Reagan campaigned against big government. It is not surprising, therefore, that he would come to embrace proposals that would reduce taxes—the most obvious and visible costs associated with government. Early in 1981 he proposed two fairly simple but substantial tax reductions. Each proposal took advantage, in part, of a public reaction against the impact of inflation on individual tax rates and on the taxation of depreciable capital.

First, he proposed to reduce individual income tax rates by 10 percent per year for three years. This so-called "10-10-10" reduction in tax rates would be the more expensive of the two proposals because it would apply to all individual income, including wages.[1] Second, he proposed to establish an accelerated cost recovery system (ACRS) that would speed up the availability of deductions allowed for depreciable assets. Under this simplified scheme, the cost of any piece of machinery or equipment, even if it might last for 8, 12, or 20 years, would be written off over a period of 5 years rather than over the life of the asset. ACRS was also referred to as the "10-5-3" method of depreciation after the number of years of life assigned to plant and buildings (10 years) and various forms of equipment (5 years and 3 years).

DEVELOPMENT OF THE 1981 TAX PROPOSALS

Despite the influence of inflation on the tax system, the proposals put forward by President Reagan were not designed after the Treasury or administration had studied ways to offset the adverse affects of this inflation. Instead, both proposals were adopted during the campaign of then candidate Reagan and adjusted barely afterwards. The 10-10-10 reduction in individual tax rates had originally been propounded within Congress by then Representative Jack Kemp (R-N.Y.) and Senator William Roth (R-Del.), while the 10-5-3 proposal was developed by a business coalition led partially by the American Council for Capital Formation, a Washington-based lobbying group. The numbers, 10-10-10 and 10-5-3, had a certain flair to them and gave the illusion that the complexities of the tax law could be described in simple terms.

Both proposals took advantage of simmering tax revolt at the end of the 1970s, itself largely influenced by the impact of inflation on tax rates and asset values. Individuals had moved into higher tax rate brackets, while businesses suffered from lower-valued depreciation allowances as inflation eroded the real value of future deductions. As noted, however, neither proposal adjusted for inflation directly. One important consequence of keeping to simple campaign promises, while avoiding any study and redesign of the proposals, was that the stage was being set for later tax reform. Had redesign been allowed, some of the major problems that remained prior to tax reform, such as the inflation-induced taxation of the poor, might have been eliminated in 1981.

Tax rates mattered greatly to President Reagan, who remembered paying the 90 percent top income tax rate in place from World War II to the early 1960s.[2] Supply-side economists, too, were concerned about tax rates and emphasized the marginal rate on the last dollar paid. Some enthusiasts, however, failed to recognize the full implication of this philosophy. Supply-side economics is closely related to the theory that only a head tax (the same amount of tax collected from each individual) is efficient. That is, the highest tax rates should be assessed on the first dollars of income—or made equal for all persons regardless of income—so that zero tax rates could be assessed on each additional dollar of income from work or saving.

Despite this inherent logic, supply-side economists in America never proposed anything nearly so drastic as a head tax. (Margaret Thatcher did succeed in getting a head tax enacted in the late 1980s, an event that some have held responsible for her downfall as prime minister of Great Britain.) In 1981, the main role of supply-siders was to provide the apologetics needed by President Reagan to justify the tax rate reductions he so fervently favored but would never be able to finance by expenditure reductions.

There appears to be a distinction between President Reagan and some of his supply-side supporters that may not have been fully appreciated at the time. President Reagan seemed to oppose all taxes, those paid at both the bottom of the income distribution and the top. This would make him more attached to reducing tax rates throughout the income distribution—a much higher cost proposition than simply reducing the top rate of tax. Later in his administration he would take further a stand in favor of increases in the personal exemption. Reductions in the bottom tax rates and increases in the personal exemption, however, have only a modest effect on marginal tax rates and, hence, on the "supply" of labor and capital. If the revenues had to be made up, marginal tax rates would usually increase, not decrease. This important distinction was barely noted in the early days of 1981.

THE NOT-SO-HIDDEN COST

When President Reagan first pushed forward his campaign proposals, there was little demand for an analysis of their effect. The Treasury Department, nonetheless, had to do its job and estimate the costs of these proposals. From the beginning, the Department published estimates that accurately indicated the large costs involved. One early published estimate, for instance, showed that when fully implemented by 1986, the individual rate reductions enacted in 1981 would cost $162 billion and the accelerated cost recovery system $59 billion (The White House 1981, p. 16). Despite pressure to lower these cost estimates (see discussion below), and the adoption of some optimistic economic assumptions by the administration, the costs could not help but be revealed.[3]

As the large costs of the program became recognized, many Democrats and Republicans in Congress tried to cut back on the proposals, in particular, by limiting individual rate reductions to one year (although the drop in the top rate to 50 percent likely would have remained). This change would allow Republicans to retain the more probusiness tax relief and allow Democrats to maintain revenues. Many in both parties would have been happy with this compromise, even though from a pure tax policy standpoint such a compromise would have favored the mismeasurement of income implied by the business changes over the simpler reduction of rates implied by the individual changes. Additional tax preferences in a world of higher tax rates would also have further exaggerated the tax shelter problem.[4]

Eventually, it became apparent that a new, popularly elected president was going to get his way. The country was tired of very high inflation rates and of the recent tax rises. The switching of political parties in the White House and the final release of the hostages from

Iran seemed to signal that it was time to try something new. President Reagan had also made a strong recovery from an assassination attempt and then boldly went to Congress to persuade them to enact his program. He also appealed to the American people, who were ready to sign on to a new initiative.

Congress eventually abandoned its cautious approach to President Reagan's proposals and went in the opposite direction. A bidding war started. Many new provisions were added to the original Reagan tax proposals, including extension of individual retirement accounts (IRAs) to higher income taxpayers who were already covered under employer-provided pension plans, a new deduction for some earnings when both spouses in a family worked (a "second-earner deduction"), an exclusion from income subject to tax of interest earned on qualified tax-exempt savings certificates ("All-Savers" Certificates), a charitable contributions deduction for individuals who did not normally itemize expenses, a credit for increasing research activities within a business, the elimination of estate taxes for a large number of wealthy taxpayers, and a number of other special preferences. The individual rate reductions were made slightly less valuable: the first rate reduction would be 5 percent, rather than 10 percent, followed by two 10 percent reductions in later years ("10-10-10" had become "5-10-10"). The net reduction in tax rates actually ended up to be about 23 percent, although inflation was to offset further some of this reduction.[5] Perhaps the most important addition of all was little noted at first: Congress required that tax brackets, the personal exemption, and the standard deduction be indexed or adjusted for inflation after 1984. Meanwhile, the accelerated cost recovery system of depreciation was not only adopted for assets purchased immediately, but was scheduled to be enhanced. Deductions would be allowed even sooner for certain assets purchased after 1984.

The Economic Recovery Tax Act of 1981 (ERTA) was to pass with all of these bells and whistles. To give some idea of its out-year impact by near to the end of the decade, the cost of the 1981 tax act was estimated for fiscal year 1990 alone at about $323 billion, or close to 6 percent of GNP (see table 12.1).

REASSESSING THE INDIVIDUAL CHANGES

To many opponents of President Reagan, the 1981 Tax Act was the chief cause of the budget deficits of the 1980s. To many of his supporters, the tax reductions represented the outstanding reform of his era. The story, however, is much more complex than either of these views allows.

On the individual side, the receipts cost of the rate reductions appears quite high when measured relative to a baseline in which then-current 1980 law would never be changed. A current-law baseline, however, involved moving individuals into higher tax brackets and significantly increasing their tax rates. Much of the 1981 rate reduction did nothing more than offset past and future increases in tax rates due to inflation or real growth in the economy.

One way of seeing how these factors combined is by examining federal individual income tax receipts, which never fell below 8.05 percent of GNP during the entire Reagan era. In contrast, these receipts were 7.94 percent of GNP in 1976—implying that the reductions never even restored tax rates to the lower level of only a few years before. After reaching their Reagan-period low point in 1984, moreover, individual rates have been increasing gradually ever since. As in periods before the implementation of indexation, individuals continue to move slowly into higher tax brackets, owing to increases in real income.

Indexing for Inflation

The major individual reform instituted in 1981 was not the direct reduction in tax rates, but the establishment of indexing of tax brackets, including, after 1984, what might be viewed as a zero bracket created by personal exemptions and standard deductions. As previously noted, this provision was not even part of the original Reagan proposals, but it has dramatically altered the nature of tax legislation ever since. No longer could Congress follow the pattern of providing tax reductions that merely offset tax increases due to inflation. By 1990, the adjustment for inflation alone was estimated to have reduced receipts by over $57 billion relative to an unindexed tax code (see table 12.1). Eventually the indexing provision will dominate all other provisions of the 1981 Act.

An alternative way of looking at the 1981 rate reduction is to compare it with the amount of receipts that would have been collected with an indexed tax system. According to estimates made by Sally Wallace, formerly of the Treasury's Office of Tax Analysis, if the individual tax base had simply been indexed for inflation in years after 1981, by 1990 receipts would have been lower by almost $180 billion.[6] In contrast, individual receipts due to all provisions of the 1981 Act were reduced by about $260 billion. Indexing since 1981, therefore, would have cost over two-thirds as much as all of the individual receipts changes in the 1981 Act, including the actual indexing that was allowed eventually to go into effect after 1984.

The 1981 Tax Act, however, was also a reaction to the significant bracket creep of the high-inflation years before 1981. Therefore, if one would have further indexed for a couple of years prior to 1981, the following conclusion is striking: *the entire revenue loss due to individual provisions in 1981 could have been achieved by nothing more than indexing the tax code for inflation from about 1979 onward.*

It is hard to believe that the nation would have gone through the 1980s with an unindexed tax code and with no tax cuts to offset the impact of inflation. The 1981 Act, of course, probably did bring about some reductions earlier than would have occurred with indexing alone. As a consequence, the opportunity for later tax cuts was essentially eliminated. The stock of debt of the country also went up faster than otherwise would have occurred if the cuts had been implemented over time—especially since the defense build up was taking place at the same time but was not being financed. The high amount of interest paid on the debt could even be argued in the long run to increase tax rates, depending upon whether one believes that these payments eventually come out of lower expenditures or higher taxes—or, what is most likely, both.

An Uneven Effect Among Individuals

The individual rate reductions did not offset inflation in an even-handed way. At the time of the Reagan tax reductions, I decided to run some of Treasury's computer models to see how tax cuts might be distributed if one really wanted to offset the inflation of the late 1970s.[7] These runs indicated that inflation increased individual taxes proportionately throughout most of the income distribution. For the vast majority of individuals in the broad middle classes, a proportionate rate reduction of 1981 was appropriate, at least if the goal was to offset bracket creep due to inflation.

However, there were two major groups for whom inflation's impact was very different: high-income and low-income taxpayers. For a person at the very highest tax rate, inflation normally cannot raise the marginal tax rate.[8] A person facing the top rate of 70 percent could not pay more than a 70 percent marginal tax rate no matter how much inflation occurred.

In 1981 many high-income individuals did not face a top rate of 70 percent, but rather 50 percent. A special provision of the tax code already attempted to limit the tax rate on earnings, or income from labor, to a maximum of 50 percent. (For many persons, the interaction among provisions resulted in a higher marginal rate than 50 percent.) For taxpayers able to use that provision, therefore, the 1981 reduction of the top rate from 70 to 50 percent often provided few additional benefits. For high-income persons with capital income, on the other hand, the lower rate was more generous. The lowering of the top statutory rate from 70 to 50 percent also effectively reduced the top rate paid on capital gains from 28 to 20 percent, since 60 percent of reported gains could be excluded from taxation both before and after the 1981 Act.

It was at the bottom of the income distribution that the combination of bracket creep and the 1981 Act was most unfair. If a taxpayer moved from paying no income tax to paying $200 in tax simply because inflation eroded the value of personal exemptions and standard deductions, a reduction in tax of 23 percent only compensated for $46 of the total increase. Moreover, the 23 percent reduction was inadequate to offset both the movement into the tax system because of inflation before 1981, and the additional tax due to inflation between 1981 to 1984, after which indexing was fully implemented.

This criticism does not apply to the 1981 Act alone. In many ways, the neglect of the poor in 1981 merely continued the trend of the late 1970s by allowing inflation to reduce the real levels of income at which tax exemption would apply. At the same time, inflation continued to force households with dependents to bear an increasing share of the total tax burden.

THE BUSINESS TAX CUTS: REVOLUTION OR PARODY OF THE PAST?

Both supporters and opponents of the Economic Recovery Tax Act of 1981 liked to claim that the business tax changes represented a revolutionary departure from the past. Supporters would proclaim, and opponents would protest, the extent and size of the new deductions. Just as on the individual side, however, the story was often exaggerated. In many ways the 1981 Act would come to repeat, even parody, the past.

Exaggerated Effects

The 1981 cost recovery provisions were hardly unique. There had already been three major reductions in the tax treatment of depreciable capital during the postwar period (see chapter 2). Proponents of the business cuts, especially those who labelled themselves supply-side economists, were especially fond of making analogies to the tax cuts and investment incentives that President Kennedy had proposed. Favoring depreciable assets had become a standard mechanism by which to reduce taxes on capital, especially as inflation accelerated or the government became enamored of the need to foster growth through the tax code. President Reagan's ACRS (10-5-3) proposals in many ways carried to a logical conclusion the precedents that had been set in prior Democratic, as well as Republican administrations. After all, if past accelerations of depreciation and enactment of investment credits had been worthwhile, then why not enact yet another investment incentive and let effective tax rates on some investments go to zero or even be made negative?

Although the costs of the 1981 program were high, they, too, could be misleading. Acceleration of depreciation allowances had an exaggerated effect on first years' revenues. That is, the reductions in tax due to the speed up of deductions would be partly offset later by the absence of deductions that had already been taken. Moreover, some speed up had always been justified by the acceleration of inflation—although explicit inflation adjustments would have been a more direct way to achieve this result and would have avoided overcompensation for inflation when inflation rates fell.

Despite the costs of the Reagan-era cuts, as a simple mathematical matter it turned out that the investment tax credit, which had first been put forward by President Kennedy, reduced tax rates on most assets by far more than the allowance of accelerated depreciation. This distinction would prove crucial later in the decade, when elimination of the investment credit, not a change in depreciation allowances, would provide the most important source of revenues by which to finance corporate rate reduction in tax reform.

Perverse Effects

While the novelty of the ACRS depreciation schedules was exaggerated by both its proponents and opponents, the new law still had a number of perverse economic effects that eventually could not be ignored. The 1981 business tax cuts contained within themselves the seeds of their own destruction. Remember that the president's package was not allowed to be redesigned to meet traditional goals of tax equity and efficiency nor to compensate accurately for inflation. As a result of the simplistic formula that was used, the benefits of the depreciation change were shared unequally among different forms of capital, and investment patterns were distorted.

Why? First, when combined with the investment credit, the new cost recovery schedules resulted in effective tax rates on new purchases of certain types of equipment that were often near zero. That is, the combination of an investment tax credit of 10 percent, plus the ability to write off the cost of equipment within 5 years, together gave allowances so generous that they were often mathematically equivalent to taxing the income from the investment at a tax rate close to zero. When these assets were purchased with borrowed dollars, the effective tax rate was negative and, thus, available to shelter other income.

Second, ACRS continued the trend of past tax preferences by putting the benefits all up front. The investment credit and the new accelerated deductions would be received in the first year or first few years of owning an asset. Since deductions and credits can only be used against other income or income tax, new businesses or businesses with current losses were put at a severe competitive disadvantage with respect to new investment. Almost none of them had enough income to make use of such generous up-front deductions and credits.

Third, the formula used to provide depreciation allowances created great disparities in the treatment of different forms of capital. The new ACRS system was especially beneficial to equipment with longer lives. Among different types of equipment, however, the provision of a common tax "life" of 5 years (over which costs could be written off) had no correspondence with the actual lives of assets. Why should an asset lasting 20 years and one lasting 7 years both be written off over the same 5-year period? This disparity meant that the return from equity investments in different assets would be taxed at different rates.

For pieces of equipment such as computers, the tax depreciation schedule was not generous at all—it did not even allow real economic depreciation. For plant and structures, which never received an investment credit, benefits of the acceleration in 1981 were also less than for most equipment. For returns on inventory investments, there was no direct benefit from tax preferences for depreciable assets.

The failure to provide benefits in a more evenhanded manner was to prove crucial later in the decade, as those industries and companies that had been left behind in 1981 were to form part of a business coalition that was to support tax reform.

TAX SHELTER BONANZA

By the late 1970s, the growth in the tax shelter market left some promoters uncertain how much further they could go. While most shelter dollars were put into oil and gas and commercial real estate, the breadth of the market at one time or another was to include investment in movies, alternative energy sources, rehabilitated structures, commodities—basically anything that lawyers could argue qualified for investment incentives. The Treasury and the IRS had already tried in various ways to prevent the expansion of the most egregious of shelters, essentially those that were abusive. Each year the threat of legislative cutback became greater.

In 1981, however, legislation moved in just the opposite direction. Because of the perverse effects just mentioned—in particular, the presence of zero or negative tax rates and the availability of up-front deductions to offset current tax liability—the feasible supply of tax shelter investments was greatly expanded.

Shelter promoters had become particularly adept at adding leverage or borrowing to the system. Because the inflationary component of interest is deductible, borrowing is effectively subsidized. Add this subsidy to a subsidy for purchasing an asset, and the tax shelter potential of leveraged investments was almost endless.

Here, then, was a tax shelter bonanza. The 1981 Tax Act compounded rather than slowed a rapidly growing problem for the U.S. economy. Moreover, it did so at a time of high inflation, thus promoting leveraged purchases of assets at the very time when changes in inflation or interest rates had increased the riskiness of such schemes.

This problem involved more than equity, or perceived equity, in the tax system. Investment in unproductive assets added to stagnation in the economy. As an example, take a piece of equipment for which excessive tax preferences were granted. Assume, as was the case for many assets in the early 1980s, that in absence of borrowing, tax preferences were equal to about 28 percent of the cost of an asset. To advocates of ACRS, this would be about enough to reduce tax

Table 3.1 EXAMPLE OF PROFITS FROM AN UNPRODUCTIVE INVESTMENT

Income or Expense	Return (as percent of asset value)
Real Income from Asset	− 9.0 percent
Interest Paid	−14.0 percent
Inflation Increase in Value of Asset	+10.0 percent
Tax Reduction on Interest Paid	+ 6.4 percent
Tax Reduction on Real Losses	+ 4.1 percent
Tax Preferences	+ 2.8 percent
Net Profit to Owner	+ 0.3 percent

rates on an equity-financed investment to zero. In a world of, say, 10 percent inflation and 14 percent interest rates, however, the leveraged purchase of this asset could produce a rate of return of a negative 9 percent and still make money for the taxpayer (see table 3.1).[9] An asset that produces a negative 9 percent rate of return, however, is equivalent to one that is not only unproductive, but feeds on and uses up the scarce resources of society. In effect, ACRS, when combined with the investment credit and the subsidy for borrowing, encouraged individuals to direct their saving away from areas where it would provide the greatest economic return and income to the economy.

The tax shelter market, which had already moved into a real growth stage in the late 1970s, now began to boom even more. Sometimes the examples were highly visible: windmill "farms" in the desert where acres of land would be covered with small windmills generating electric power, usually at far greater cost than other utilities; and "see-through" buildings where one wall of an old building would be propped up until new construction containing that wall would be allowed to qualify for "rehabilitation" credits. Sometimes gyrations in markets such as commodities were related to tax shelter demands in those markets. The savings and loan fiasco and the bank failures of the late 1980s were also partly driven by the tax-related attempts to build more and more commercial real estate on a sheltered basis, even when markets had already been saturated.

At the corporate level, shelters were also more visible than ever. New lease arrangements created under the 1981 Act allowed corporations to sell negative tax liability they could not use themselves. Under so-called "safe-harbor" leases, other corporations could buy tax benefits by taking only minimal ownership of another company's assets and then "leasing" the assets back to the user and true owner.[10]

The purchasers of these negative tax liabilities might then pay little net tax—having cancelled their positive debt to the government with the tax benefits from the leases.

As noted earlier, tax shelters were beginning to swamp the IRS. By 1985, for instance, over one-eighth of the technical staff devoted to examining tax returns directly (the examinations staff) was devoted to the tax shelter program, and the fraction was continuing to grow. In the meantime, the early Reagan administration attempted to cut back on the overall size of the IRS, only later to reverse its position for both revenue and administrative reasons.

What Was Different About the Tax Shelter Market in the Early 1980s?

As stressed before, the tax shelter problem cannot be laid solely or even principally to the 1981 Tax Act. In truth, the structure was already in place for the creation of shelters even before 1981, as witnessed by the market's expansion up to that time. What, then, made tax arbitrage so different after 1981 that it was to provide the major momentum for tax reform later in the decade?

First, the enactment of the 1981 tax breaks was done in a way that made a mockery of traditional tax principles. Unlike many previous subtle and hidden attempts to grant special favors, here was a wide open and readily acknowledged attempt to create zero or negative effective tax rates on an economy-wide scale. Many taxpayers began to believe that the government favored the purchases of shelters. No longer did people need to fear disputes with the IRS. The government seemed to claim, at least temporarily, that what was good for the shelter market was good for the country.

Second, throughout the 1970s and 1980s, lawyers, brokers and other tax experts had steadily enhanced their ability to take advantage of nuances and new tax breaks in the tax code. Even though the original fixtures were put in place as early as the 1960s with the enactment of the investment tax credit and some increase in deductions because of the impact of inflation on interest rates, the learning curve was exponential. The rapid progress in the use of computers added greatly to the ability to sell shelters. The arithmetic behind tax preferences was easier to reveal than ever before, and the ability to engage in transactions, even across countries, at times became almost instantaneous.

Third, there was a continual increase in the amount of debt available to finance leveraged purchases of tax-preferred assets. The reasons for this increase are complex and can only be summarized here. The increased availability of loanable funds can be traced in part to the ability of taxpayers to effectively lend to themselves, as when they deposited money in an Individual Retirement Account, while their bank then lent that money back to a similar group of customers. Mainly, however, the postwar era was to witness a dramatic increase in the amount of private debt in the economy, and most of this was household, non-corporate, and farm debt, not corporate debt. In the 1960s and 1970s, the growth in private debt substituted for a decline in public debt relative to the economy. In the 1980s, however, more borrowing became possible because of an increase in the amount of financial assets that would be lent by individuals through intermediaries. Prior to that period, available loans were limited in part by interest rate ceilings on deposits—one of the principal sources of loan dollars (Steuerle 1990b).

Regardless of the reasons, the increased amount of loanable funds was to finance much of the expansion of the tax shelter market up until the late 1980s, when the tax code finally clamped down on these shelters, and the growth rate in the availability of loanable funds began to slow for other reasons as well.

IT DOESN'T ADD UP

To this point I have emphasized the tax issues related to the 1981 Act. Yet the impact on the overall budget of the numbers coming out in 1981 cannot be ignored: they didn't add up. The cost estimates originally provided by the Treasury, the Joint Committee on Taxation, and the Congressional Budget Office were remarkably accurate. While those opposed to the tax cuts sometimes singled out their magnitude for criticism, we have already seen how, over a several-year period, taxes fell only moderately as a percentage of income. But when added to the cost of the defense build up, and the limited amount of expenditure reduction coming out of 1981 legislation, the deficit was destined to skyrocket absent only some phenomenal increase in economic growth that could have provided some offset. The package, as a whole, simply didn't add up.

There were early warnings that this problem would be dodged by playing games with the numbers. When Reagan's tax and fiscal program was presented to the Treasury for estimation, it produced estimates of the cost of the tax program that, when combined with the rest of the package, would result in very high out-year deficits.

Here it is important to note just how executive branch projections are made. The Office of Tax Analysis (OTA) in the Treasury Department makes estimates of revenues given a particular set of laws and economic assumptions about gross national product, inflation, interest rates, labor market participation, and so forth. At the same time, the expenditure agencies and departments of the government perform a role similar to OTA's—with the exception that they must submit these numbers to the Office of Management and Budget (OMB) to be added together. OMB then adds up the expenditure estimates to get an expenditure total, compares these numbers with the revenue total from the Treasury Department, and makes deficit projections.

Note the crucial role played by the macro-economic assumptions. These assumptions are put forward by the Office of Management and Budget, in combination with the Council of Economic Advisers and the Office of Economic Policy in Treasury (the "Troika"). What happens when the first set of estimates produces results that are not politically attractive? The scenario is usually the same. In both Democratic and Republican administrations, the first question that comes back to Treasury is: can't your revenue estimators change their numbers? OTA's response has always been that it will give the best estimates it can and will not change them for political reasons.[11]

At this point, political recourse is made elsewhere in the system. OTA does not control economic assumptions. These can be changed by OMB, with the consent of the Chairman of the Council of Economic Advisers and the Assistant Secretary of the Treasury for Economic Policy. These economic assumptions, then, are the numbers that are adjusted. Inflation rates might be raised to yield revenues in excess of the increase in cost of expenditure programs. More likely, the estimate of real growth in the economy will be increased in a way that yields additional projected revenues, but little in the way of additional expenditures. At another level, corporate profits might be assumed to rise faster than the income of individuals. If profits are taxed at a higher rate than individual income, then revenues go up even without a change in assumptions about real growth in the economy.

The process still creates problems for the political budgeteers, who often have multiple targets for real growth, deficits, inflation, and other parameters that are mutually inconsistent. Changing one economic assumption often moves one target in the "right" political direction, but another in the wrong one, or can have other undesirable features. Multiple scenarios are then proposed. Eventually there is some recognition that not all political targets can be met, and last minute compromises attempt to minimize, rather than eliminate, all political damage. In his book, David Stockman, the Director of OMB in 1981, revealed some of the wrangling over economic assumptions in 1981 and the final acceptance of what later became known as the "Rosy Scenario."

That some executive branch officials agreed to this charade helps to explain why increased reliance was placed upon the Congressional Budget Office for budget estimates during the tax decade. In fairness, most members of the executive branch do not participate in the game, and in many years of the 1980s the estimates were made honestly and even with a good deal of forecast accuracy. Moreover, even in 1981 the efforts of OTA and the other agencies insured that estimates would be consistent, even if based upon rosy economic assumptions.[12] The remnants of the 1981 fiasco, however, were to hurt the executive branch's credibility throughout the decade.

Much of the problem is that the system is unclear about ultimate responsibility. If a president ever said that he wanted the best set of economic assumptions possible, and did not want them to change to meet some other political goal, a good deal of the problem could be solved. The process could also be changed by setting economic assumptions through other means or in other settings, for instance, by acceptance of impartial economic assumptions determined before the rest of the budget process begins.

Consistency and Accuracy of Numbers

The inadequate concern carried beyond poor economic projections. One of the first warnings that truth was to be determined by the bottom line, not by the facts, came early in 1981. When a president makes speeches, the accuracy of numbers is often sent around to the departments for checking. In one of Ronald Reagan's most famous speeches, his address to the nation on February 5, 1981, he argued that "Prior to World War II, taxes were such that on the average we only had to work just a little over 1 month each year to pay our total federal, state, and local tax bill. Today we have to work 4 months to pay that bill." The actual figures were that total taxes as a percentage of GNP had approximately doubled, not quadrupled, during that period—from about 14 percent of GNP in 1937–1939 to a little less than 27 percent in 1978–1980 (see appendix table A.1).

When the White House speechwriters first sent this speech to OTA for checking, OTA kept responding that the numbers were wrong: taxes prior to World War II were much higher than the numbers used by the President. Every time this response was sent back, another request was sent over to check the same numbers. Apparently, the numbers were the president's own, and no one had the nerve to tell him they were wrong. Finally, one request was sent through the Office of Economic Policy, which proceeded to verify the correctness of the numbers. When I asked how they could possibly accept this deception, the response was the following: "Well, the president didn't exactly say how long before World War II!"

This lack of concern for whether the numbers added up correctly is more than of anecdotal interest. It was quickly to have an impact on future policy. It meant that a much needed part of any conservative revolution—the elimination of inefficient programs—did not appear to be needed to pay for other parts of revolution. It meant that truthful claims would become so jumbled with distortionary claims that important information would become lost. Until the problem could be overcome, the Executive Office would be unable to pull together the broad-ranging types of reforms that required consistent and unbiased analysis, estimation, and consideration of alternatives.

When information is misleading, logic almost inevitably implies that there will be contradictions. It didn't take long for some of these contradictions to appear, as the very next year Congress and the president would agree to pass a major bill that in many ways went directly against some of the presumed accomplishments of 1981.

Notes

1. The mathematics of the proposal were that rates would be reduced each year to 90 percent of their previous level. Hence, taxes would be reduced to $.9 \times .9 \times .9$, or 72.9 percent of their original level. The proposed reduction in taxes was actually 27.1 percent (100 percent minus 72.9 percent), not 30 percent.

2. In comparing notes as to why they favored reform, Senator Bradley (D-N.J.) stated, "Mr. President, you came to this [tax reform] because you were an actor who paid at the 90-percent rate; that's why you want a lower rate. . ." See Birnbaum and Murray (1987, p. 26).

3. In the Treasury Department, the Office of Tax Analysis forms the economic arm

of the Office of Tax Policy, which is in charge of the administration's tax policy efforts. The Office of Tax Analysis makes the estimates of the receipts of the U.S. government and of the revenue costs of tax proposals, and prepares tax studies for both Republican and Democratic administrations, develops the models and data files by which to examine the impact of tax changes, and performs economic analyses of proposals. The Office's insistence that the integrity of the cost estimation function be maintained was often misunderstood by those who wanted it to show low costs for favored proposals.

4. Shelters would be encouraged further by the maintenance of higher tax rates, which increase the value of the deductions.

5. The net reduction in tax is actually about 23 percent rather than 25 percent. Taxpayers' liabilities were reduced, first to 95 percent of their original level, then to 90 percent of the new level, then to 90 percent of the previous level. Thus, excluding other economic changes such as inflation, their taxpayers' burdens ended up at 77 percent of their original level.

6. These calculations do not even include the additional $10 billion in tax reduction that would have taken place with indexing for real growth over and above inflation.

7. I performed these runs to simulate the effect of inflation on tax increases faced by individuals. Essentially, statements of income and expense were increased in line with inflation, and then changes in taxes over income were calculated.

8. Inflation can raise the average tax rate by pushing a larger share of income into the higher tax rate brackets.

9. See Steuerle (1985b, p. 104). The calculation assumes that tax preferences (credits and accelerated depreciation) are designed to provide a tax break that is available regardless of actual inflation, interest rates, and return from the asset. Tax preferences here are assumed to offset a tax rate of 46 percent (the corporate rate in 1981) times a 6 percent real rate of return, or 2.8 percent. Then the taxpayer can make a net profit if the real rate of return from the asset (in the example, a negative 9 percent) and the after-tax interest payments (14 percent × [1 − .46]) are offset by the tax preferences, plus the additional tax write-off on the real losses (.46 times the negative 9 percent), plus the inflationary increase in value of the asset.

10. If the government wants to provide incentives for certain equipment purchases, a strong economic argument can be made to apply that incentive equally to corporations with and without tax liability. Nonetheless, the appearance of corporations buying and selling tax liabilities called into question the fairness of the underlying tax structure.

11. Technical review will always be performed, but it almost never results in change of any significance. Indeed, the change is as likely to go in one direction as the other.

12. A secondary debate was whether the Treasury's Office of Tax Analysis adequately took into account so-called "feedback" effects from growth in the economy that derived from tax reductions. As it turns out, OTA did nothing more than prevent double counting and force the presentation of consistent numbers. The "Troika" had to make projections of phenomenal economic growth under the president's plan in order to show small deficits in future budgets. The feedback effect, therefore, was already in the numbers by being built into the economic assumptions. By assuming that growth would be 4 percent per year with enactment of the president's program, rather than, say, 3 percent, additional receipts of tens of billions of dollars for the government were projected.

Misleading attacks on OTA were to last throughout the 1980s and were printed repeatedly in such places as the editorial pages of *The Wall Street Journal.* One attack associated OTA and CBO with the Kremlin.

The strange irony was that OTA never had control of these "feedback" effects, whereby lower taxes led to economic growth which, in turn, led to higher tax collections. It merely had control of the machinery to make revenue estimates consistent with assumptions on the state of the economy. Supply-siders and others who wanted to show feedback effects simply needed to present to the public two sets of economic assumptions—one with the policy they favored and one without. Revenue, as well as expenditure effects, would have followed.

Chapter Four

THE PRELUDE TO REFORM: 1982–84

The Reagan administration had put a great deal of effort behind its 1981 proposals, and it claimed that it had achieved significant legislative success. The core of its success, however, was in reducing tax rates, extending depreciation allowances, and increasing defense expenditures. Despite the rhetoric on both sides of the aisle, neither the Congress nor the administration succeeded in reducing other expenditures more than modestly, and even here much of the reduction was in subsidies provided to state and local governments. Moreover, the bidding war on the tax bill had added to costs. At the end of the process, almost everyone knew that in budget terms the numbers simply didn't add up.

Almost everyone. David Stockman writes that "After November, 1981, the administration locked the door on its disastrous fiscal policy jail cell and threw away the key. The President would not let go of his tax cut. Cap Weinberger hung on for dear life to the $1.46 trillion defense budget . . . Deaver, Meese, and the others ceaselessly endeavored to keep all the bad news out of the Oval Office and off the tube. The nation's huge fiscal imbalance was never addressed or corrected; it just festered and grew" (Stockman 1986, p. 13).

"By 1982," Stockman continues, "I knew that the Reagan Revolution was impossible," and began working on "reducing the size of the national's fiscal disaster."

The 1981 proposals of the new administration, especially with respect to tax policy, had come mainly out of campaign promises. With the exception of Stockman's temporary but soon disillusioned belief that he had figured out a way to use budget machinery to restrict expenditure growth, no major initiative had been developed within the executive branch itself. Little effort had been made to study the details of programs and how programs could be made more efficient, fairer, or simply better run. Recall on the tax side of the budget that the proposals were so simple that they could be identified with simple numbers such as 5-10-10, the percentage cut in individual tax rates, or 10-5-3, the new lives into which almost all depreciable assets would fall.

The next three years were to witness a significant change both in the direction of tax policy and in the source of new initiatives. Once again, tax policy would dominate the agenda, but in an unexpected way: the enactment of a major tax increase in each of the three years. Legislative peacetime income tax increases, however, were almost unknown after World War II.[1] Leadership for the details of initiatives was seldom to be provided by the president and the White House. Real responsibility was to rest with the Republican Senate and with a commission designed to deal with the possibility that the Social Security program might have insufficient funds to meet its obligations. Within the administration, political forces were split: some proclaiming the need for further tax cuts, and others working to try to reduce the deficit. The administration would waffle in its role. It did not want to take responsibility for any tax increases, but some of its members wanted deficit reduction that might include some tax increase. The president's public position was that he opposed all taxes, but he eventually accepted many increases. In this situation, the visible leadership role was often left to others.

THE TAX INCREASES BEGIN: 1982

Less than two months after the victories of 1981 were still being celebrated, work was already underway on reducing the looming federal deficit. In mid-year of 1981, as had become the annual custom, both the administration and the Congressional Budget Office (CBO) made new estimates of the budget situation through a "midsession" review of the budget. This meant that by late-summer to early-fall of 1981, the deficit debate would be renewed. On September 10, 1981, the CBO testified before Congress that $80 billion deficits loomed for 1982 and that expenditure cuts of $100 billion would be needed if the budget were to be balanced by 1984 (Berry and Dewar 1981). Although the CBO's economic assumptions also quickly turned out to be quite rosy, both Congress and the administration began to admit that the budget situation was in need of correction even before a recession hit in late 1981.

On September 24, 1981, the administration came out with a fall

initiative that would cut the deficit further, mainly through a reduction in entitlements, across-the board cuts, "future saving to be
identified," and even some paring of defense appropriations. Measures also included about $22 billion in tax increases over a period
of slightly more than two years. The proposals were never called
"tax increases," but rather "revisions in the tax code to curtail certain
tax abuses and enhance tax revenues" (The White House 1981). Senate Republicans, in particular, Senator Pete V. Domenici (R-N.M.)
and the Senate Budget Committee, also began their own efforts at
deficit reduction and prepared legislation that called for a $60 to $80
billion tax increase over the following three years, along with a number of other expenditure reductions (Edsall 1981).[2]

These 1981 efforts stalled mainly over disputes as to the amount
of tax increase that might be allowed. At one point, the president
declared that he had "no plans for increasing taxes in any way,"
only to be contradicted by his press spokesman, who indicated that
the president still planned to ask Congress for $22 billion of tax
increases first proposed in September (Bacon 1981).

By the beginning of 1982, the administration moved even further
toward proposing some amount of tax increase. The president's budget document itself was to contain proposals—many of which were
first revealed in the fall of 1981—that would increase tax revenues
by over $20 billion per year, or more than half of 1 percent of GNP.
These proposals included improved tax enforcement and revisions
that centered on the taxation of business income. In the latter category were such items as a minimum tax for corporations and dis-
allowance of certain deductions taken before contracts were completed
and payments were made to the contractor. Almost all of the proposals were revenue-raising rather than revenue-losing.

The Initiative Switches to Congress

There was no strong presidential push behind these proposals, and
they were not given much attention by the public or the press. Nonetheless, they signaled some willingness within the administration to
worry about the upcoming deficits. To Congress, therefore, fell the
task of taking up the gauntlet to try to reduce the deficit. In particular,
Senator Robert Dole, then chairman of the Senate Finance Committee, began the arduous task of grafting together a package of proposals
that he could get through the Senate. He was supported with technical assistance by the increasingly important congressional staff of
the Senate Finance Committee and the Joint Committee on Taxation

and, within the administration, by the Office of Management and Budget and the Office of Tax Policy within the Treasury Department. Thus was born the Tax Equity and Fiscal Responsibility Act of 1982 (TEFRA).

The design of TEFRA began with some of the proposals in the president's budget. But then it went much further. Compliance and collection procedures were given special prominence through expanded information reporting and increased penalties. For instance, only 60 percent of reportable capital gains were estimated to be actually reported on individual income tax returns. Taxpayers were either negligent or noncompliant on the rest. TEFRA gave Treasury permission to require brokers to report the gross receipts of customers from the sales of capital assets. Withholding of taxes on interest and dividends was also enacted, but later retracted. Life insurance company taxation was partially reformed. Excise taxes and employment taxes for unemployment insurance were increased. Other reforms were also enacted in such areas as leasing and Medicare coverage of federal employees.

The Beginning of a Reversal of Actions Taken in 1981

TEFRA also began the process of reversing some of the actions taken in 1981. While the 1981 Tax Act had allowed higher income individuals greater opportunity to take deductions for deposits to individual retirement accounts, TEFRA was to place restrictions on the benefits available to high-income individuals from other pension plans. The 1982 Act also reduced, rather than increased, the tax benefits from investment. First, the value of investment tax credits was reduced slightly.[3] Second, recall that the very generous depreciation allowances granted in 1981, when combined with the investment tax credit, often provided the equivalent of negative tax rates on the returns from assets. Slipped into the 1981 agreement were further, very expensive accelerations of depreciation allowances that were to have begun in 1985 and 1986. These accelerations, whose costs would have risen to over $18 billion by 1987, were repealed.[4]

Another slight reversal from the rhetoric of 1981 was to take place in the Highway Revenue Act of 1982. Through an increase in excise taxes on gasoline, the Department of Transportation was able to obtain funding for further work on the nation's highway and transit systems. President Reagan had at first opposed any mention of a tax increase (Stockman 1986, p. 139), but later was to allow that some increases in taxes (highway taxes that might also be considered user fees), as well as government expenditures, could be enacted. The reality of running government programs impinged itself once again upon the tax policy process.

A Focus on Revenues

Political overstatements in 1981 led to an assumption by many that domestic spending had been drastically reduced. While growth rates had been reduced in some expenditure programs, others were still growing rapidly. In 1982, this misguided perception—propounded by Democrats and Republicans alike—actually weakened the administration's ability both to reduce expenditures and raise taxes to pare the budget deficit. TEFRA 1982 turned out to be only the first of many bills in the 1980s that would achieve deficit reduction by increasing taxes more than reducing or reforming expenditures. In part this was due to the nature of the budget process. The tax changes were often permanent in nature, whereas expenditure cuts frequently involved nothing more than promises in future years to cut back on programs. In addition, many expenditure programs were still "off the table"—defense because of the president's desire to increase expenditures, and entitlements such as Social Security, where spending was often set by formulas that required no voting for appropriations from year to year.

Perhaps the most important reversal was in the president himself. Earlier in 1981 President Reagan had reacted strongly against the attempt of David Stockman to try to cut back on expenditures hidden in the tax code, attacking the whole notion of tax expenditures as a "liberal myth" (Stockman 1986, p. 131) and failing to recognize that cutbacks in tax expenditures often served exactly the same conservative purpose as cutbacks in direct expenditures. In signing the 1982 bill, the president had begun the first of many acceptances of efforts to "enhance revenues," eliminate "tax loopholes" and "unintended benefits," favor "compliance measures," and "curtail tax abuse."

SOCIAL SECURITY REFORM: 1983

The year 1983 was the year of Social Security reform. From the beginning, many in the Reagan administration viewed Social Security as a portion of the budget in need of paring. Disability payments were considered too high by some, spouses' and students' benefits were thought unnecessary by others, and early retirement was viewed by others as an option that should be curtailed. However, early attempts in 1981 to try to cut back on benefits created a storm of controversy and failed miserably (Stockman 1986, pp. 181–193). Part of this failure was predictable. Prior to his election, President Reagan had spoken out so strongly against Social Security that he was distrusted by many. On the opposite side were strong constituencies who considered the benefits of the program almost sacred. Politically it was said that programs for the elderly were untouchable.

Part of the failure, however, was again due to bad planning and organization. During 1981 the administration held some internal meetings on Social Security reform with some political officials from the White House, the Department of Health and Human Services, and the Social Security Administration.[5] In attendance were many new political appointees with strong but sometimes unchecked views on what was wrong with the system. The newcomers were so distrustful of the entire civil service that they prevented many of the most talented individuals in the executive branch, including top analysts from the Social Security Administration, from attending these meetings. Valuable information was thereby precluded through inadequate use of staff. The controversy that eventually surrounded the proposals that were tentatively released, therefore, was due not simply to the difficulty and sacredness of the Social Security issue; it was also due to bad planning and the forwarding of some poorly designed proposals.

The Social Security issue, however, could be forgotten neither by the administration nor its opponents. Increasingly, projections began to show that Social Security likely would not have enough funds to pay out benefits during the mid-1980s. In the September 1981 fall budget program noted earlier, the president proposed the establishment of a bipartisan task force that would develop a "permanent solution to the problems facing the Social Security system" by January 1983. This political solution was accepted and a bipartisan commission, headed by Alan Greenspan, was created. Once again, responsibility for studying the problem fell outside of the executive branch.

What forced both the administration and Congress to accept some solution was the threat that if something were not done, benefit checks would not be paid in the very near future. For the most part, therefore, the recommendations of this commission were accepted by both political parties. The net effect of the bill that was enacted was substantial (and, at its peak, would increase Social Security revenues over expenditures by $31.0 billion in fiscal year 1989).[6] One of the principal changes for the short run was to accelerate tax rate increases already scheduled for 1990 into earlier years of the 1980s. In effect, there was no permanent increase in tax rates in the 1983 legislation. Employer and employee Social Security tax rates for 1990 and beyond were to end up at the same level as had been scheduled under the 1977 Carter administration reforms.

The Social Security Amendments of 1983 achieved a fair degree of other reform. First, new federal civilian employees and employees of non-profit organizations were required to join the Social Security system and be given the same tax treatment as extended to most other employees. Second, tax rates for self-employed individuals were revised so that they paid approximately the same total tax rate as applied to employees. Perhaps the most important tax reform was that Social Security benefits, which formerly had been exempt from taxation, became partially taxable for higher income beneficiaries. By the 1990s, these other tax changes were to result in an increase in revenues of almost $24 billion on an annual basis, or close to half of 1 percent of GNP.[7]

President Reagan was converted to reform of Social Security taxation on the basis of a tax expenditure argument. Rather than view the taxation of benefits as an increase in taxes on Social Security beneficiaries, he became persuaded that it was a reduction in net benefits, or net expenditures, under Social Security.

Because of the Social Security Amendments of 1983 and the 1977 Social Security Amendments, the 1980s were to witness significant Social Security tax increases. Between 1980 and 1990, the combined employer-employee tax rate by itself was to increase from 12.26 to 15.3 percent of wages. This increase by itself would eventually raise revenues by more than $70 billion on an annual basis for 1990 and beyond, and would represent the dominant tax increase of the tax decade. When the other tax amendments of 1983 are added in, Social Security taxes were increased by over $85 billion per year. Of course, this was not a new trend. The 1980s were almost identical to the four decades before—witnessing an increase in tax rates of about 3 percentage points, as well as other structural reforms to make the system solvent.

The 1983 Social Security Amendments repeated the pattern of 1982 in relying more upon tax increases than expenditure decreases to achieve deficit reduction. Expenditure reductions, in fact, were confined almost entirely to a six-month delay in benefit increases, and the eventual increase in the normal retirement age to age 67, to be phased in gradually between 2000 and 2022. This last adjustment had been long expected, but was still far less than adequate to compensate for the increase in costs that had been imposed over time due to the increased lifespan of individuals. Over the period 1983 to 1989, tax increases were to provide almost three-fourths, or $110.5 billion of the $148.5 billion of changes in Social Security receipts and payments (see table 4.1). Over the long term, the tax increases were to provide almost 62 percent of the total reduction in the Social Security deficit.

MORE TAX INCREASES AND DEFICIT REDUCTION: 1984

At the beginning of 1984, the administration's budget submission again included net tax increases. One novelty in the submission for the next fiscal year, 1985, was the proposed capping of tax benefits for employer-provided health benefits—a reform not only of tax policy, but of health policy. The president, who in earlier years had rejected a similar proposal because he viewed it as a tax increase, was now persuaded that it was not fair that a wage earner with cash wages should pay substantially higher taxes than one with income in the form of fringe benefits such as health insurance. Note again the president's conversion to standard tax policy principles and traditional tax expenditure analysis.

A modest attack on tax shelters was also to make its way onto the agenda, with such lead-ins as "The administration proposes a number of changes that will curtail transactions that generate unintended tax benefits or form the basis for tax shelter schemes" (OMB 1984, pp. 4–10). Thus, while increasing taxes might not be acceptable, it was allowable to eliminate "unintended tax benefits" and "tax shelters"— the absence of which had the effect of increasing tax revenues. While the 1984 proposals only contemplated a moderate counterattack, it was becoming clearer that tax shelters had grown to such a point that no one of any political philosophy could ignore them entirely.

Structural tax reform of a detailed nature also made its appearance, particularly in the effort to change the way in which the income of life insurance companies would be measured and taxed. This turned out to be only one of many efforts in the 1980s to reform the taxation

Table 4.1 ESTIMATED CHANGES IN SOCIAL SECURITY* RECEIPTS AND BENEFIT PAYMENTS RESULTING FROM THE 1983 SOCIAL SECURITY AMENDMENTS

	Total 1983–89 ($ billions)	Total long-range cost effects (percentage of payroll)
TAX (AND COVERAGE) CHANGES**		
Accelerate tax rate increases on wages and salaries	39.4	.03
Increase tax rate on self-employed	18.5	.19
Cover new federal workers and all non-profit employees	21.8	.38
Prevent termination of state and local employees and accelerate collection of state and local taxes	4.2	.06
Tax up to half of benefits for high-income employees	26.6	.61
Subtotal for tax changes	110.5	1.27
BENEFIT CHANGES		
Raise normal retirement age to age 67	—	.71
Delay benefit increases by 6 months	39.4	.30
Other benefit changes	− 1.4	− .22
Subtotal for benefit changes ...	38.0	0.79
TOTAL***	148.5	2.06

Source: Committee on Ways and Means (1990a, pp. 28–29).
*Social Security here includes Old Age and Survivors Insurance (OASI) and Disability Insurance.
**Coverage changes primarily raise tax collections, although there are also some benefit increases.
***Excludes changes in general fund transfers for military service credit and reimbursement from general fund for unnegotiated checks [total = $17.7 billion for 1983–1989 and .03 percent of payroll for long-range costs].

of financial institutions. By this time, too, the growth in the use of tax-exempt bonds for private purposes was so great that curtailment was inevitable. The administration again made some modest proposals with respect to tax-exempt leasing and restrictions on the extent to which state and local governments could float nontaxable bonds to finance private industrial development.

Reality of Budget Deficit Sets In

The proposals for tax increases were made necessary by the reality of the budget. Any administration must present budgetary figures that show the deficit coming under control. By the beginning of 1984, of course, not only had many of the costs of the 1981 Tax Act been incurred, as projected, but the deficit had been increased significantly by the shortfall in revenues created by the recession of 1981–1982. In addition, partly due to the efforts of Martin Feldstein, then Chairman of the Council of Economic Advisers, the "Troika" had decided to use realistic economic assumptions and to abandon the "rosy scenarios." Chairman Feldstein also succeeded in getting the administration to propose a "Contingency Tax Plan" that would involve a surcharge in case the budget deficit exceeded 2.5 percent of GNP.

Despite these budgetary pressures, the administration chose not to exercise a principal leadership role in 1984. The president gave little public support to these tax proposals, especially the contingency tax plan. Excluding that plan, the other proposals would increase net revenue by only a few billion dollars or a tiny portion of the budget deficit, and even those gains would be offset by proposals for tuition tax credits and tax breaks for businesses set up in low-income areas designated as "enterprise zones." Most of the administration's efforts were directed at taking tax reform proposals out of the presidential campaign. This move was supported by President Reagan's request at the beginning of 1984 that Treasury perform a tax reform study that would be delivered after the election. In spite of this lukewarm environment, Congress was again to take the initiative in tax legislation.

Take the initiative, indeed! Led by Senator Robert Dole of the Senate Finance Committee, Congress eventually was to put forward a myriad of tax changes under the Deficit Reduction Act of 1984 (DEFRA). Following in part the format of TEFRA 1982, efforts were made to improve tax compliance by extending information reporting to items such as state and local tax refunds. Excise taxes on distilled spirits and other items were increased, a number of corporate transactions and sales of assets were made taxable, contributions and benefits under pension plans were further limited, and tax-exempt leasing was restricted. The aggregate volume of certain private activity bonds sold by state and local governments (e.g., certain industrial development and student loan bonds) were capped or limited.

Various tax shelters again came under attack. So-called "tax straddles," for instance, had become too popular for the legislature to ignore anymore. A person could essentially buy and sell rights to future commodities in a way that created equal gains and losses— like flipping a coin and betting on both heads and tails. The taxpayer would then take losses on whichever "leg" of the straddle generated a loss, use that loss to offset other capital gains that otherwise would be taxable, and then defer recognition of the "leg" with a gain to future years. DEFRA 1984 also attempted to place some control on the growing market for "abusive" or fictitious shelters that existed on paper but often had no real investment associated with them.

Further cutbacks were made on the changes enacted in 1981. Depreciation lives were extended for real property. The 1981 Tax Act had also provided that, beginning in 1985, there was to be an exclusion from taxation of a certain portion of interest income up to $6,000 for married couples. This was repealed before it was implemented.

A cutback on the benefits of income averaging was to raise several billion dollars per year.[8] So-called "accounting changes" also began to get much more attention. These changes, falling under technical headings such as "premature accruals," "deferred payments for use of property and services," and "capitalization of construction period interest and taxes," usually dealt with inconsistent accounting practices whereby deductions were being taken while income (or increases in asset value) was not being currently taxed.

By fiscal year 1990, DEFRA was to raise $31 billion on an annual basis. While the revenue pick-up was not quite as large as that created by TEFRA 1982, in many ways DEFRA went beyond the earlier act by relying more upon reform of the tax base and less upon changes in tax compliance or simple elimination of provisions enacted in 1981 for implementation at a later date. Like the 1982 and 1983 bills, however, the emphasis was more on taxes than on expenditures. Tax expenditures remained easier to reform than many types of direct expenditures.

LESSONS FROM THE PERIOD

As a whole, the period 1982 to 1984 represented an historical turnaround in postwar tax policy. All in all, the various tax acts passed in this period were to raise over $108 billion on an annual basis— or over 2 percent of GNP—by fiscal year 1990. Other than excise taxes, very few changes involved increases in tax rates themselves.

Most involved improvements in tax compliance, expansion of the tax base, and retrenchment on the provisions of 1981.

Even with all these changes, however, the nation's fiscal house remained in disorder. The calendar year 1984 witnessed the continuation of the defense build ups and was the first full year during which the 1981 individual tax cuts were implemented. The projected economic growth rates from 1981, however, had never materialized, and the nation was only in the second year of a recovery from a deep recession. Not only were deficits quite large by this time, but many of the 1982 and 1984 reforms were inadequate for dealing with the problems they purportedly addressed. Thus, while some tax rates on returns from some investments had been prevented from going more negative, many remained negative. Private-purpose tax-exempt bonds continued to grow, and the tax shelter market flourished. The growth rate in learning how to manipulate the tax code was much higher than the government's reaction rate to these legal attacks on the nation's fiscal house. Tax shelters, tax-exempt bonds, and tax straddles were only the leading edge of a continually growing problem.

Yet the handwriting was clearly on the wall for those who wanted to see it. Although the rhetoric in 1984 was largely the same as in 1980 and 1981, in practice the world had changed. Revenue increases on the order of 1982–1984 had never before been passed in absence of war or major crisis. In many respects, the events of 1982–1984 demonstrated that 1981 represented less of a beginning of a new period than the ending of an old one. The 1981 tax cuts brought down the final curtain on a long-running play. The Economic Recovery Tax Act of 1981 was the last of the major postwar tax bills that involved tax cuts, and were passed under the supposition that the future would eventually take care of the cost. The years 1982 to 1984, therefore, presaged the dawn of a different era of financing.

The turn-around of the president was also important. While not leading the charge, even President Reagan seemed to have become converted between 1982 and 1984 to accepting attacks on various loopholes and tax expenditures hidden in the tax code. Certainly, he found such attacks preferable to increasing tax rates or repealing the indexing for inflation (a back door way of increasing rates). Then again, why shouldn't he? Recall that tax reform is as much a conservative notion as a progressive one. Without necessarily comprehending why, the administration and the Congress were having more success in reducing expenditures hidden in the tax code than in reducing direct expenditures.

The 1982–1984 period had also witnessed a passing of responsibilities. After 1981, the White House would take less of a role in designing major legislation and selling it to the public. Between 1982 and 1984, the leadership was mainly provided by other actors within the Congress and a bipartisan commission. Of course, none of these bills could have been enacted without the president's tacit support or willingness to let the responsibilities be delegated.

A Vacuum?

Leadership on taxes had moved from the White House to other parts of the government, but in the process the momentum for reforming programs had been lost. By 1984 there was a vacuum to be filled. Even the 1984 campaign stressed little more than a defense of what had taken place in 1981. The administration essentially had no major domestic agenda.

Stuart Spencer, a California political consultant who attended a meeting of key political strategists mapping Ronald Reagan's second campaign, was later recorded as saying, "The problem is we've been talking to everybody at the White House over the past few days— and the Reagan Administration fired all its bullets very early and very successfully in the first two years. All their plans, all their priorities, all their programs. The most striking thing I discovered is that they don't have a goddam thing in the pipeline. They don't have an idea" (Mayer and McManus 1988).

Notes

1. In 1985, John Witte noted that, up until the early 1980s, "The only legislated peacetime tax increases in U.S. history have been the Revenue Act of 1932, a slight one-year increase later in the 1930s, and a relatively modest and mostly administrative increase in 1982" (Witte 1985, p. 249).

2. See, also, Dale Tate, "Dispute Over Tax Increases Stalls Action on 1982 Budget," *Congressional Quarterly*, November 7, 1981, p. 2164.

3. The amount of expenditure to be depreciated was adjusted partially for the size of the investment credit. If a taxpayer spent $100 on an asset and received a $10 credit, a new basic adjustment only allowed depreciation on $95 of the asset's value.

4. See Joint Committee on Taxation (1982). For discussion of change in the ACRS system of depreciation, see pp. 39–40.

5. I represented the Treasury Department at some of these meetings.

6. See OMB (1988, p. 4–4).

7. *Ibid.*

8. This cutback demonstrated for me the haphazard way in which research could have an impact on policy. See Steuerle, McHugh, and Sunley (1978). This article, when first published, was almost ignored. Later it was presented by Peter Davis, an economist who worked with both the Joint Committee on Taxation and the Senate Budget Committee, to Senator Dole's staff in its search for revenue-raising ideas.

Chapter Five

A NEW ERA OF DECISION MAKING

Even while Congress was debating whether to pass the 1984 Deficit Reduction Act, work was proceeding slowly on what was to become the Tax Reform Act of 1986. The goal was actual reform of the tax system, not deficit reduction through tax increase, as in 1982 and 1984. Yet, the 1986 Tax Reform Act was more kindred to those of 1982 and 1984 than to those of the earlier postwar period, when practically all tax bills and tax reform proposals had involved significant losses of revenues.

For some, the turnaround after 1981, including the movement away from revenue-losing bills, is easy to explain. President Reagan increased deficits significantly early in 1981, and those large deficits caused a stalemate in policy. The implied conclusion is that once these deficits are reduced, the United States will return to the type of policymaking that prevailed in the 1960s and 1970s. This view is fundamentally wrong, as I will demonstrate in this chapter. It is now important to pause in our chronological tale to see why the nation was moving to a new era of decision making and how the arithmetic miscalculations of 1981 only speeded up the process. The new era was already making its presence felt by the late 1970s and would have appeared no matter who was elected president.

THE SEARCH FOR NEW SOURCES OF FINANCING

Despite the magnitude and intensity of tax negotiations in the 1980s, the decade often saw overall federal policy dominated by stalemate. Fairly limited choices were made as to how the government might reorient its efforts toward the most pressing of current needs. This stalemate was reflected in an inability to adequately bring down the size of the deficit, tremendous difficulty in passing expenditure legislation to deal with the problems of the day, and severe revenue constraints on all tax and expenditure bills. This period of government muddling, and how the 1986 tax reform and 1990 budget reform were able to break temporarily through the stalemate, cannot be understood without a broader historical perspective as to the events that led there.

There is a balance sheet requirement imposed on tax and expenditure decisions. An expansion of an expenditure program typically implies 1) higher taxes or 2) reductions in other expenditure programs. Deficits can be increased temporarily, but then interest costs of the government rise. These payments of interest or debt retirement, too, must also be financed through higher taxes or reduced expenditures down the road. No amount of political maneuvering can avoid this basic accounting identity—although a carefully designed program might improve economic performance along the way and make the task less arduous. In many ways, the budgetary stalemates that stretched from the late 1970s through 1990 can best be explained in terms of these balance sheets. The old ways of achieving balance and adapting to the current needs of government were gone, while new ways could only be found with much struggle.

In the United States in the 1930s and 1940s, there was significant expansion of government expenditures, particularly on the defense build up for World War II. This expansion was initially paid for through sizable tax increases and sizable increases in the national debt.

After the war, focus shifted toward expansion of domestic programs. New means of financing these changing priorities were required, and the balances were provided in four principal ways. First, especially in the early postwar era, there was a large and unexpected decrease in the value of outstanding government debt due to rises in the rate of inflation. Interest rates were often low or negative in real terms. For instance, a 3 percent return on older obligations would continue to be paid even though inflation rates had risen to 4 percent or more. In effect, there was a large implicit tax on holders of old government bonds.

Second, there was a significant decline in the size of the defense budget relative to GNP, with exceptions for the Korean and Vietnam Wars and for the slight build up in the 1980s. If one draws a trend line through the cycles, however, the decline in defense stands out clearly as a major source of funds for growth in outlays for domestic programs.

The third and fourth ways of providing balance were through significant tax increases. Both were noted in chapter 2. Bracket creep in the individual income tax raised individual tax rates, while continual and little-debated increases in Social Security tax rates were often enacted either to pay for expanded benefits or, as in 1977 and 1983, because of a requirement to keep the trust funds solvent.

Until the 1980s, these four sources of funds did not simply pay for expansions in domestic expenditures. They also paid for a variety of changes in tax policy. Parallel with debates on expansion of expenditures on Medicare, Social Security, federal aid to education, welfare relief, and so forth, were debates on tax reductions. Accompanying each tax reduction was also a series of tax provisions or preferences designed to provide new sources of subsidy or expenditure through the tax code. Of course, while a tax bill might temporarily reduce revenues, over a several-year period the loss was paid for by bracket creep and Social Security tax increases. Within a few years after a tax cut, revenues would be as high as ever.

The Demise of the Easy Financing Period

As the nation approached the late 1970s and early 1980s, all of these sources of financing for expenditure or tax changes were reduced in importance or eliminated. First, the stock of debt relative to GNP had already declined significantly, making the impact of inflation on that stock less important relative to the economy. Additionally, modest increases in the inflation rate—and the accompanying inflation tax they involved—had been abandoned by the late 1970s as useful tools of fiscal or monetary policy. Interest rates rose to well in excess of the rate of inflation.

Second, defense expenditures declined in importance relative to GNP, making declines in defense a less important source of revenue for domestic expenditures. By the late 1970s, President Carter was proposing increases, not declines, in the defense budget's share of national output.

Third, bracket creep in the individual income tax was reduced greatly through indexation for inflation, passed in 1981 for implementation after 1984. The eventual enactment of indexation had become almost inevitable by the late-1970s.

Fourth, the five-decade expansion of Social Security tax rates was drawing to a close. The 1980s were to see the last of the regular 3-percentage-points-per-decade increase in Social Security tax rates. For the first time in the lives of most Americans, no such increase

would be scheduled for the 1990s. By the late 1980s, in fact, the Social Security debate had been turned on its head, and Social Security tax reductions, not increases, were being discussed seriously for the first time since the early years of the program.

This story, of course, is simplified. While past multi-decade trends were clearly waning in importance, there still can and will be cycles during which old sources of funds become temporarily available. The growth in the stock of debt in the 1980s, for instance, offers the temptation in the 1990s to reduce the real stock through inflation. After the defense build up of the early- to mid-1980s, the late 1980s and early 1990s have involved a decline in defense spending relative to GNP. Some might also argue that the retirement of the baby boom generation should be paid for through another Social Security tax increase. And, of course, policymakers might try to raise tax rates by paring back the indexation of income tax brackets. Regardless of possible cyclical changes, however, these sources of revenue are no longer almost automatic nor, more importantly, are they likely to be as large relative to the economy.

The elimination of all four of these sources profoundly affected the political process under which tax and expenditure policy proceeded. The bottom line was this: changes in priorities had always required trade-offs, but past sources of funds to pay for new priorities were increasingly unavailable. The nation was at the end of the "Easy Financing Period" of the postwar era.

This new world was starting to become apparent in the late 1970s. The declines in the value of debt relative to GNP were beginning to end, and increases rather than decreases in defense expenditures relative to GNP received bipartisan support. Social Security reform still meant tax rate increases in the 1977 agreement, but one could see that even those increases were soon going to bump up against limits. Even the 1983 Social Security agreement did not increase tax rates in the long run, but instead turned to other tax changes and raised the retirement age after the turn of the century. Quite significant bracket creep was allowed to take place at the end of the 1970s, but here too a taxpayer revolt indicated that the situation could not continue indefinitely.

Policymaking institutions within the executive branch and Congress were not yet ready for the changes about to be forced upon them. When President Carter asked the Department of Health and Human Services for a deficit-neutral welfare reform bill, for instance, he was rebuffed both by Congress and his own appointees, who argued that reform had to involve significant increases in outlays and in the deficit.

In the 1980s, President Reagan supported a new set of priorities: to reduce taxes and to increase defense expenditures. One can agree or disagree with those priorities, but some shifting of demands by voters or their representatives was almost inevitable with the election of a new president. Congress, of course, balked at paying for new priorities by reducing other expenditures, while President Reagan balked at increasing taxes since one of his priorities was lower taxes. With the adoption of indexing of tax brackets in 1981 (effective beginning in 1984), and with the last Social Security tax rate increase scheduled for 1990, however, no one could rely upon the old sources of funds to pay for the new changes in priorities either immediately or even down the road.

The implications were felt in legislation enacted throughout the 1980s. As will be seen, tax reform would have failed right from the start if it had tried to rely upon the old (tried but untrue) method of paying for reform through a revenue-losing bill. Every tax rate reduction or increase in personal exemption had to be paid for through a reduction or elimination of some special preference or deduction.

Legislated Elimination of Fiscal Slack

During the early postwar era, the availability of different sources of funds insured that, whatever the current deficit, within a few years there would be an excess of receipts over expenditures if current law was maintained. As long as this fiscal slack was available, it was possible to enact legislation that appeared to have only winners—beneficiaries of added expenditures or reduced taxes. As we have seen, by the end of the "Easy Financing Period," the funds that created this slack were beginning to dry up. Even without this source of pressure, however, policymakers had become increasingly adept at enacting legislation that allowed programs to grow without any current legislation and at eating up any possible future fiscal slack long before it became available.

Expansion by formula was sometimes a key.[1] Formulas were set so that benefits would rise over time even in absence of any legislation. A related phenomenon was the growth of "entitlement" programs that could be cut only through explicit legislation, as opposed to discretionary programs that require explicit annual appropriations to be funded. Entitlements supposedly derived from a "social contract" to pay future benefits on the basis of a formula fixed in the past. Allen Schick (1990, pp. 123–126) similarly points to "sticky expenditures"—entitlements, obligated bonds, long-term commitments—that respond only weakly to contraction policies. A number of programs were also designed with different types of "open" commitments: an absence of legislated limits on what would qualify for the particular government expenditure or subsidy. For instance, many governmental loan programs were designed with few or no limits on how much agencies could borrow, while Medicare and Medicaid continually accept a variety of new medical procedures that are supported because of the open nature of what qualifies as medical care.

Actually, none of these terms—entitlement, sticky expenditure, open commitment—is sufficient to define all the ways that programs could be crafted to maintain built-in growth or contain future contraction. Defense agencies, for instance, sometimes attempted to spend more on equipment than manpower because they believed that the building of the equipment required a multi-year commitment toward spending in future years.

The games, moreover, were hardly confined to the direct expenditure side of the budget. Each of the methods of maintaining or increasing funding for direct expenditure programs had a parallel on the tax side. Many tax expenditures, for instance, might be labeled as tax entitlements rather than discretionary tax expenditures. Preferences, such as those provided to owner-occupied housing or to employer-provided health insurance, expanded along with growth in housing and health expenditures. Except for provisions that had to be extended every few years, the level of tax expenditure was almost never determined currently by policymakers. In a sense, the "appropriation" for 1985 or 1989 was set by legislation enacted as long ago as 1935 or 1954. Once an exclusion or deduction was granted for a given category of activity, its cost would often expand along with the level of that activity in the economy.

The movement toward three- and five-year budgeting actually helped formalize the ways in which Congress would appropriate away any future year's slack between revenues and expenditures. Under multi-year budgeting, it was true, programs could no longer be designed in ways that ignored costs beyond the first year. At the same time, multi-year budgeting gave members of Congress information on exactly how much spending might take place or how little revenues needed to be raised. Often Congress created negative fiscal slack after the window period strictures were removed. For instance, a tax expenditure might be limited for five years, then its cost be allowed to rise significantly. In fact, for a member or committee of Congress not to take advantage of possible spending on favored programs in the out years usually meant that some other member or committee spent it instead. In this manner, Congress continued to eliminate fiscal slack in future years and, by the same token, its own future ability to act.

THE POWER OF THE TAX-WRITING COMMITTEES

It might be expected that in this new era the tax-writing committees would wane in importance. After all, the easy sources of financing were gone, and the fun of enacting tax reduction bills was no longer available.

In fact, just the opposite occurred. We have already seen how the tax-writing committees proceeded almost without pause from the 1981 Tax Act to major tax increases in 1982 and 1984. In fact, *in every major budget, expenditure, and tax bill of the 1981–1990 period, the tax-writing committees turned out to be a major, and often the dominant, participant.*[2] A complaint voiced after the 1982 experience was that the tax increases were never balanced by promised reductions in expenditures. A similar complaint was later to be heard in a 1987 deficit-reducing package, when a member of the Ways and Means Committee argued that 80 percent of the deficit-reducing decisions were being made in that committee rather than in other committees in the House. (Dan Rostenkowski, the committee chairman, responded to that complaint with the quip, "You wouldn't have it any other way.")

Few seem to understand why so much policy—not just tax, but deficit reduction, labor, family, housing and other expenditure policy—falls within the bailiwick of the tax writers. Yet the lessons that can be learned are extraordinarily important. In fact, they tell us not only how tax reform could be made to succeed, but give us guidance as to how to structure future governmental efforts to reorient itself to the current needs of society.

The power of the tax-writing committees is related directly to the way they are organized. One source of power is obvious: they control the entire revenue side of the budget. In addition, about one-third of expenditures and subsidies fall into the tax code. Take an executive branch department such as Housing and Urban Development. Its housing budget is dwarfed in importance by the housing provisions in the tax code. Or compare the business provisions under the purview of the Department of Commerce with those business decisions affected by the tax code. And so on.

Maybe those expenditures ideally don't belong in the tax code. But look what they do to the decision-making process in government as a whole. Because so much falls under the purview of the tax-writing committees, members of these committees are forced to deal with the balance sheet aspect of almost everything they do. In effect, when they enact a credit for education or welfare, when they enact a tax break for pensions or some business interest, when they subsidize energy or transportation, they are eventually going to have to pay for these decisions. Every tax break has to be paid for by other changes somewhere in the tax system. In effect, these committees were organized in a way that made it possible to deal with the trade-offs required in the new era.

The tax-writing committees also have important jurisdiction over many direct spending programs, a consequence of their obtaining jurisdiction over the many insurance and welfare programs initially enacted in the Social Security Act of 1935.[3] The balance sheet requirements imposed on the tax writers in effect is extended far beyond the tax code. John Cogan (1988, p. 56) estimates that in 1982, the Ways and Means Committee controlled 36.7 percent of total outlays and the Senate Finance Committee 40.9 percent.

The only other congressional committees with a similarly large breadth of responsibility over direct spending are the appropriations and budget committees.[4] The outlay control of the appropriations committees, however, has to a certain degree been transferred to other committees.[5] Again, according to Cogan, by 1982 the appropriations committees controlled only 43.6 percent of total outlays, not much more than the tax-writing committees. The appropriations committees also have no control on the other half of the budget: the revenue side.

The budget committees have partly come in to replace that gap, but at a cost of further splitting power and, therefore, the ability to deliver packages. The budget committees, too, have to worry about how expenditures and taxes balance. To date, their influence has been wielded primarily through overall constraints on the size of the deficit, although they have always needed the support of both the House and Senate leadership, as well as that of other strong committee chairpersons. The budget committees also lacked the power and the oversight responsibility to change the details of programs sent to them by the expenditure committees. Moreover, the jurisdictional line between the budget committees and the appropriations committees remained fairly arbitrary.

The breadth of the budget and appropriations committees' responsibilities, therefore, was sometimes matched by a shallow depth. As a result, they remained much weaker than the tax-writing committees. Tax-writing committees could easily override (or, at least, pay for) the special interest provisions of any subcommittee. Both the budget and appropriations committees, however, had to constantly bargain with other expenditure committees over authorization of funds and the allocation of special interest provisions, and at times with the tax-writing committees over the provision of revenues.

Elaborate committee and power structures always stifle decision making. The tax-writing committees, despite many inefficiencies and an unwieldiness that would offend almost any private sector manager, were still much leaner and more efficient than the expenditure committees. This is one major reason that the former dominated congressional decision making, not just with respect to tax bills per se, but budget bills such as in 1982 and 1984 and, as will be seen, in later years as well. Try to make sweeping exchanges in expenditure programs, and no one member of Congress—not even the Majority leader of the Senate or the Speaker of the House—could deliver. Try the same within the tax-writing committees, and the chairmen, whether Republican or Democrat, could and often did deliver.

Therefore, after 1981, if there was to be another major successful initiative from the Reagan administration it is not surprising that it would once again involve taxation and go through the tax-writing committees. As will be seen, however, this also implied a number of restrictions. For instance, it was often impossible to make exchanges of tax programs for expenditure programs that would have involved other congressional committees. The relative power of the tax-writing committees helps explain not only how tax or tax expenditure reform was possible, but also why many related expenditure reforms and trade-offs could not be achieved.

PREVIOUS FISCAL AND TAX REFORM EFFORTS

In the new era, balance sheet requirements would be recognized explicitly, and power would move toward those parts of government with enough breadth of responsibility and depth of authority to be able to respond to the new challenge. In what may at first appear a contradiction, the difficulties of passing legislation in the new era and of paying directly for changes, in some ways actually enhanced the possibility of enacting tax reform. Why?

Tax reform was hardly a new idea. There had been a long history of failure in achieving tax reform. A Brookings Institution study published in the mid-1970s by two long-time advocates of tax reform had adopted the title *Federal Tax Reform: The Impossible Dream?* (Break and Pechman 1975). From 1982 onward, moreover, the country was in the middle of a budget crisis, old sources of funding to support shifts in priorities were drying up, and there was no money available to pay for reform.

Three decades of postwar experience had created the conventional wisdom that all reforms of expenditure programs or of the tax system didn't have to be financed, and that the public needed to be converted through additional give-aways. In particular, expenditure or tax bills would be passed in a way that implied that there were few or no "losers," that is, that no one paid for governmental action. What the conventional wisdom ignored, however, was that the availability of easy money was a major source of funds for deform, as well as reform. The spending of money to try to buy reform became confused with reform itself. Previous reform efforts, thus, actually floundered between the dual goals of tax reform and tax reduction. What typically happened was that the tax reduction goal quickly took precedence.

Consider the 1963 tax reform effort initiated by President Kennedy. Tax reform was only part of the initial package. This tax cut was to represent the great victory for applying Keynesian theory to a peacetime economy, with tax reduction proposed as a way to spur the economy. President Kennedy's 1963 tax message to Congress led off with appeals "to step up the growth and vigor of our national economy" and complaints that "our present income tax rate structure now holds back consumer demand." Only later did he note that "*in addition* [emphasis added], the present tax code contains special preferences and provisions, all of which narrow the tax base."[6]

Following the presidential proposal, much debate ensued over the demand-creating thesis. In the midst of this debate, the administration was eventually asked which it preferred: the tax reductions or the tax reform. The latter was said to be getting in the way of the former. The choice was made to abandon horizontal equity and efficiency goals to achieve what was believed to be a victory for Keynesian and macroeconomic theory—the deliberate use of tax cuts as a fiscal policy tool.

As an interesting irony, it might be noted that investment incentives were first enacted in 1962 as the initial stage of the attempt to spur the economy. At the time, macroeconomic objectives were given precedence over more narrow concepts of tax reform or ideal tax bases, and there was little notion that these investment incentives might come to be viewed as deform. (Of course, with active fiscal policy they could be easily eliminated once the economy expanded.) In the 1986 reform effort, one of the major reforms was the elimination of the investment credit first enacted in 1962.[7]

In 1978, the Carter administration was also to put forward a tax reform initiative that failed.[8] Again, much of its political effort was spent in providing for the more popular tax reduction part of the package. Congress again accepted the tax reduction, while performing little in the way of reform. In some cases, such as capital gains, it even increased the amount of exclusion provided under current law.

The extent of these previous reform efforts should not be exaggerated. President Kennedy's base-broadening and equity proposals could be summarized under only 9 headings on about 4 pages. Taking into account the new investment incentives, net base broadening was only to amount to $3.4 billion.[9] President Carter's 1978 proposals contained only $9 billion of "revenue-raising reforms," but $25 billion of net tax reduction.[10] In the latter case, this may be somewhat misleading. By the time the proposals came out, Congress had already convinced the White House to minimize its reform efforts.

It has been noted that the 1981 tax reductions were in many ways a parody, a carrying to an extreme, of these previous tax reform efforts, in particular, the Kennedy round of tax reduction. Investment incentives were not only going to be provided, they were going to drive many tax rates to zero or below. Accelerated depreciation would be so accelerated that the term "depreciation"— implying an actual measure of income loss due to change in value—would be dropped in favor of the term "cost recovery." Base broadening would be abandoned not just early on, but altogether.

Most of all, macroeconomic policy would not only be dominant, but one didn't even need to check down the road to see if the deficit increase was temporary or permanent. This was the biggest mistake of all. Whether or not the tax cut of the early 1960s represented good macroeconomic policy, the availability of future automatic sources of funds meant that there was no permanent increase in the deficit. The 1981 cut, on the other hand, was enacted in an era when automatic sources of funds would no longer be available in future years. Throughout much of the post-World War II era, the continual focus on macroeconomic issues actually made it easier for policymakers to avoid making hard choices and decisions. Macroeconomic fiscal policy almost always translated to tax reduction, regardless of whether the underlying apologetics were Keynesian or supply side in orientation. Other issues, particularly issues of fairness, efficiency, and administration, were disdained as institutional, structural, and micro issues not worthy of attention.[11] After all, it was argued, additional growth through the changing of one simple variable—the deficit in the early 1960s or tax rates in 1981— would swamp all these other mundane issues of efficient government. Tax reform would represent a fundamental departure from that earlier view, not so much by rejecting the importance of macroeconomic policy, but by refocusing attention on the basic purpose of government. After all, macroeconomic fiscal policy is a by-product of tax and expenditure policy, not the other way around.

Notes

1. Social Security presents a classic example. The benefits paid to each generation of workers were purposely designed to be increased over time by a formula that adjusted payments to growth in wages. Barring the complications of demographic cycles and changes in rates of inflation, wages usually grow as fast as the economy—thus, so do benefits. Through such devices, Social Security's level of existing benefits relative to the economy usually represented a minimum bound that would be made available in absence of legislation. New legislation could increase benefits as a share of national income, but decreasing those benefits was argued to go against a social contract by "cutting" (growing) benefits.

2. The dominance of the tax-writing committees was reflected in their ability to deliver a bill, not necessarily in their internal control over its contents. In 1981, for instance, the campaign proposals of Ronald Reagan comprised the principal components of the tax cut that was finally adopted—probably against the wishes of the average member of both tax-writing committees. Moreover, the chairpersons at that time were unable to stop the Christmas tree add-ons, reflecting some weakness on their part. In 1982, the Republican head of the Senate Finance Committee had greater ability than the Democratic head of the Ways and Means Committee to develop a bill. Regardless, it was through the tax-writing committees, not other parts of Congress, that this deficit-increasing, then deficit-decreasing, legislation flowed. Moreover, the tax cutting parts of the president's 1981 program proved much easier to enact than the expenditure reduction parts.

3. The programs established by the Social Security Act of 1935 and Amendments of

1939 include Old-Age and Survivor's Insurance, Unemployment Insurance, Aid to Families with Dependent Children, and grants to the states for maternal and child welfare, public health, and aid to the blind. These programs were placed under the jurisdiction of the tax-writing committees for a number of reasons. At the time, there was serious doubt as to whether these programs could get past the conservative Supreme Court. The government's case for Social Security's constitutionality rested almost entirely on the government's power to tax. Financing the major Social Security programs through their own separate taxes helped drive this point home. The separate tax elements of these programs made them natural candidates for the taxwriting committees' jurisdiction, while giving Social Security to the taxwriters would reinforce the link between these programs and the government's constitutionally-granted power to tax.

The decision to put Social Security in the hands of the taxwriters also involved a strategic judgment by President Roosevelt with regards to congressional politics. Because the chairmen of the taxwriting committees had given a lukewarm reception to the Social Security Act, its drafters hoped to bypass them and put it under the jurisdiction of a special committee. Roosevelt, however, correctly believed that putting the tax-writing chairmen in charge of Social Security would win their support and loyalty to the program.

Over the years, new programs such as Disability Insurance and Medicare were placed within the boundaries of Social Security so that they might benefit from the lustre and popularity of the "social insurance" label. Thus, they too were assigned to the tax-writing committees.

See Derthick (1979, pp. 38–47). Also see *The 50th Anniversary Edition of the Report of the Committee on Economic Security of 1935 and Other Basic Documents Relating to the Development of the Social Security Act* (Washington, DC: The National Conference on Social Welfare, 1985).

4. The House Committee on Energy and Commerce actually has enormous jurisdiction as well, but much of it is regulatory. Again, this helps explain why a member of this committee would attempt to achieve policy goals through regulation even when it would be more efficient to operate through direct taxes and spending. Each committee attempts to achieve objectives through the instruments at its control, not necessarily through those instruments that are most appropriate.

5. Cogan (1988) notes that Congress has tended to spread spending jurisdiction among an ever-increasing number of committees since 1932, when the Reconstruction Finance Corporation was created and financed outside the normal appropriations process.

6. *President's 1963 Tax Message.* Washington, D.C.: Superintendent of Documents, 1963, pp. 1–2.

7. Herbert Stein provides further explanation for the neglect of equity principles in the Kennedy tax cut: "The only possibility of holding the next tax cut to the neighborhood of $3 billion was to accompany the rate reduction with major revenue-raising 'reforms' or 'loophole-closings.' Indeed, this was the Treasury's intention. But each of these reforms would be unpopular with someone. The loopholes were not in the tax law by accident; someone had wanted them and the Congress had agreed. Once the President had proposed and promised rate reduction, and described it as terribly important, where would be the compulsion on Congress to enact the reforms? It could only be in the sentiment for balancing the budget. But this sentiment was not strong enough for the task. Therefore the administration, having opened the door, was led unavoidably to large net tax reduction" (Stein 1969, p. 411).

8. Lesser independent reform attempts were made between 1962 and 1978, also with mixed results. "The final [1976 tax reform] Senate bill . . . was unsatisfactory to both the reform liberals and such conservatives as James Buckley (I-N.Y.), who lamented the revenue loss and the structure of the bill as 'the worst possible collection of tax

preferences for the lobbied interests.' The liberals, in a last-ditch act of defiance, proposed the word 'reform' be dropped from the title of the act . . . the bill accounted for a greater cut in taxes than any bill to that time . . . the reduction was estimated at $15.7 billion for fiscal year 1977 and $11.6 billion for 1978'' (Witte 1985, p. 194). Again, despite the size of the bill, it did not fully offset bracket creep from previous years.

9. *The President's 1963 Tax Message*, pp. iii, 3, and 19.

10. *The President's 1978 Tax Program.* Washington, D.C.: Department of the Treasury, 1978, p. 2.

11. The fault lay not just with the politicians. Many academic researchers failed to get involved in detailed structural issues, partly because they were ignorant of the many details of tax and expenditure law and often couldn't incorporate such details into their simple models of the economy, even if they were aware of them. In a self-deceptive way, issues became defined as unimportant because they weren't in one's economic model.

Chapter Six

CONSENSUS AND DIVERSITY

The movement to a new era of decision making required new trade-offs to achieve reform. Reform could not be bought or attained through give-aways. At the same time, the tax-writing committees were the one part of the Congress not only able but required to engage in making broad trade-offs among a wide variety of tax and tax expenditure programs. These factors provide the setting under which tax reform could be considered in the 1980s, but they do not explain how opportunities for reform expanded nor how leadership could bring forces together to take advantage of these opportunities. This chapter examines the opportunity for developing liberal-conservative coalitions behind reform and for making use of the diverse, sometimes contradictory tax reform proposals and movements of the early 1980s.

THE FORMATION OF LIBERAL-CONSERVATIVE COALITIONS

Certain events encourage a governmental response. Although many tax practitioners decried the continual enactment of tax legislation in the 1981–1990 decade, what they often failed to realize is that much legislation was a reaction to forcing events. Yet action-forcing events and even crises also present opportunities. The nature of the reaction and the contents of the bills are initially indeterminate. The governmental response may deflect attention elsewhere, may be weak or minimalist, may go further and seek to prevent the repetition of problems in the future, or may even move beyond the initial set of problems to other fundamental or underlying issues. Tax reform took the last route.

At the time of tax reform, there were several events for which a response was invited. Medium-size hemorrhages were demanding attention. State and local governments increasingly were using federal subsidies to take over the private lending market. Having discovered that the advantages of borrowing at a tax-exempt rate need not be confined to traditional state and local government investment functions, these governments were besieged by private investors seeking an expansion of state and local governments' role as financial intermediary. And why not? Who wouldn't want to borrow at 7 percent when riskless investments in bank accounts were paying 10 percent? Congress had made partial attempts to stem this hemorrhage in 1980, 1982, and 1984, but the legislation was too minimalist and ineffective. Increasingly, policies were channeling investment on the basis of bureaucratic rules and access to selected networks of state and local government decision makers. Economic returns from the investment were of secondary importance. Everyone wanted access to subsidized state and local government borrowing, whether for investment, mortgages, industrial or commercial development, or other activities.

Other medium-size hemorrhages were occurring. Certain types of profit-sharing, pension, and individual retirement accounts were being utilized much more than expected and were reducing revenues.[1] Installment sales—selling an asset but deferring capital gains taxation by recognizing the gains only in installments over time—were growing as a mechanism by which to reduce current taxes. Many financial institutions were growing in importance in the economy, but were paying little federal tax on their income.

Still, these medium-size problems might have been ignored longer or attacked through a more modest bill, perhaps on the order of the tax bills of 1982 or 1984. Two major problems—1) the taxation of the poor and of families with dependents and 2) tax shelters and tax arbitrage—were more serious and provided more of an opportunity, as well as a need, for major surgery. From these issues developed the liberal-conservative coalitions that eventually united behind tax reform. Once there was a public commitment to tackling these problems, it became increasingly difficult for any politician in a leadership position to leave to fester sores for which clear-cut cures had been offered.

The Turnaround on Taxation of the Poor and Families

The first major problem attracting attention was the growth in income taxes paid by the poor and households with dependents. Surprisingly, these increases in taxes were never the explicit result of a direct decision-making process, but rather the accidental by-product of other decisions.

As summarized in chapter 1, the decline in the value of the personal exemption was the single most important change in the individual income tax base over the entire post-World War II era. By itself, this one change practically paid for all of the other erosions of the individual income tax base during those decades. By the late 1970s, inflation accelerated this decline.

Income tax burdens on the poor were increasing significantly as this population moved from being nontaxable (in zero-rate brackets) to being taxable (in positive rate brackets). By the early to mid-1980s, some organizations began to use the higher burdens to lobby for greater tax relief for the poor. Some were spurred by further political considerations and by a belief that the 1981 tax bill greatly favored the wealthy. As already noted, however, the trend toward increased taxation of the poor had started long before the 1980 election.

It might be thought that income taxation of the poor would be opposed by a majority of each political party. Yet a strange mixture of policymakers had indirectly united against attacking the increased tax burdens placed on the poor. One group argued that the rapid rate of tax increase in the late 1970s was justifiable as a means of bringing the budget under control. After the deficit was increased in 1981, they felt even more strongly about the need for tax increases. Allowing personal exemptions to erode over time was a major source of increased revenues, as it increased the taxable income of all taxpayers, not just those at the bottom of the income distribution.[2] A second group was composed of some (but not all) supply-siders and capital formation advocates. They understood that reducing taxes at the bottom of the income distribution often did little to decrease marginal rates. Given a total level of revenues to be obtained, marginal tax rates on average might even increase if top rates were raised to pay for a reduction in lower rates. Take the case of a single individual with an annual income of $50,000. The same amount of tax is collected from this individual if he pays 20 percent on all his income or 25 percent on income over and above a nontaxable amount of $10,000. A more progressive system has higher marginal tax rates.

These proponents of allowing tax-exempt levels to erode, therefore, ranged across the political spectrum. Remember that no legislative decision was required to allow these burdens to increase. Reversing the trend, on the other hand, would require a vote to increase the deficit or make someone else pay for the switch.

As a result of this unwillingness to abandon the status quo, taxes on the poor were allowed to increase throughout the late 1970s and early 1980s. Here I must turn to an anecdotal story that shows just how unexpected and accidental can be the impact of policy analysis on the views of policymakers. In 1982 I was asked almost as an afterthought by Rudolph Penner, later director of the Congressional Budget Office, but then at the American Enterprise Institute, to write an article on the taxation of households of different sizes as part of a book on the taxation of the family. His main interest in the book initially was the tax treatment of single versus married taxpayers.

What I discovered in doing this research was a logical consequence of the previous research on changes in the tax base and on taxation of the poor, but one that was never explicitly noted: the decline in the value of the personal exemption increased taxes most for those for whom the exemption was most important, those with dependents. Thus, heads of households and those filing joint returns who had dependents had borne much greater increases in taxes in the postwar era than had other households. On a variety of equity criteria, I concluded that this relative shift in burdens resulted in a tax system that did not tax equally those with equal ability to pay, but instead taxed most heavily those with dependents.

While my related research on the taxation of the poor had received only moderate attention, to my surprise this corollary 1982 research was to be picked up by *The Wall Street Journal, Forbes,* and *The Washington Times,* among others, and eventually made the banner headline in *USA Today.* (Of course, none discussed the more theoretical and difficult parts of the research.) This publicity helped attract the attention of liberal and conservative politicians in both political parties. Quoting this research, for instance, Senator Daniel Patrick Moynihan (D-N.Y.) argued strongly for an increase in the personal exemption in a book on the family and, later, in his support for the tax reform bill on the floor of the Senate.[3] By the same token, Representative Jack Kemp (R-N.Y.) was to incorporate substantial increases in the personal exemption in his tax reform proposals. Perhaps most importantly, Bruce Chapman, who became director of Planning and Evaluation in the White House office (and who earlier had been connected with the American Enterprise Institute, which published the research) raised the issue with the president. Chapman later wrote me that "Had I not read your paper . . ., I would have missed what became the core argument of the family initiative I urged on the President, and which he adopted—and there never would have been a presidential decision to double the personal exemption" (letter to author, July 28, 1985).

Due to Chapman's efforts, the president came out in favor of a substantial increase in the personal exemption. This proposal quickly became the Reagan administration's principal initiative to help the "family."[4] Unfortunately, the initial rumblings in favor of increasing the personal exemption were to come at a time when the budget deficit increases from the 1981 changes were becoming apparent to all. Those concerned with the deficit were not about to spend tens of billions of dollars more on increasing the personal exemption.

Here we must note again the important shifting of President Reagan's policy positions—in this case, from proposals more focused on the top rate to concern over taxes at the bottom of the income distribution, albeit in the context of the family. As in the case of his acceptance of "loophole" closing measures in the 1982 and 1984 acts, he was once again being converted to the tax reform cause.

The turnaround, nonetheless, was to cause some difficulty among those who were most concerned with reducing the top or marginal rate. Lower taxes at the bottom almost inevitably means higher marginal rates, especially when comparing tax rate structures of equal yield.

The appeal to President Reagan, perhaps, was to his opposition to taxes in any form or shape. In 1981 he had supported an across-the-board cut in tax rates, but not increasing personal exemptions or minimum amounts of income that would not be subject to tax. At the time, he apparently thought that this was a fair way for the tax reduction to be shared. The cut, however, had been determined politically in the campaign, and it proved impossible to pass through other information on alternative ways the cut might be achieved. Thus, in 1981 there was little use for evidence that, as an offset to past inflation, the poor deserved a much greater proportion of the total cut. Since the president's aversion to taxes was more fundamental than his understanding of supply-side theory, his later concern for the impact of inflation on the value of the personal exemption should not be surprising.

The combination of concern for the poor and concern for the "family" resulted in the formation of the first of two major liberal-conservative coalitions that later would prove crucial to tax reform. Between 1982 and 1984, however, the coalition had nowhere to go because it had no way to pay for these changes. Congressional attention had turned toward deficit decreases, not increases. One possibility, then considered unlikely, still beckoned. If it were possible to incorporate concerns for the poor and for families into a more comprehensive tax reform effort, might not some of the revenues from base broadening be used to support reduced taxation of the poor and of households with dependents?

Addressing Tax Shelters While Lowering Tax Rates

By the mid-1980s, a second major hemorrhage was attracting more attention. Tax shelters and tax arbitrage were deterring growth, reducing public confidence in government, significantly increasing the complexity of individuals' financial affairs, and destroying the ability of the IRS to effectively administer the tax laws. To see how far these shelters extended by the mid-1980s, Susan Nelson of the Treasury Department and I initiated some studies with the IRS to see who was investing in these tax shelters. Many of the purchasers turned out to be middle-income savers who were sacrificing higher yields in favor of only moderate tax saving. Even students with little tax liability were found to be investors in many shelters. The system of financial intermediation was failing in its function of directing saving toward optimal economic investment. Along the way billions in savings were being lost simply in payments to shelter promoters and organizers, and a number of individuals were being sold investments that were clearly not in their self-interest.

Bad and inefficient investment, new administrative problems for the IRS, and misleading investment advice for many Americans of modest means were not enough by themselves to spur Congress to action. The constant trumpeting of the tax shelter industry, on the other hand, aroused many to react against the basic unfairness of the existing system. Of course, simply going after tax shelters alone might not be enough to unite a coalition into attacking the status quo. If a drastic paring of tax shelters could be combined with tax rate reduction, however, there might be formed a second liberal-conservative coalition to help provide the majority necessary for legislative action.

In several respects, the core of this coalition had been around for years. Economists trained in traditional public finance principles had been taught how the unequal treatment of different sources of income led to inefficient patterns of investment and consumption. The literature on this subject stretches back to the beginning of the income tax.[5] The basis for broad-based taxation had been popularized in economics books and texts by individuals ranging from Henry

Simons (1938) at the University of Chicago to Richard Musgrave (1959) of Harvard University to Office of Tax Analysis alumni Joseph Pechman (1983) and Richard Goode (1976), who published their work at The Brookings Institution.

Within the government, the Office of Tax Policy at the Department of Treasury had become an institutional base for promoting the view that different forms of income and consumption should be treated equally for both efficiency and equity reasons. The office, comprised mainly of economists and lawyers trained in public finance and tax law, gave testimony year after year about the difficulties created when income from different sources was taxed differentially. This same office had been in charge of previous tax reform efforts under such presidents as Kennedy and Carter. Influential alumni of the office, such as Stanley Surrey at Harvard, Milton Friedman at Chicago, and the authors mentioned above, continued to promote this view.[6]

While this academic support helped, it was not new. An important addition to the mixture, however, was a president who objected most strongly to high tax rates. Although some political officials (including the president, who initially attacked the idea of "tax expenditures" as a liberal myth) had prevented the 1981 process from drawing a connection between rate reduction and base broadening, it was an obvious and logical one. By 1984, the president had come to support tax reform principles, whether purposively or not, when he supported attempts to reduce tax "abuses."

To form a coalition of those favoring lower rates and those favoring base broadening, there needed to be some agreement as to which parts of the base would be reformed. Issues such as fringe benefits and other middle-income preferences had never been able to carry the day and, indeed, were to fail again by the time the 1986 reform effort was over. We have already noted that the Kennedy and Carter efforts at tax reform were quite modest in size. The principal difference in the 1980s, therefore, can probably be attributed to concern over the widespread pattern of tax evasion, legal or otherwise, generated by the tax shelter industry. It was this problem, as much as any other, that finally allowed sufficient support to be roused to carry the tax reform banner.

In a sense, the promoters of the 1981 Tax Act must be given some of the credit for tax reform. By overselling what had been achieved in 1981 and by advertising the zero or negative tax rates on many types of investment, they made it easier to organize a revolt against what had been done. After all, taxpayers could hardly have been pleased with messages about the number of individuals and corporations with significant positive income paying no tax.

In some cases, of course, the net tax benefits of tax preferences were less than might at first appear. Corporations, for instance, were doing nothing more at the corporate level than was already occurring at the individual level through the purchase of assets of non-corporate businesses and of little-used vacation homes. That is, the corporations were simply engaging in the tax arbitrage and tax shelter opportunities that were already quite common at the individual level. Many of these corporations could claim correctly that in many cases the tax benefits were passed on to consumers in the form of lower prices or lease rates. No matter. The appearance of these zero tax rates was devastating to public relations.[7] Whatever the economic justifications for low taxes on corporations, such a theory would be hard to reconcile with the existence of a tax that purported to tax away 46 percent of corporate profits.

Available information on partnership activity began to provide support for the reformers. Between 1965 and 1982, the number of partnerships reporting net losses grew from 229,000 to 723,000, while the number of partners (individual owners of partnerships) in all partnerships grew from 2.7 to 9.8 million. Net "losses" reported in oil and gas partnerships grew from $128 million to $13.2 billion, and in real estate from $619 million to $23 billion. Together, oil and gas and real estate partnerships accounted for about 60 percent of all losses reported on partnerships. And the growth rate was phenomenal. New public offerings of partnerships grew from $38 billion in 1979 to $64 billion by 1982 (Nelson 1985, pp. 58–59).

Eliminating individual and corporate shelters, while lowering rates in the process, gradually became a trade-off that could be made to appeal to a large number of conservatives and liberals. A building up of this second coalition for tax reform would eventually prove quite potent. Even opponents of reform could not comfortably argue for higher tax rates as a means of supporting a growing tax shelter industry that enabled many wealthy individuals and corporations to pay no tax.[8]

THE DEBATE EXPANDS

The growing problems of the tax system served as a catalyst for the development of tax proposals in the early 1980s. While these proposals varied widely, they succeeded in raising the level of the debate on tax reform and increased the opportunity for initiating a tax reform effort that would succeed.

Consumption Taxes and Flat Taxes

Many proposals went beyond traditional income tax "reform." By the late 1970s and early 1980s, a number of economists had revived and expanded interest in consumption or expenditure taxes as a replacement for income taxes. Although such taxes may be thought to be the antithesis of income taxes, in fact, a comprehensive consumption tax would in many cases work similarly to a comprehensive income tax. Both move toward uniformity of treatment, but in different ways. The comprehensive income tax would ideally provide uniform treatment of all income regardless of source or consumption use. The comprehensive consumption tax, on the other hand, moves toward uniform treatment of income *spent* for consumption, regardless of source or use. Capital income would be treated uniformly by being taxed at a zero rate.

The difference is obviously important: under an expenditure tax, income saved would not be taxed until consumed. For some economists, this would make the tax system more neutral between consumption today and consumption tomorrow. For others it would provide an undue benefit to higher-income individuals and exempt many capitalists from paying tax even while enjoying the benefits of U.S. citizenship. This debate was often to sidetrack the tax reform process.

In terms of forming coalitions for reform, however, many consumption tax advocates recognized the need for eliminating special preferences in the tax code—at least those that did not apply to capital income. They also favored taxing capital income at a uniform rate, although that rate was at zero percent. Thus, they sought after many of the same efficiency goals favored by comprehensive income tax enthusiasts.

Another, related set of proposals centered around applying a flat or proportional rather than progressive rate of tax to the tax base. This type of proposal is as old as the field of economics. Indeed, Adam Smith proposed a proportional tax on income on the grounds of fairness. The application of progressivity to the income tax, with tax rates rising as incomes rose, had been a bone of contention since the enactment of an income tax in this country.

The new "flat tax" advocates had more in mind than elimination of progressivity. They also objected to the various exclusions, deductions, and credits in the income tax. That is, they took up the tax reform goal of base broadening as a way of showing how low a flat rate might be. In addition, simplification could be achieved through the elimination of many special provisions, as well as through the application of a single rate of tax. One important simplification is the collection of tax from payers and the elimination of many filing requirements. For instance, if everyone owes exactly 15 percent of interest income as a tax, a bank could pay the tax without sending statements to individuals, while individuals would not need to report this income on their tax returns.

Some proposals combined elements. One widely publicized "flat tax" proposal was really a combination of a consumption tax and a flat rate tax proposal (see Hall and Rabushka 1983). This proposal was to evolve over the years. As it turns out, many proponents claimed that they favored a single, flat rate of tax when what they sought was a two-rate structure: a zero rate on the first dollars of income (or consumption) and a single positive rate on the remaining income. The zero rate effectively would reduce taxes for the lowest income individuals. Of course, a two-rate structure eliminated many of the administrative simplifications possible with a perfectly flat tax rate.

In September 1982, the Assistant Secretary of the Treasury for Tax Policy, John E. Chapoton, was called to testify on flat-tax approaches to reforming the income tax system (Chapoton 1982). While the Treasury laid out many important equity, efficiency, and simplicity issues, the principal impact of the testimony came from clarification of the amount of redistribution that would take place under a flat tax. For instance, with a single uniform rate of tax on all income, taxes on the highest income individuals would be reduced by 61 percent, while the taxes on those with incomes between $5,000 and $10,000 would be increased by 149 percent. While the results varied somewhat by type of proposal—that is, by whether or not there really was to be a two-rate structure— the testimony made clear that a flat tax by itself involved more redistribution from poor to rich than the country was likely to tolerate or desire.[9]

Treasury also took the opportunity to present other options that accepted the "flat tax" label, but weren't "flat" at all. In particular, the testimony showed that it was possible to reduce tax rates significantly by treating income uniformly, yet without abandoning progressivity. The uniformity goal of a flatter rate tax system (i.e., the traditional income tax reform goal) was shown to be a viable option for those who would be a little less pure about how flat "flat" was meant to be.

Both flat rate taxes and consumption taxes have many merits that are not examined here.[10] By the same token, it would be a mistake to treat various proponents as having identical goals. Some probably cared more about reducing taxes on capital owners or on higher income individuals, while others were more concerned about efficiency and simplicity.

Bradley-Gephardt, Kemp-Kasten, and Other Congressional Proposals

To the reader unfamiliar with the ways of Washington, the way in which proposals are put together may appear a trivial issue. But it is important to know that few proposals initiated within Congress are developed with significant refinement—partly because few do more than cut taxes or raise expenditures for a select group of taxpayers. As a result, they are normally full of holes. Revenue sources are ignored or left inadequate, administrative details are ignored, distributional results are unsaleable, and so forth. Remember that most proposals are mainly developed to make a political point, not necessarily to move toward enactment of a comprehensive policy change. Moreover, sometimes when members of Congress seek technical help, it is only to find an ex-post justification for what they already advocate. Some are unwilling to accept information as to the real costs of what they are undertaking without making accusations against the bearers of the news.

Between 1982 and 1984, a number of congressionally developed proposals also began to receive attention. The most important of these, known simply as "Bradley-Gephardt," was put forward by Senator Bill Bradley (D-N.J.), who then secured Representative Richard Gephardt (D-Mo.) as a cosponsor. Unlike most congressional bills, it was able to deal with many separate details and yet remain grounded in technical realism.

Senator Bradley's public leadership role on tax reform has been well recognized, but this book's emphasis on the organization of policy would be incomplete without noting two important technical reasons why his proposal received and maintained more attention than others. First, the proposal turned back toward the notion of a comprehensive but progressive income tax. Whatever one thinks of the merits of flat taxes and consumption taxes, there already had been an acrimonious debate over how generous the 1981 tax cut had been for the wealthy. Proposals that abandoned a progressive income tax never had a chance of passage. A comprehensive income tax proposal, on the other hand, did not face the same hurdle. The Bradley-Gephardt proposal further dodged distributional issues by accepting the existing amount of progressivity already in the income tax. By passing over the issue of whether to tax the rich more or less, the proposal concentrated on more equal treatment of equals, or equal taxation of those with equal incomes. The proposal became a vehicle by which to offer and concentrate on the simple trade-off of lower rates for expansion of the tax base.

Secondly, Senator Bradley engaged experts and staff who could put together a proposal without too many hidden pitfalls. The proposal was largely developed by tax experts who could provide considerable technical expertise on how to pull disparate parts together.[11] The help of the Joint Committee on Taxation, which serves the congressional tax-writing committees, was crucial in allowing Senator Bradley to obtain accurate revenue estimates and distributional tables.

The Bradley-Gephardt proposal was to be followed by a whole slew of congressional bills favoring tax reform, including the so-called "Kemp-Kasten," "Roth-Moore," "Nickles-Siljander," and "DeConcini-Shelby" bills. Of these other bills, Kemp-Kasten was to command the most attention for several reasons. It put supply-side advocates such as Representative Jack Kemp (R-N.Y.) behind the base-broadening aspect of reform. It meant that a portion of the Republican party would favor reform. A significant portion of all bills, moreover, contained identical elements, thus helping to create a coalition in favor of certain tax changes that would allow lower tax rates. Finally, Jack Kemp was a Republican who would run for president and who sought a leadership role in the Republican Party. The White House, therefore, felt the threat of his competition as much as that of the Democratic Party.

Some Common Themes

Perhaps the only theme truly common to the tax proposals of this period was the exchange of lower rates for a broader base—a traditional theme, but one applied more consistently to labor income and uses of income than to the taxation of capital. A lesser consensus was obtained in other areas. Tax shelter and tax arbitrage problems of the day were clearly a concern, and a lowering of tax rates would lessen this problem by making deductions less valuable. Some consumption tax proposals and congressional proposals, however, were so generous to capital income receipts that they would have expanded rather than contracted the shelter market. Except for some of the flat rate tax proposals, the desire to achieve fairer taxation of the poor or taxation of the family was also fairly widespread. The implications and details of many, if not most, proposals were not drawn out, and a number of them promised more rate reduction and lower taxation of capital than could be financed by the base broadening proposed.

Notes

1. So-called 401(k) plans became quite popular with employees, especially those at higher wages. Individual retirement accounts had exploded since the 1981 Tax Act extended their availability to all taxpayers, regardless of their income level or whether they had available another pension plan from an employer.

2. See the discussion in chapter 1 about the revenue limitations of a progressive tax system. Allowing personal exemptions to erode moves the system toward a more proportionate, higher revenue-raising structure.

3. See Moynihan (1986), and *Congressional Record*, June 10, 1986, p. S7151.

4. It is also likely that the research on taxation of the family was accepted because it was published under the auspices of the American Enterprise Institute, where Rudolph Penner, the editor, then resided. Recall that the earlier research on the taxation of the poor had not received a similar reception. One of the more unfortunate aspects of policy-related research is that it tends to get labeled as conservative or liberal depending upon which research institute publishes the research.

5. For a detailed discussion of the historical development of the American income tax and the role of equity principles, see Witte (1985).

6. Conlan et al. (1990, p. 242) note the importance of experts: "The movement for tax reform rested above all else on the shared conviction of knowledgeable experts that the federal income-tax system had grown indefensible from the standpoint of professionally salient values."

7. For a discussion of some of the most egregious examples of corporate tax sheltering and how they were publicized, see Birnbaum and Murray (1987, pp. 9–11).

8. Birnbaum and Murray discuss the formation of this coalition in a related way. "Reform was also achieved because it combined goals that were important to both political parties. Ending loopholes for the privileged had long been the desire of some Democrats. But the 1980s also saw the emergence of a new wing of the Republican party that was crucial to tax reform's success—the supply-siders, whose influence grew dramatically after President Reagan's election and who were passionately committed to lowering tax rates. These activist-conservatives had no deep interest in closing loopholes, but if that was the only way to pay for lower rates, they were willing to go along. By combining with the older Democratic reformers, they created an impressive bipartisan coalition" (Birnbaum and Murray 1987, p. 186).

9. Among others, John Wilkins, then director of the Office of Tax Analysis, deserves special credit for pulling together this testimony.

10. For a more elaborate treatment of these issues, see chapter 12 in Steuerle (1985b).

11. Credit here goes mainly to Joseph Minarik, then at The Urban Institute, and Randall Weiss and James Wexler, then at the Joint Committee on Taxation, with Gina Despres leading the Senator's own staff efforts.

Chapter Seven

THE ORGANIZATION OF THE 1986 TAX REFORM: EVOLUTION AND IMPLICATIONS

In his State of the Union address at the beginning of 1984, President Reagan asked that the Treasury Department prepare "a plan for action to simplify the entire Tax Code" and that "specific recommendations be presented [to him] by December 1984." Notice the nuances in the words. No proposal was to be put forward, simply a plan for action. The recommendations were to be made to him, not necessarily to the public, and were not to be put forward until after the 1984 election. This hardly sounded like a mandate for major reform, nor did its drafters necessarily intend it to be one.

In hindsight, many of the actors in tax reform claimed to have a strong idea of just what was to develop.[1] At the time, however, the only clear direction was that there was to be no tax reform debate during the election.

During the State of the Union address, congressional laughter greeted the president's request. Some members of Congress were probably thinking that the give-aways of 1981 went in exactly the opposite direction of tax reform. The post-election delivery date did not go without notice. Was this request even serious? Tax reform had been tried so many times before, why would it succeed now?

LACK OF DIRECTION

The president's cautious statement gave little basis on which to proceed. It wasn't even clear if an honest proposal could be drafted without offending some top officials in the administration. Tax reform in the mid-1980s was no more or less feasible than welfare, health care, or educational reform in the early 1990s. It takes more than a consensus that something is awry to enact reform of any major governmental system. The president had requested a study, but that was hardly enough.

Congressional and presidential requests for studies are a dime a dozen. While they can be invaluable vehicles for forwarding a reform agenda, many are ignored. Others are put together in such a way that they fail to help move the process along. Many plans for action end up to be nothing more than requirements for still further study. Other requests get involved in such partisan internal wrangling that an administration is unable to put forward any study or set of suggestions. It was little surprise, then, that few expected anything to come of this request for a "plan for action" on the tax front.

Consider some of the other studies that the president or Congress had requested during the 1980s. The collapse of the early Reagan administration effort to reform Social Security has already been noted. In a later State of the Union address, President Reagan was to ask for a study of welfare reform, a request that was never really met. A new federalism initiative had also been tried, producing another set of failed proposals. And a presidentially mandated health study was delayed and then watered down greatly to ensure that there was no political nor legislative reaction.

On top of everything else, in 1984 the debate over the meaning of "reform" swirled in every direction. The administration was still strongly defending its 1981 tax cuts while signing legislation in 1982 and 1984 that contradicted some of the 1981 effort. Many wanted to extend the 1981 cuts further. The flat tax debate continued apace, and some felt that the time had finally arrived for its adoption. Several members of the administration, such as David Stockman at the Office of Management and Budget, were trying to focus the debate on deficit reduction. Bradley-Gephardt, Kemp-Kasten, and other congressional proposals had either been put forward or were still in various stages of development, but they had design problems and had many important differences among them.

The treatment of capital income—"expensing" of capital costs, adopting a consumption tax, or eliminating taxes on capital income—was an especially acrimonious issue. Some supply-side enthusiasts were supportive of almost any approach to lowering capital income taxes, including many that created even more negative tax rates on equipment and on capital purchased with borrowed money. Some continued to argue that a larger deduction for purchases of capital would pay for itself through feedback effects on the economy.

Another group, which usually discounted the supply-side rhetoric with respect to the deficit, still believed that lower taxes on capital and business were vitally important. This more traditional group included many business lobbyists and economists who placed significant emphasis on "cost of capital" or tax rates on capital income. In contrast to supply-siders, they usually worried little about higher rates of tax on workers and non-capital income. According to this pro-capital thesis, the tax changes in 1981 may have been too extensive—but on the personal income side, not the business side. Advocates of lower taxes on capital sometimes favored investment credits and special business incentives and sometimes wanted to replace the income tax with a consumption tax. They comprised a significant percentage of economists in such influential organizations as the National Bureau of Economic Research.

Opposition to a broad-based income tax that taxed capital income included many high-level administration officials. The Office of Economic Policy within Treasury contained political appointees who identified themselves as "supply-side" economists. Moreover, the reality was that lower or zero taxes on capital income were logical political extensions of the 1981 changes. After all, the investment credit, plus rapid depreciation, had already reduced the effective tax rate on many types of equipment to almost zero even before borrowing was taken into account. For many, this tax rate needed to be maintained and, if at all possible, made even more negative.

Many advocates wanted to go all the way to "expensing" of capital purchases—writing off costs immediately rather than depreciating costs more slowly over time. Others, such as Martin Feldstein, then Chairman of the Council of Economic Advisers, were willing to keep an investment credit and vastly accelerated depreciation allowances even if they needed to be supported with higher corporate rates. One argument here was that investment subsidies favored new capital, and high corporate rates collected taxes from returns to capital that already existed. In effect, the investment credit-high tax rate argument tries to "surprise" owners of old or existing capital by hitting them with a tax, then exempting new types of investment or saving from that tax. The attempt to impose rent controls for existing housing stock operates in a similar fashion. Of course, the logic of this argument can be used to favor even higher tax rates and higher investment credits than existed in the early 1980s.[2]

Finally, tax reform would go against standard operating procedures and ways of doing things. Why reform the tax code and raise the opposition of the many interest groups that would lose out? For some this would be political suicide. Tax reform also lacked political reality to those who believed that reform at best was incremental—a nibble here and there when defenses are down. A large number of politicians, as well as academic researchers, felt that focus should be on only one or two important variables such as the size of the deficit, not on the redesign of hundreds of tax code provisions.

FORMATION OF A PLAN

In March 1984, I returned to the Treasury Department from a year of studying capital income taxation and other issues at The Brookings Institution. Partly because I proceeded to lay out the initial plan to pull together a tax reform study, the role of organizing the tax reform work fell into my lap, and I became the Economic Coordinator of the Project for Fundamental Tax Reform. The following comments, therefore, are flavored by my personal involvement in the events of that time.

The emphasis here is fairly narrow. It is on the ways in which the organization of the 1986 tax reform was to constrain the succeeding process. Some of the successes and failures will be contrasted in later chapters with the ways in which the 1990 budget reform was organized and the ways future reforms of both taxes and expenditures might be developed.

A Game Plan

As noted, a temporary stalemate resulted from the swirling debate in 1984 and the question of whether the request for a study should even be taken seriously. Several weeks after the president's address, the project had not really gotten off the ground. And yet people weren't exactly waiting for something to do. The crafting of the 1984 tax bill itself began after the presidential request for a tax study, and its enactment into law later in the year required significant efforts to implement its new requirements and to write interpretive regulations. There was a temptation, moreover, to focus on what "was" rather than what "might be." While a person could make a difference working on the 1984 Act, the study called for by the president might simply be one more of an endless list of ineffectual or unheeded studies.

The process was also floundering because of vague lines of authority and the lack of any definition of reform. Throughout the system everyone was waiting for instructions from the top, which were never to come.

Former Treasury Secretary Donald Regan once commented that President Reagan never really advised him on how to spend his tenure as secretary. "To this day I have never had so much as one minute alone with Ronald Reagan! Never has he, or anyone else, sat down to explain to me what is expected of me, what goals he would like to see me accomplish, what results he wants. Since I am accustomed to management by objective, where people have 'in writing' what is expected and explicit standards are set, this has been most disconcerting. How can one do a job if the job is not defined?" According to Regan, "[t]his excerpt from a note I wrote to myself in a spiral notebook late in the second month of the Reagan Administration is interesting as commentary on the nature of the 40th presidency and as a prophecy of things to come of my own life in Washington" (Regan 1988, pp. 38–40).

Regan's lack of job definition, however, was a two-edged sword. In many cases neither the president nor the White House staff can or should be expected to know the important nuances of how policies relate to one another, limits on administration, and how the legislative process works in particular areas of policy. No one has all the needed information. Indeed, my experience in working under four presidents (and watching many tax and expenditure reforms flounder, including the Carter tax reform effort) is that the process is often destroyed when there are too many, not too few, bright individuals who want to kibbitz in the process too early. The movement toward committee decision making at the top, rather than delegation of authority to specific individuals or agencies, often results in no consistently developed plan ever being presented. As a result of default, rather than more sinister reasons, important information is prevented from ever getting to decision makers. Comprehensive studies of what needs to be done are often never allowed to be completed. Put simply, if President Reagan had not delegated authority to the Treasury Department to perform the tax reform study, there would be no tax reform today.

Despite Secretary Regan's call for a job description, in the case of tax reform it wasn't even clear what was to be done. Sensing the many reasons for a void, I decided one day to put a plan of action on the table. Relying upon files gathered over a number of years and a comprehensive review of many studies, I proposed to set a process in motion through the development of a comprehensive list of over 20 major "modules" that were to be studied and from which proposals were to follow. Modules centered around issues such as itemized deductions, fringe benefits, low-income exemptions and deductions, depreciation and investment credits, energy and minerals taxation, and international issues.

Breaking the issues up into separable topics provided a way for the decision making process to begin. The goal of each module would be to discover ways in which the current system departed from a comprehensive income tax. Sometimes it was easy to attach a list of proposals to the module—proposals that would help move toward equal treatment of income, regardless of source or use. Consumption tax options were also included, where appropriate. In other areas, it was clear that adequate analysis had never been performed or integrated, and that much work remained. Fortunately, the professional economists and tax lawyers in the Office of Tax Policy had both the talent and the dedication to provide the analyses needed.[3]

To get around one major source of stalemate on whether to further lower the tax on capital income or to move toward a consumption tax, the modules would be taken to the secretary one at a time—with the non-capital income issues coming first.[4] This would emphasize the common base-broadening themes running through the income tax, consumption tax, and flat tax proposals.

Next, to provide maximum flexibility and to defer judgment on the overall process, tax rates would be set at the end of the process. This would allow incremental decision making on base-broadening issues. Equally as important, it would encourage Secretary Regan not to reject reform proposals early on before seeing how much rate reduction could be generated. The secretary's initial acceptance of the elimination of some tax preferences for strong constituencies such as the elderly set the stage for acceptance of many other attempts to broaden the base. It also meant that no particular issue needed to be decided on grounds of progressivity, as the overall progressivity of the system would be set at the end through adjustment of the rate schedule. If the secretary decided to eliminate the subsidy, later rate adjustments would cancel out the distributional effects of that decision.

At the time of the Treasury study, the future of tax reform was very uncertain. The experiences of 1982 and 1984 had led me to what I called a "hopper" theory of reform. The more good things that get into the hopper, the more good and the fewer bad things emerge in the legislation when Congress finally, often suddenly, decides to act. This meant that far more than an academic study would be required. What I suggested was a second volume, a "how to" manual on just how changes would be implemented—a suggestion that was incorporated into the second volume of the Treasury's original study. For instance, it wouldn't be adequate to state that families with equal incomes should be taxed equally. Instead, detailed rules for the operation of trusts and the treatment of family member income would have to be developed.

Finally, to make the study as comprehensive as possible, I attempted to pull every idea I could from the staff on ways in which the tax base was incomplete or overstated. This included addressing the problems of income that was unduly subject to tax more than once, as well as income on which no tax was paid.

Comprehensive Reform

Past tax reform proposals generally had resulted from a process in which individuals sat around a table and picked out a few tax expenditures to eliminate. This was a variation on what former presidential press secretary Brady referred to as BOGSAT—a "Bunch Of Guys Sitting Around a Table." Typically, the largest expenditures got the most attention.

There were several problems with this method. The tax expenditure list was quite incomplete. It failed to take into account negative expenditures, as when income was subject to taxation twice. Because so many sources of business income were subject to double taxation, this bias tended to make the method anti-business. Most important, by confining the process to a few individuals, the method often ignored the ideas and knowledge of others.

Comprehensiveness, on the other hand, had several benefits. First, it offered the possibility of attacking the small problems, the ones usually ignored when focus was only centered on major items. Many provisions, though not large in terms of their impact on the budget, are needlessly complex. Indeed, whatever their other benefits, their small size often makes it difficult to justify the additional complexity or cost imposed upon taxpayers and tax administrators. Many of the problems of the federal government today stem from the unwillingness of policymakers to deal with thousands of issues that, one by one, can be considered minor, but together bog down taxpayers and bureaucrats alike in an endless maze of complexity.

The second advantage of a comprehensive tax study was a political one. Comprehensiveness may have tended to gore more oxen, but it had a positive side: the opportunity to convince some of the public that the effort was sincere. Tax reform would be an attack not on particular groups or individuals, but on the inefficient and unfair preferences that provided some partial benefits to all citizens. Many taxpayers would only be willing to pay the price of tax reform if they believed that they were not being singled out, but were being treated fairly relative to other groups. In any case, the more comprehensive the tax reform proposal, the more rates could be lowered.

Finally, a comprehensive study, even if it led to no action, might restore to Treasury Department officials the ability to state more openly what they believed to be in the public interest. For a number of years, the Treasury Department had been forced to take the more political role of not testifying against congressional bills and other proposals that it had determined to be inefficient or unfair. The fear was that forthright testimony would only gain the enmity of special interests and, if a proposal was likely to pass anyway, the administration could not share the credit. The Treasury Department and the executive branch, however, have a responsibility to present what they believe to be in the public interest, even in losing endeavors. When the Treasury Department fails to serve that role on tax issues, often no one in the tax process is left to fill in the gap.

FURTHER STEPS

Although a comprehensive review of the tax code would provide a direction for the study, other important steps were crucial to the way it would be received and to how the debate itself would evolve.

Establishing Principles and Constraints

One of the most important initial steps was to set forward principles around which the tax reform process would evolve. Among the most powerful of these principles was fairness, as defined by equal treatment of equals or equal taxation of those with equal ability to pay tax. Efficiency was also a major goal: the elimination of means by which the tax code arbitrarily tended to favor one form of investment or consumption over another. Lower tax rates were also favored on efficiency grounds. Measuring income correctly in a world of inflation was argued to improve both fairness and efficiency. Fair treatment of families was included to deal with the concern over "family" issues, and it was argued that those in poverty should not be subject to income taxation. The goal of simplicity was used to justify proposals to eliminate many parts of the code that failed to meet other goals. Of course, these goals could at times conflict. Some reforms, for instance, might require that income be calculated more accurately, even at the cost of additional complexity.

Putting forward principles may appear to be an idealistic effort in a political process. Certainly some of these goals were forgotten, or at least partially ignored, on the way toward tax reform. Yet they provided powerful direction to the process and limited the efforts of those who wanted to move beyond what the principles would allow. Who could easily argue that individuals with equal incomes should pay unequal tax (except in special situations where, despite equal incomes, individuals are not equally situated)? Principles allowed reformers to take the high ground and required special interest groups to make the case that the principles didn't really apply to them.

Two constraints on the reform process served the above-stated principles. First, revenue neutrality meant that revenues were to be neither greatly increased nor decreased as a result of the reform process. Second, distributional neutrality meant that the distribution of tax burdens among income classes was not to change significantly. These revenue and distributional neutrality constraints were largely pursued to prevent policymakers from diverting their attention from the tough choices necessary to reduce inequities and promote the efficient allocation of resources.

Focusing on equal treatment of equals and efficiency rather than revenue raising meant some members of interest groups would be offered rate reduction that would more than compensate for their losses of deductions, while for others, the reverse would be true. This bargain effectively prevented many of these interest groups from uniting against reform. Not all businesses, for instance, would support tax reform, but the offering of significant rate reductions won the support of a large number with few preferences under prior law, or who were tired of tax games and wanted to get back to the basic task of making new and better products.[5]

These constraints had an enormous impact on the subsequent process, a fact that was understood by only a few at the beginning. Taken together, the two constraints implied that revenue neutrality had to be maintained in each income class.[6] A change in one tax provision could easily require several other amendments to be enacted simultaneously to restore the amount of revenues collected from each of the income classes.

These constraints were to become especially binding later in the process when legislators predetermined the top rate or other parts of the rate structure before deciding on the extent of base broadening.

With Treasury's initial effort, the rate structure remained variable until the end of the process, so it could be restructured to compensate for any particular amendment. At later stages in the process, however, parts or all of the rate structure would become fixed, causing enormous agony among legislators over how to make up for revenue losses associated with restoring certain special interest provisions.

Collecting and Analyzing Data

Another formidable task remained. Vast quantities of data needed to be assembled and analyzed.[7]

Traditionally, the Treasury's Office of Tax Policy and the IRS's Statistics of Income Division produce data files that are used by Treasury and the Joint Committee on Taxation to analyze tax bills and to present tables on the distribution of changes in taxes by income class. These distributional tables often prevent policymakers from making a system much more regressive. In addition, since the tax reform package was to be distributionally neutral, data to justify that claim was required.

Very early on I discovered one problem that had to be eliminated if we were to rely upon these distributional tables. (David Brockway, then chief of staff of the Joint Committee on Taxation, was separately to perform a similar calculation when the proposals reached Congress.) Limiting tax shelters was one major area in which base expansion could be achieved at the top. Tax shelter losses, however, tended to be reflected as losses from partnerships or other unincorporated business. These losses ended up lowering the measure of adjusted gross income and expanded income, the traditional measures used for classifying taxpayers by income and showing distributional effects of tax bills. Tax shelter owners often appeared to be in the low- or middle-income brackets when their income was accounted for in this manner. It was necessary, therefore, to make sure that negative statements of taxable income from these shelters did not result in a misclassification of these owners within economic income classes.

The solution used at Treasury was to impute to the individual tax model the various items on partnership and other returns that resulted in these negative statements. Such items included accelerated depreciation and deductions of the inflationary component of interest. The Joint Committee on Taxation was to address the same issue, but to use a different approach. Facing the same dilemma, they decided for classification purposes to treat all negative statements of total partnership income as equal to zero (e.g., a taxpayer with $200,000 of wages and $100,000 of partnership losses would be classified as having $200,000 of income). The advantage of this method is that it avoids the difficulties with the imputations made by Treasury. One disadvantage of the method is that it doesn't account for the fact that not all partnership losses are bogus. Still, without either improvement in the economic income measures, it would have appeared as if closing down tax loopholes increased taxes on the "poor."

Dealing with Bradley-Gephardt, Kemp-Kasten, and Other Congressional Proposals

Although congressional proposals offered a possible base of support for tax reform, the Treasury's proposals would have to be more thorough, more developed, and closer to what could be drafted than the congressional proposals. This is not so much a criticism of congressional proposals as a reflection on the power of the executive branch to pull together the needed personnel and expertise to develop major reform packages.

There were a number of problems with the congressional plans, many of which were in the process of revision at the same time that the Treasury study was being developed. First, they were not comprehensive enough. None dealt with abuses deriving from entertainment deductions or deductions for "seminars" on cruise ships. Income shifting through children was ignored. Neither did these proposals touch on complicated issues such as multiperiod production (whereby deductions are taken before income is realized), deductions by banks carrying tax-exempt bonds, the taxation of life and property and casualty insurance companies, international tax issues, the windfall profits tax, tax penalties, and a whole host of other provisions. (For a detailed comparison of proposals, see U.S. Department of the Treasury 1984, vol. 1, pp. 169–183.)

Second, some of the proposals lost revenues and often gave far more away at the top of the income distribution than elsewhere. The Kemp-Kasten proposal was a case in point. The give-aways were so great for some items of capital income that a significant deficit increase would have resulted from enactment of the bill as it was written. Interest was also deductible, even though the many purchases of equipment would face negative taxes under the bill.

As mentioned earlier, the Bradley-Gephardt proposal was much more forthright in meeting revenue and distributional constraints. However, it too was not sufficiently comprehensive. One of its major revenue-raising features was to convert all itemized deductions into credits by allowing them to be deducted at only one tax rate.[8] While this might be justifiable for some purposes, it made little sense with respect to legitimate deductions to reach the tax base. A person with $1,000 of interest income and $1,000 of interest expense, for instance, would pay more tax than someone with no interest income and expense. The proposal eliminated the indexing of tax brackets for inflation, thus providing for significant tax rate increases over time. Another major source of revenues was to eliminate the exclusion for employer-provided health benefits. This exclusion was clearly inefficient, but with no replacement program there was a danger of increasing the number of uninsured Americans. As a practical matter, this exclusion was not going to be eliminated, so large, alternative, sources of funds were necessary. Bradley-Gephardt also did not increase the dependent exemption. As a result, a number of larger poor households with dependents would have been subject to income taxation.[9] Because Bradley-Gephardt also repealed indexation of tax brackets, the number of poor persons subject to taxation would have been scheduled to increase over time, and tax rates on all taxpayers would have risen rapidly in a manner similar to the 1970s.

As mentioned earlier, at a political level, it was decided that Treasury would not publicly criticize these proposals, since their sponsors were potential allies.

SOME IMPLICATIONS OF THE PROCESS

Initial principles, constraints, data development, and comprehensiveness all helped determine the direction of the tax reform process. The goal of rate reduction, combined with the constraints of revenue neutrality and distributional neutrality prevented the process from deviating too far from its original path. Here are a few examples.

Abandonment of Consumption Taxes

Although advocates of consumption taxes and of expensing for capital equipment were to oppose many parts of tax reform, they were never able to come up with viable alternatives. One major reason was that such proposals would involve significant reductions in the tax base. In a revenue-neutral proposal, this would mean higher rather than lower tax rates. In a distributionally neutral proposal, it would also mean significantly higher top rates on both individuals and corporations. Finally, many consumption tax advocates were not willing to bite the political bullet of treating borrowing and lending consistently—that is, eliminating interest deductions if interest payments were to be made nontaxable, or requiring that loans (negative saving) be made taxable if positive saving was to become deductible.

In practice, consumption tax advocates and those who wanted to significantly reduce taxes on capital income often confined themselves to attacking the tax reform effort. They were almost never willing to spell out the rate, revenue, and distributional implications of their alternatives. Nor did they concern themselves with "technical" matters such as how to restructure tax treaties with other countries, none of which has ever been able to implement a full-scale consumption tax. Between the original Treasury proposal and the final tax reform act, these proponents thought they obtained a small success in accelerating deductions for depreciable capital, but it was a Pyrrhic victory because they they did this in a way that led Congress to pay for the change by actually increasing tax rates on capital income.

Abandonment of Investment Policy Through the Tax Code

One of the major difficulties with the changes in depreciation allowances put into the Economic Recovery Tax Act of 1981 was that the same rate of depreciation was applied to almost all equipment no matter how fast it actually depreciated. This created incentives to buy different types of equipment for tax rather than economic reasons. Once the principles of equity and efficiency were adopted in tax reform, it was inconsistent to maintain a depreciation system that created very different rates of taxation on equal amounts of income. A new depreciation schedule, one more related to actual depreciation, was required.

In addition, the investment credit adopted in the 1960s had the same problem: it resulted in very uneven rates of taxation on different forms of capital equipment. A simple example illustrates these distortions: the individual investing $100 in an asset lasting 7 years, then taking the earnings and depreciation from that asset to buy another asset lasting 7 years, will receive two investment credits— twice as many as the investor buying only one asset that lasts 14 years.[10] The principles of tax reform required that the effective tax rate on income from all assets be made more equal by either amending or abandoning the investment credit.

Since significant rate reduction was a target of reform, it was not surprising that modest reform of these existing capital income provisions would prove inadequate. Elimination, not merely reform, of the investment credit quickly became necessary to finance the rate reductions that were to apply to the corporate sector. Maintaining that credit, or providing for expensing and other consumption tax goals, would have required higher tax rates. The goal of lower rates strongly supported abandonment of the implementation of investment policy through the tax code.

Abandonment of the Regressive Taxation Favored by the Extreme Wing of the Supply-Side Movement

Absent base broadening, it is almost impossible in a revenue-neutral bill to reduce tax burdens for the poor without increasing average marginal tax rates in the economy. This problem is inherent in the design of both welfare and income tax systems. Higher marginal tax rates in turn affect incentives, a concern to supply-siders, and raise the marginal effective tax rates on capital income, a concern to those who want to lower the cost of capital. The ways out of this dilemma are to reduce expenditures or, in the case of capital, to shift even more of the tax burden to labor. Another alternative is to broaden the tax base but, in truth, the funds provided by base broadening can almost always be used to meet supply-side or cost of capital goals if those funds are not spent on low-income individuals.

Many of those opposed to increases in personal exemptions recognized this trade-off from the start. Indirectly, however, they were put in the awkward position of voting for maintaining or expanding the increases in taxes on low-income individuals.

It would be unfair to state that the majority of those who called themselves supply-side advocates opposed reduction in taxes on low-income individuals. This group, like many other groups that become defined by narrow criterion, was quite split. Nonetheless, acceptance of tax reform objectives clearly contradicted the more extreme version of supply-side economics, which would place the highest tax rates on the first dollars of income, not the last.

Significant Base Broadening for High-Income Individuals

Outside of reductions in taxes for low-income individuals, tax reform came to be popularly defined by what happened to the top rate. Few paid attention to all of the other rates faced by taxpayers. Newspaper headlines would blare out proposed changes in the top rate, while ignoring altogether other parts of the rate schedule. To better understand how constraints on the process worked, focus must turn toward the high-income group.

As stated earlier, the goals of revenue neutrality and distributional neutrality imply revenue neutrality for *each* income class. Therefore, a drop of about one-third in the top rate required about a 50 percent expansion of the tax base for the group of taxpayers paying that rate of tax.[11]

What became obvious was that there were limits on the means that could be used to expand the tax base for high-income individuals. Much of the income recognized at that level came from dividends and interest. Since dividends were subject to double taxation and interest was fully taxed on both real and inflationary components, no expansion of the base was possible here. If anything, the proposition that real income should be taxed only once meant that that portion of the base should be contracted. Four major options were left.

Capital gains also stood out as a source of income for taxpayers at the top tax rates and, indeed, Treasury's initial study proposed full taxation of real capital gains. While full taxation of gains that were real (not due to inflation) would have offset almost all of the revenue pick-up from elimination of the capital gains exclusion, it would not have resulted in a full offset for high-income groups because they tend to recognize greater-than-average amounts of real relative to inflationary gains.[12]

On the deduction side of the ledger, the search for revenue sources from high-income taxpayers led quickly to a second large item: deductions for state and local income taxes. If they could be limited, the lower federal rate for high-income taxpayers would be easier to justify, although the effective state tax rate would have been higher.[13] In the tax reform process, Treasury was slow to abandon proposals to eliminate these deductions, in part because of an understanding of their effect on the distributional analysis and on high-income taxpayers.

Limiting the use of tax shelters presented the third major area in which base expansion could be achieved at the top.

A final method of achieving some rate reduction at the top came from the eventual shift in taxes from individuals to corporations. In effect, a portion of the reduction in the top rate could be justified without any individual base expansion at all. While this shift was eventually used to justify some one-third of the reduction in the top rate, it did not occur until the end of the initial Treasury process. After base broadening decisions had been made, it turned out that setting a top individual and corporate rate close to each other would require higher corporate and lower individual rates. Because of an unwillingness to expand the base in other areas, however, this shift quickly became a necessary political component of all the bills.

ONWARD TO ENACTMENT

The Treasury Department's proposal (Treasury I) underwent several reincarnations after its release—the administration's or president's proposal (so-called Treasury II); the Ways and Means bill; and the Senate Finance bill—before passage of the final Tax Reform Act of 1986. The process in each stage was remarkably similar. First, public responsibility for carrying forward with the project primarily rested with one person. Second, the process always involved a series of steps: give-aways designed to appease some of those who would be offended, the publication of distributional and revenue tables showing that the package had become regressive and lost revenues, and the offering of a new package that would restore revenues and progressivity—but with some new bells and whistles.

The Treasury II effort was led by new Treasury Secretary James Baker, who had traded positions with Donald Regan, who became White House Chief of Staff. This exchange not only insured the commitment of the administration to tax reform, but put the new secretary in the position of wanting to show that he could deliver on what had quickly grown into the major policy initiative of the administration in 1985 and 1986. Baker relied heavily on Richard Darman, who became Deputy Secretary.

The Bipartisan Effort and the Compromises

When the bill went to the Ways and Means Committee, Chairman Daniel Rostenkowski next took on the responsibility for ensuring that the project not be dropped. Partly because tax reform promised more equal treatment of equals, reduced taxation of the poor, and an attack on tax shelters, it almost became impossible for him to imply that he, his committee, or the Democratic House would be the source of failure. The move toward bipartisan effort was enhanced when Rostenkowski

went to the White House and offered to deliver up a bill if President
Reagan agreed not to attack the House bill while it was being ne-
gotiated.

At the Senate Finance Committee, responsibility fell on Chairman
Robert Packwood (R-Or.). Neither he nor his committee were known
as fans of comprehensive reform, but again the onus of failure—the
inability to reduce rates, cut back on tax shelters, and help "families"—was one that he could not accept.

The process was often acrimonious. The beginning of each stage
involved a set of give-aways. Soon thereafter distributional and revenue tables would show that the package had become regressive and
lost revenues.

At this point, the staff of the Treasury or the Joint Committee on
Taxation would come under attack for carrying the news. In two examples, David Brockway and Randy Weiss, leaders of the Joint Committee, came under direct and public attack by the chairman of the
Senate Finance Committee (Birnbaum and Murray 1987, pp. 213–218).
In the end, however, these attacks would prove useless, and there
would begin a widespread search for new, alternative sources of revenues—although seldom would previous give-aways be abandoned.

The compromises along the way, of course, had their toll both on
reform and on those responsible for the succeeding package. The
route from the Treasury study to the president's proposal began with
the usual give-away of items both small and big. It was felt that issues
such as tax preferences for religious clergy were too small to fight,
while other groups such as veterans were too powerful. Significant
attempts were also made to appease those who wanted to protect
capital, oil and gas, and certain other industries. Early business supporters of tax reform, on the other hand, did not want to give up rate
reduction. Two proposed solutions in the Treasury II package were
to impose a "windfall profits tax" on old capital and to deny transition rules, thus attacking old investments as well as new ones.[14]

In Ways and Means, Chairman Rostenkowski knew that the windfall profits tax on old capital would not work. In addition, he could
not obtain a majority unless he gave up the revenues gained through
denial of state and local tax deductions. A significant portion of his
solution was to grant less generous depreciation allowances, to increase tax rates both directly and through reductions in the income
levels at which different rate brackets would begin, and to grant Ways
and Means Committee members smaller special interest provisions.

Senator Packwood, in turn, now faced higher rates than the administration or the Republican Senate would support and a dwindled

list of unused reform options by which to pay for changes. He also granted members various revenue-losing provisions in exchange for their support. His initial solution to this revenue dilemma was to try games such as the denial of sales tax deductions to businesses— a denial that would require businesses with zero income to pay income tax. His final solution was to turn to proposals that had been prepared by the Joint Committee on Taxation on the full taxation of capital gains, restrictions on the use of Individual Retirement Accounts (IRAs) for higher income taxpayers already covered under employer-provided pension plans, and additional denials of loss deductions in any investment that looked like a tax shelter.

Additional Sources of Revenue

In sum, the additional sources of revenues that paid for the give-aways between Treasury I and the end of the whole process fall mainly into four categories: higher tax rates, double taxation of certain forms of income, new base expansions, and complex, back-door provisions.

Higher tax rates were achieved in several ways. A promised increase from $1,000 to $2,000 in the personal exemption was implemented over time rather than immediately and without indexation for inflation during the phase-in period. In real terms, the net increase was smaller than proposed initially. Tax rates below the top rate were also raised at times. A proposed tax rate of 25 percent for many middle-income individuals became converted to a rate of 28 percent by the time of final passage. Less base broadening was thereby required in middle-income brackets.

Double taxation of income was an especially popular means of amending the reform proposal. Proposals to move away from double taxation of corporate income—that is, to tax income once when earned by the corporation and then again when paid out as dividends— were reduced drastically, then eventually abandoned altogether. Indexing of capital gains for inflation was eliminated, then replaced in the final bill with full taxation of all nominal gains, even those due to inflation. Proposals to index depreciation allowances were also eliminated. Rather than allow real depreciation to be claimed, these changes resulted in understatements of depreciation in later years. However, the additional revenues also helped support the higher-than-real depreciation allowances in the early years.

New base expansions were few in number. In the bill to come out of the Senate, some restrictions on IRAs and the full taxation of capital gains can be listed, but the capital gains adjustment did not account for inflation. Moreover, the revenue pick-up from expanded gains taxation was modest, since taxpayers had the option of realizing fewer gains to avoid this increase in tax rate on actual realizations. This issue would continue to haunt tax politics for the rest of the decade.

Complex, back-door provisions became the real art form of the later process. In a number of cases, these provisions were to set many of the policy dilemmas and debates of the next few years. The Senate Finance Committee, for instance, wanted to claim that it had reduced the top rate to 28 percent. But it couldn't come up with enough base broadening to justify the change. As a result, it created a fourth rate of 33 percent, and then called it something else—a "phase out of the benefits of the personal exemption and the bottom tax rate." This indirect increase in marginal tax rates on many high-income individuals resulted from attempts to phase out the "benefits" of the 15 percent bracket and the personal exemption. This was to create what was called a "bubble" effect—tax rates of 15, 28, 33, and 28 percent; marginal tax rates actually fell at the highest income levels after rising in a bubble fashion at preceding income levels.[15]

Even more popular were increasingly complex means of imposing minimum taxes and limits on loss write-offs.[16] Almost none of the tax increase was attributed to those individuals who actually had real losses. Because the Joint Committee did not adopt the Treasury method of imputing to partners particular preferences and special tax breaks, any proposal to cut back on those breaks directly would not show up in the tables. As a result, the more complex and indirect methods of changing the tax system appeared distributionally superior to the direct methods of achieving the same goals.

The new alternative minimum tax was to define not only special tax breaks as "preferences" subject to minimum tax, but was to include such items as personal exemptions, state and local taxes, some interest deductions allowed on second mortgages, and much more. Taxpayers were often required to calculate depreciation and other allowances two different ways and then pay the higher tax that resulted. In addition, these calculations had to be kept for years, as the taxpayer might recapture these accelerated payments of tax when the process reversed itself, as when an initially faster depreciation schedule left fewer later allowances. Businesses were required to pay tax on the higher of taxable income or income reported on financial returns, even when there was no special tax preference involved. This was a reaction to the populist sentiment that corporations reporting positive financial income should pay tax on that income.[17]

Although many of these changes whittled away at tax reform, they could not eliminate its basic premise. The political process followed first by Secretary Baker and Deputy Secretary Darman of the Treasury Department, then by Representative Rostenkowski of Ways and Means, and finally by Senator Packwood, still required maintaining the most basic goals of tax reform. Substantial erosion was allowed around the edges but, by the same token, enough political support was garnered to attain passage.

Notes

1. See, for instance, former Secretary of the Treasury Regan's comments in Regan (1988, pp. 202–203).

2. One dilemma for those favoring investment incentives was where to stop. For instance, should tax rates be allowed to be negative? A consumption tax would maintain tax rates at zero. Because of tax arbitrage, an investment credit system might maintain a positive tax rate for equity investments and a negative tax rate for investments purchased with borrowed dollars.

3. Giving full credit is impossible. Some of the personal involvement of political appointees is detailed in Birnbaum and Murray (1987), and Conlan et al. (1990). Facing space limitations of their own, however, these authors were not able to give adequate attention to the extraordinary importance of Assistant Secretary John E. (Buck) Chapoton's laying of the groundwork and of his influence with the Treasury Secretary and the White House; of Assistant Secretary Ronald Pearlman's ability to deal with an extraordinary number of details and the extent of his true bent toward reform; and of Deputy Assistant Secretary Charles E. McLure's tireless, subtle, yet convincing argument of the tax reform cause. These three individuals were all forceful advocates for reform and, most importantly, helped convince Secretary Regan to back a strong reform effort. Their successors, Assistant Secretary Roger Mentz and Deputy Assistant Secretary Don Fullerton, faced much difficulty in keeping together a coherent plan in the face of many administration and congressional attempts to make decisions that could not be technically implemented. Where credit has been especially lacking is with respect to the civil servants of the Treasury Department and the staff of the Joint Committee on Taxation. Although it is probably unfair to single out only a few individuals, it would be even more unfair not to mention the Treasury's Thomas Neubig and Geraldine Gerardi, who volunteered to meet with me daily to coordinate the effort, and Victor Thuronyi, who constantly came forward to help with the writing and analysis. Without their voluntary efforts—none were obligated to help in this way—it is unclear whether the Treasury Department would ever have been able to get off the ground. Dennis Ross, later to become a Deputy Assistant Secretary, made a brilliant effort to help write up, draft, and coordinate much of the legal work.

4. The Treasury Department group involved in discussing these modules with the secretary included Assistant Secretary for Tax Policy John E. (Buck) Chapoton and, later, Ronald Pearlman; the Deputy Assistant Secretary for Tax Analysis, Charles McLure; the Assistant Secretary for Economic Policy, Manuel Johnson; the Undersecretary of the Treasury, Beryl Sprinkel; Commissioner of the Internal Revenue Roscoe Egger; Deputy Secretary Tim McNamar; Assistant Secretary for Legislative Affairs Bruce Thompson; Assistant Secretary for Public Affairs and Public Liaison Alfred Kingon; and Thomas Dawson and Chris Hicks, who worked as close aides in the Executive Secretary. See Birnbaum and Murray (1987).

5. Among the many business supporters of tax reform were companies in electronics and technology, most retail establishments and sellers of services, food and beverage companies, and many others who benefited little from existing tax preferences. Household names such as General Motors, IBM, and Sara Lee were also active supporters at various stages.

6. Again, there was an exception. The goal of removing the poor from the income tax rolls required that the tax system be made more progressive at the bottom. This goal overrode the distributional neutrality constraint.

7. The success of this effort was due in large part to the efforts of Susan Nelson of the Office of Tax Analysis, who initiated an effort to insure that the data sets being developed could properly account for many of the changes we were proposing.

8. In effect, the deductions would be allowed against only the first tax bracket. For example, if the tax rate schedule provided for a 15 percent tax rate on all income up to $50,000 and a 28 percent tax rate on all income in excess of $50,000, Bradley-Gephardt would allow itemized deductions only against the 15 percent rate. Under the old law, before taking $10,000 of medical deductions, someone with $100,000 of taxable income would have $90,000 of taxable income.   Under Bradley-Gephardt, $50,000 would be taxed at the 15 percent rate, $40,000 at the 28 percent rate (as under old law), but the medical expenses, now no longer fully deductible, would be taxed at a 13 percent rate (the difference between 28 percent and 15 percent).

9. Bradley-Gephardt concentrated relief at the bottom through increases in the standard deduction. This deduction was not adjusted for number of dependents. Poverty measures indicated that for a family just above the poverty level, an additional member adds $2,000 to the income necessary to keep that family out of poverty. Without a personal exemption of $2,000 or more, therefore, at some point larger size households might be in poverty, yet still subject to income taxation.

10. The interested reader might look ahead to table 8.2 or 9.1 for the variance in tax rates on different types of investment in the period before tax reform.

11. Let B be the base taxed at 50 percent. If the rate is dropped by one-third to 33 percent, then the base must expand by 50 percent for the same amount of taxes to be collected. In other words, $.5 \times B = .33 \times ([1.5] \times B)$.

12. There are two reasons for the higher returns of higher income individuals. First, suppose two individuals in the same income situation both invest in the stock market, and one succeeds in generating significant gains, while the other does not. Measured prior to their investment, they look the same. Measured at the end of the year when filing their tax returns, the one with a higher rate of return on the investment is the one who falls into the higher income class. Second, even if one only looks at income excluding capital gains, real gains relative to nominal gains are still skewed toward higher income classes. Among the reasons for this latter result are greater risk-taking at that level, better management of portfolios, or simply better knowledge of the markets.

13. The argument for limiting state and local income taxes went far beyond rates. Should the federal government, for instance, subsidize state taxation? Should the states give a deduction for federal taxes? These and other issues of fiscal federalism were raised in the course of the ensuing debate.

14. As originally put together, the windfall profits tax that was suggested by Economic Policy Office of Treasury would have imposed a several percentage point increase in corporate tax rates on any company that held any depreciable capital. The Tax Policy Office managed to remove this version and to make the proposal more oriented to the amount of depreciable capital held. The final proposal, however, remained both unfair—the tax rate would have been too high—and essentially unsaleable.

15. This debate, too, was to carry forward to later years. Amendments were made in

1990 in the structure of the top rate, but the attempt to impose those rate increases through the back door were maintained.

16. The means by which the Joint Committee performed distributional analysis also supported the political tendency to deal with some issues through the back door—through increases in minimum taxes and limitations on write-offs of "passive" losses and interest payments. Note what happened when limits were imposed on the extent to which business losses could be taken or when minimum taxes were imposed. The Joint Committee imputed these increases in taxes almost entirely to high-income individuals.

17. Citizens for Tax Justice, a labor-backed, Washington-based organization, had significant influence here through the publication of tables relating tax liability to financial income.

Chapter Eight

WHAT WAS ACHIEVED IN TAX REFORM?

The political process succeeded in derailing only part of the tax reform effort. In general, it was impossible to move far from the overall principles and constraints set out at the beginning of the process. Once it became clear that an administratively feasible system could be designed that would lower rates and eliminate shelters, remove the poor from the tax roles, and treat individuals with equal income more equally, no one wanted to be known as the person who stood in the way of this effort and caused it to fail.[1] The organization of tax policy in the U.S. concentrates decision making in the hands of the president, the Treasury secretary and the chairpersons of the tax-writing committees. This concentration implies that at each stage of reform—Treasury II or the president's proposals, the House Ways and Means bill, and the Senate Finance bill—failure could have been attributed primarily to one of them. Even if all were dubious about reform at one time or another, none wanted the onus of failure pinned on him.

The entire tax reform process took almost three years. It was never directed to meet short-term goals; rather, it was aimed at correcting some of the long-term distortions created by the tax laws. This reform effort started and concluded with the basic premise that the purpose of any tax system—indeed, the very reason for its existence—is to raise revenues. It is only reasonable to require that the system also create minimal distortions and inefficiencies in the long run. Despite the slow speed of the political process—often, yesterday's problems, not today's, were being solved—tax policy since World War II had been used increasingly as a short-term economic tool.[2] Overemphasis on this one aspect of tax policy in turn had prevented policymakers from dealing with longer-run issues.

The simple recognition of the basic purpose of a tax system must be listed as one of the major achievements of the tax reform effort.

The historian Elliot Brownlee states the case quite strongly. "It can be argued that, as a result of the bipartisan effort, the Tax Reform Act of 1986 advanced a process of restoring to federal taxation the sense of balance sought by the founders of the republic. The Act represented a major step in the elimination of tax-based privilege, while reaffirming the duties of citizenship" (Brownlee 1989, p. 1620).

In the end, the Tax Reform Act of 1986 represented one of the most sweeping tax code changes in the history of the country. Certainly, it involved the largest reshuffling of incentives and priorities ever achieved in a roughly revenue-neutral act. This chapter provides an assessment of what was achieved, while the next chapter focuses on what was left undone and what new problems were created.

MORE PROGRESSIVE TAXATION AND IMPROVED INCENTIVES FOR LOWER INCOME WORKERS

In the end, tax reform was probably mildly progressive or at least distributionally neutral. Table 8.1 shows the distribution of individual income tax returns as reported by the Joint Committee on Taxation after enactment. A number of caveats to this table must be

Table 8.1 PERCENTAGE CHANGE IN 1988 IN INCOME TAX LIABILITY UNDER THE TAX REFORM ACT OF 1986

Income class (thousands of 1986 dollars)	Percentage change in income tax liability 1988	Average income tax rate (percent) Prior law	1986 act
Less than $10	−65.1	1.6	0.5
$10 to $20	−22.3	5.7	4.4
$20 to $30	−9.8	8.3	7.5
$30 to $40	−7.7	9.5	8.7
$40 to $50	−9.1	11.1	10.1
$50 to $75	−1.8	13.3	13.1
$75 to $100	−1.2	15.7	15.6
$100 to $200	−2.2	19.3	18.9
$200 and above	−2.4	22.8	22.3
Total	−6.1	11.8	11.1

Source: Joint Committee on Taxation (1987, pp. 17–18).
Note: These figures do not take into account certain provisions affecting individuals. Thus, total tax reductions are somewhat different from what is indicated in this table.

expressed. The tax cuts at the top do not take into account individuals' abilities to avoid increased capital gains tax by reducing the amount of gains realized. The percentage cuts at the bottom, on the other hand, can be misleading because average income tax liability in the $10,000 and under range was only $60; hence, a 65 percent cut amounted to only $39 per tax return. Corporate tax increases were not included, which would probably raise tax liability more in higher income classes. Despite these caveats, most estimates of tax reform have indicated a mild increase in progressivity.[3]

Tax reform succeeded in reducing the taxation of the poor and low income individuals through three different changes: increases in the personal exemption from $1,080 in 1986 to $2,000 by 1989 for all taxpayers and their dependents; increases in the standard deduction, which reduces taxable income for all taxpayers who do not itemize or declare interest payments, state and local taxes, or other allowed deductions (for a married couple, the standard deduction was increased from $3,660 in 1986 to $5,000 by 1988); and significant expansion, as well as indexing for inflation, of an earned income tax credit (EITC) given to low-income workers with children. When fully phased in, the expansion and the indexing together raised the maximum credit (from $550 in 1986 to $874 in 1988), while the credit did not phase out completely until income exceeded $18,576 (IRS 1988, vol. 1, p. 145).

The first two of these provisions raised the tax-exempt level of income to about the poverty level for households of almost all sizes. At low-income levels above poverty, the average tax decrease was also significant, primarily because these two provisions considerably reduced the amount of income subject to taxation.

The change in the earned income tax credit (EITC) ensured that the tax cuts for lower-income individuals were concentrated on workers. For households with both labor earnings and children, the EITC can be viewed as providing either outlays from the government or offsets against income and Social Security taxes. In 1989 about $4 billion in additional outlays or reduced tax collections was needed to pay for the earned income tax credit. While the maximum credit amount was raised, it was only returned to the real level that applied in 1975, the first year that the credit was available. Because of the increase in the income levels at which the credit began to phase out, however, it was now made available to full-time workers at minimum and slightly higher wages. Under old law the credit had phased out completely or substantially for such workers, making it a credit for part-time or part-year workers. The 1986 EITC expansion was also to set a precedent for further increases that would be enacted in 1990 (see chapter 11).

When compared to an expansion of welfare programs, the net impact of these changes should have been to increase the overall incentive to work for those who have a discrete choice between working and not working. As taxpayers moved into the phase-out range of the earned income tax credit, however, combined direct marginal tax rates, including state income tax rates, rose as high as 45 percent. Of this total, 10 percentage points were contributed by the EITC phase-out alone, while the remainder was roughly composed of 15 percentage points of Social Security taxes (including the employer's share), 15 percentage points of federal income taxation, and about 5 percentage points of state income taxation in a typical state. In the EITC phase-out range, marginal rates were higher under the new law than before, so that here the new EITC reduced the marginal incentive to undertake more work.[4]

In terms of base broadening, there were few reforms that applied at low-income levels. The extra exemption for the elderly was replaced with a less valuable increase in the standard deduction. Because of the increase in the personal exemption for all taxpayers and the nontaxability of most Social Security benefits, however, the elderly still maintained lower taxes than other taxpayers in equal situations, although the disparity was lessened.

One change—full taxation of unemployment insurance—complemented the tax reductions applying to low-income persons. Under old tax law, priority in taxation was given to low-income unemployed persons over low-income workers. Under the Tax Reform Act of 1986, poor workers not only pay significantly less tax than in prior years, but pay no higher tax than unemployed persons with the same amount of income. Although many unemployed may not pay any more tax in total—other increased benefits may offset the loss of nontaxation of unemployment insurance—their *relative* incentive to work is still improved. Thus, lower (or negative for some EITC recipients) rates of tax on earned income, plus higher or more equal rates of tax on unemployment income complement each other in improving work incentives. The trade-off of lower tax rates for a broader base, of course, is the essence of tax reform.

Some comparisons give an idea of the magnitude of the overall changes in the taxation of poor and low-income workers. For a married couple with two dependents, the tax threshold was about $7,980 for 1986, but rose to $12,800 by 1988 under the new law. This tax threshold was above the estimated poverty threshold of $12,092 for the same year (U.S. Bureau of the Census, various years). If the earned income tax credit is included in the calculations, the changes are more significant. For instance, the average income tax rate (income taxes, less EITC, divided by income) at the poverty level dropped from 3.3 percent in 1986 to minus 5.3 percent in 1988. Thus, at poverty levels, the EITC might be viewed as offsetting some Social Security tax as well as income tax.

The Trend to Tax Low-Income Workers

At low-income levels above poverty, the changes were still significant but less dramatic. From an historical perspective, the 1986 Tax Reform Act only partially offset the trend to raise taxes on low-income workers. Federal income tax rates on a family of four at one-half median income, for instance, were zero until 1960. Inflation and real growth then began to push the one-half median income family into positive tax brackets, and previous tax reforms were insufficient to compensate for the increase. By 1985, the average tax rate reached 6.5 percent. Under the 1986 tax act, the average rate initially dropped to about 5 percent, but then rose again to 5.5 percent by the end of the decade. At this income level, there were no earned income credits available to offset Social Security taxes. The combined employer-employee Social Security tax rates rose from 4 percent in 1955 to 13.4 percent in 1984, when the tax reform study was underway, and then to 15.3 percent in 1990.

These tax decreases, of course, need to be put into perspective. Tax reform raised the personal exemption to $2,000 by 1989, but at that time it would have taken a personal exemption of almost $7,500 to offset the same relative amount of income as the $600 personal exemption did in 1948.[5] In addition, Social Security tax increases continued almost unabated. For a family of four with taxable earnings from labor equal to one-half the median income, Social Security taxes and federal income taxes together accounted for 5 percent or less of income before 1960. In 1990 these taxes equalled 20.9 percent of income.

IMPROVEMENTS IN THE ALLOCATION OF ASSETS

One major benefit of the 1986 Tax Reform Act was a significant improvement in the allocation of assets and investment within the economy. The government greatly reduced its role in directing which industries and which types of business activity should be favored and which should be penalized. Effective tax rates across assets were made more equal.

Table 8.2 presents estimates of effective tax rates on new or marginal purchases of assets for different asset types and categories. These calculations take into account both corporate and personal taxes or returns from these assets.[6] As can be seen, prior to the Tax Reform Act of 1986, the principal differences in effective rates across assets were among equipment, structures, and inventory, and less among different types of equipment or among different types of structures. Much, but not all, of the variance in effective tax rates could be attributed to the investment tax credit, which was made available to equipment but not structures, and was not adjusted in the case of equipment according to the economic depreciation rate or life of the asset. Most types of equipment are shown to have tax rates of about 7 percent before 1986; under inflation assumptions lower than the 4 percent used in the table, the effective tax rate begins to go negative. Structures, on the other hand, average about a 35 percent tax rate under pre-tax reform law, while for inventories the rate is 58 percent.

Under tax reform, the differences in effective rates were narrowed considerably. Fewer distinctions were made among types of equipment or between structures and equipment. Thus, the tax rate on investments in structures were approximately 39 percent, while on equipment the average was 38 percent. The tax rate on inventories was also reduced and made closer to returns on other assets.

Human and Intangible Capital

Not shown in the table is another form of equalization of effective tax rates that is important to the economy but difficult to measure under traditional procedures. Economists have long recognized that investments are made not just in physical assets, but in research, better management, and human capital. Payments for these intangible forms of capital are difficult to calculate separately from other wage payments. In the case of invention and ideas, the common concept of "investment" may be inadequate to describe, much less measure, a process that may involve little in the way of monetary investment in labor or capital in the traditional sense.

Many of the most dynamic companies in an economy pay the statutory tax rate on the returns to their ideas and advances in knowledge and procedures. That is, such advances are often associated with very high rates of return to the companies that succeed. In part, the high rate of return is related to the risk of the ventures. These high rates of return cannot be offset by investment credits or other preferences that are only associated with gross purchases of physical assets. Nor does "expensing" or immediate write-off of wage payments result in a much lower rate of tax, because the riskier investments tend to generate a higher rate of return and because the tax law grants very imperfect loss offsets.[7]

New Business Versus Old Business

Closely related to the discrimination under old law against dynamic and successful firms was a broad discrimination against new firms, as well as against certain older firms that had not been profitable for a number of years. For a given marginal investment, both types of firms were made to face higher tax rates than most established firms. Thus, new or formerly nonprofitable firms had to achieve a higher-than-normal return from an investment in order to compete (Steuerle 1983). The reduced threat of entry into the market of new firms may have lessened the efforts made by existing firms to take advantage of the latest technologies and market opportunities.

Two common features of postwar investment incentives were that they were available only as tax reductions and were available almost immediately, either at time of investment or soon thereafter. These features implied that any tax saving would be mainly received by those firms with enough outside income to make full use of the credits and accelerated deductions. New firms could seldom make use of such incentives because new equipment could not be expected to return enough output in so short a period of time to create sufficient taxable income to offset the accelerated deductions or to generate sufficient tax liability to offset credits against tax. Some established firms with little income were also denied tax benefits, as existing lines of business generated inadequate taxable income to allow full use of incentives for marginal investments.[8]

This helps explain why some companies in basic industries supported a tax reform that eliminated the investment tax credit: they felt they were at a competitive disadvantage with respect to new investment since they already had a large carryover of unused investment credits from previous years. Potential new firms, of course, are always unrepresented in the political process because they don't yet exist.

Here is an example of the discrimination under the old law. At a zero inflation rate, an asset generates output valued at about 31 percent

Table 8.2 TOTAL EFFECTIVE TAX RATES ON CORPORATE INVESTMENT, BY BROAD ASSET TYPE AND BY INDUSTRY
(percentage)

	Old law	Treasury[a]	Administration[a]	House	Senate	New law
Total	38	34	30	40	39	41
By Asset Type						
Equipment & Structures	29	33	25	38	37	39
Equipment	11	33	24	39	34	38
Structures	38	33	26	37	38	39
Inventories	58	35	44	47	47	48
By Specific Asset Type						
Equipment						
Automobiles	7	34	26	45	40	46
Office & computing equipment	8	35	26	41	42	42
Trucks, buses, & trailers	8	34	25	39	39	41
Aircraft	7	34	25	45	36	41
Construction machinery	7	33	24	33	35	35
Mining & oilfield machinery	7	32	24	41	34	40
Service industry machinery	7	32	24	38	34	40
Tractors	7	32	23	41	34	38
Instruments	13	31	22	42	34	39
Other equipment	7	37	26	42	33	38
General industrial equipment	12	32	23	40	32	37

Metalworking machinery	7	31	22	38	30	35
Electric transmission equipment	25	37	25	45	39	44
Communications equipment	7	34	24	29	30	30
Other electrical equipment	7	34	24	38	30	35
Furniture & fixtures	7	33	23	38	30	34
Special industrial equipment	7	32	22	36	29	33
Agricultural equipment	6	31	22	36	28	33
Fabricated metal products	19	31	21	35	32	40
Engines & turbines	32	34	24	44	42	46
Ships & boats	6	34	23	39	35	42
Railroad equipment	27	32	22	35	33	29
Structures						
Mining oil & gas	16	28	10	11	19	20
Other	48	39	34	44	45	46
Industrial structures	44	36	31	41	43	43
Public utility structures	28	31	18	36	34	37
Commercial structures	41	34	29	38	40	41
Farm structures	42	34	29	38	40	41

Sources: Jane G. Gravelle (1984 and 1986).

a. Calculations for Treasury and administration proposals assume that taxation of dividends on existing shares does raise overall effective tax rates on capital.

Note: Calculations assume a 4 percent inflation rate and separate marginal tax rates for corporations, interest income, dividend income, and capital gains. Only effective tax rates on corporate investments are shown here, but the effective tax rates include both corporate and personal taxes. Investment is financed one-third by debt.

of the initial price of the asset over a two and a half year period if it depreciates at 10 percent per year and yields about a 4 percent real return over and above depreciation. Yet under old law, tax deductions and credits could offset income equal to 80 percent of purchase price over the same period. Since the income from the asset is less than half of the allowed offsets, only the established firm with existing flows of taxable income could make full use of the deductions and credits.

The new law reduced some of the disparities between new and established firms. After passage, deductions in the first two and a half years only offset income up to 56 percent of the purchase price. Thus, while discrimination against new business was not eliminated, it was lessened considerably. Most of the change between the two laws was due to the repeal of the investment tax credit. The greater leveling of tax rates faced by new and old businesses served to enhance productivity, in part by making potential new businesses a more likely source of competition for established businesses.

INVESTMENT IN MORE PRODUCTIVE ASSETS

Perhaps the major improvement in the tax bill was brought about by a significant restoration of the market incentive to invest in the most productive assets. This restoration was dramatized by the reduction—absent significant inflation—in the incentive to invest in unproductive assets.

Investment in assets with less than maximum productivity is encouraged whenever some assets are tax-favored. At the extreme, investment in unproductive assets can even become profitable when one of two conditions holds: the effective tax rate on equity-financed investments is negative, or the after-tax real interest rate is negative.[9] In the latter case it is through leveraging—borrowing (or selling short a tax-disfavored asset) to purchase another asset that is relatively tax preferred—that the taxpayer can profit on an after-tax basis even when the asset itself produces a negative rate of return.

The 1986 tax act took two important steps to considerably reduce the probability that the conditions necessary for unproductive investment would hold. First, the investment credit was eliminated. As long as the investor writes off no more than the real cost, acceleration of depreciation allowances can never result in a negative tax rate on equity investments in depreciable assets. To understand this, note that expensing is equivalent under most conditions to a zero tax rate. Any acceleration less than expensing requires that the purchase price be written off over a period of time rather than immediately and, therefore, results in a positive tax rate.

The second step made in the tax act was to lower the marginal tax rate. This makes the tax consequences of any miscalculation of income less important. In the case of interest, the failure to index (both in old and new law) means that the subsidy given to borrowing (or the penalty for lending) is equal to the tax rate times the inflationary component of the interest rate. That subsidy declines when either the tax rate or the inflation rate decreases.

It is apparent that negative after-tax interest rates can induce investment in unproductive capital. When borrowing takes place, the investor must receive a return from the investment itself that is greater than or equal to the after-tax interest rate. If the after-tax real interest rate is positive and real, then the after-tax return from the investment itself (calculated without regard to the borrowing) must also be positive in real terms, else the borrower-investor will not earn enough to pay the after-tax interest rate. When, however, the after-tax interest rate is negative in real terms, the investor may profit personally from investment in an unproductive asset, that is, one with negative real rate of return.[10]

For the interest rate to be positive and real for most business investors, it must be at least twice the rate of inflation when the tax rate is 50 percent, but only one and a half times the inflation rate when the tax rate is 33 percent.[11] As an example, at an inflation rate of 10 percent, the interest rate must be 20 percent or more to prevent the taxpayer with a tax rate of 50 percent from investing in unproductive assets and activities. At an interest cost of exactly 20 percent, the tax deduction pays for one-half of the interest rate or 10 percentage points of cost, while inflation covers the remaining 10 percentage points. Correspondingly, the required interest rate is only 15 percent at a tax rate of 33 percent. Similarly, at an inflation rate of 4 percent, the required interest rate falls one-quarter from 8 percent to 6 percent when the tax rate falls from 50 percent to 33 percent (see figure 8.1).

Not only does the interest rate required to prevent investment in unproductive assets fall with the drop in tax rates, but the new tax rates most likely reduce the interest rate as well. Starting at a given before-tax interest rate, lower tax rates initially increase the after-tax interest rate. As a result, the demand curve for borrowing should initially fall and the supply curve of saving in interest-bearing assets should initially rise. Both movements tend to reduce the interest rate.

Figure 8.1 INTEREST RATES NECESSARY TO PREVENT UNPRODUCTIVE
INVESTMENTS

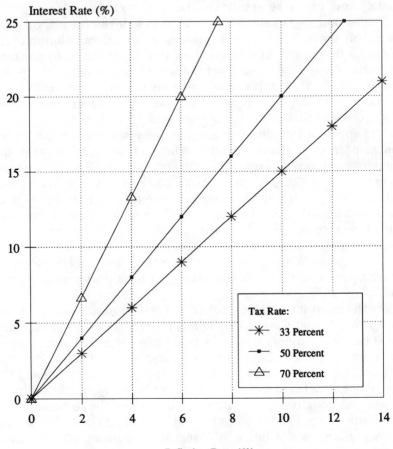

Inflation Rate (%)

Source: Author's calculations (see note 11 of this chapter).

The Attack Against Tax Shelters

As indicated above, when the tax rate on the investment asset was
negative, or the after-tax interest rate was negative, a major problem
arose: the investor could profit from unproductive investments with
negative returns to the economy. Since tax shelters leveraged tax
advantages by both borrowing and purchasing assets that benefited

from credits and early write-offs of expenses, the required before-tax return was often negative.

The 1986 Tax Reform Act significantly reduced the amount of money flowing into such shelters, just as it reduced many other tax arbitrage opportunities, by lowering tax rates and by making the effective tax rate positive for equity investments in various assets. In addition, the Tax Reform Act made a series of additional attacks on shelters by limiting deductions from passive investments,[12] by restricting investment interest payments in excess of investment income, and by deferring many deductions through minimum tax rules. While these latter approaches were often cumbersome and inefficient, they too reduced the flow of monies into shelter investments. An entire industry promoting inefficient investment was almost dismantled, and tax planners and lawyers typically would tell clients that shelter planning was severely restricted.

In many ways, under the 1986 Tax Reform Act, individuals were treated more like corporations: where taxable income from a designated grouping of investment assets (e.g., all passive income for the individual, all income within the corporation for the corporation) is negative, deductions often cannot be used fully. They can be carried over until such time as enough positive taxable income is generated from investments within the same grouping.

LOWER INDIVIDUAL MARGINAL TAX RATES

As advertised, tax reform did succeed in lowering the *marginal* tax rates faced by individuals. *Average* individual rates also dropped, but this can be misleading since average corporate rates increased by a similar amount. Marginal rates were able to drop at the same time as average rates without major revenue loss largely because of the expansion of the tax base.

Figure 8.2 updates figure 2.3 to show the percent of returns taxed at various marginal tax rates. As can be seen, by the time tax reform was almost fully implemented in 1988, marginal rates were lower everywhere, but especially for returns at the very highest levels.

Figure 8.3, in turn, updates figure 2.4 to show estimates of marginal rates for taxpayers at half-median, median, and twice median income (of four-person families). Here it is even clearer that the drop in marginal rates by 1988 was most extensive at median and twice-median income. At half-median income, the increases in personal

Figure 8.2 CUMULATIVE PERCENT OF FEDERAL INCOME TAX RETURNS
TAXED AT OR BELOW EACH SUCCESSIVE MARGINAL RATE

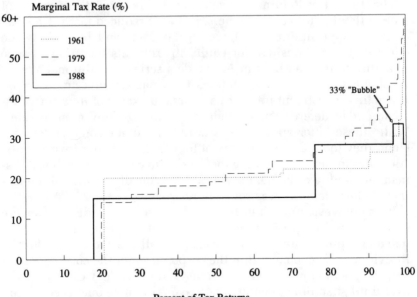

Percent of Tax Returns

Sources: Author's calculations based on data from the Bureau of Economic
Analysis, *Survey of Current Business*, various years, and unpublished data; the
Internal Revenue Service Statistics of Income Division, *Individual Income Tax
Returns*; and Steuerle and Hartzmark (1981, p. 153).

exemptions and standard deductions tend to drop average rates, but
not marginal rates.

REDUCED INFLUENCE OF TAXES ON CONSUMER AND PRODUCER CHOICES

The benefits of lower marginal rates of tax derive not from the lower
rates per se, but from the fact that lowering the rates reduces the
impact of taxes on the decision making of both business managers
and individual investors. While the Tax Reform Act of 1986 did
eliminate a number of special preferences, deductions, and exclusions, many were also retained. The lower rate of taxation, however,
meant that the value of deductions was calculated at a rate of 33

Figure 8.3 FEDERAL INCOME TAX RATES FOR A FAMILY OF FOUR AT
VARIOUS INCOME LEVELS, 1955–1990

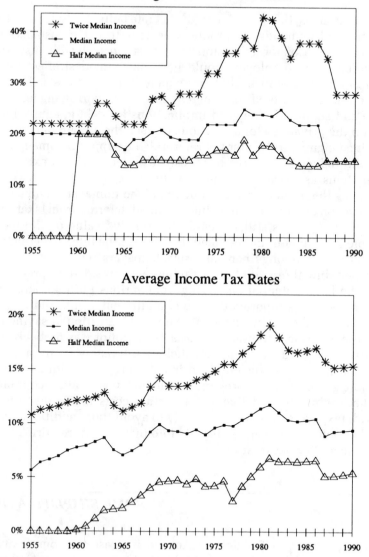

Marginal Income Tax Rates

Average Income Tax Rates

Source: U.S. Department of the Treasury, Office of Tax Analysis (Allen Lerman); U.S.
Bureau of the Census, *Population Reports*, Series P-60, various years; and author's
calculations.

Note: see appendix table A.3.

percent or less for individuals and 34 percent for most corporations. Thus, when choices remained between nontaxable and taxable items, the tax consequences of alternative consumption or production patterns was reduced.

In some areas, the reduction in the tax rate helped lessen excessive, tax-induced demands for products or activities. For instance, the reduced value of the exclusion from taxation of health insurance provided by an employer should have had a modest effect on restraining increases in health care expenditures and costs. The rate reduction also lowered the inherent subsidy to borrowing and may have had significant long-run implications for debt-to-equity ratios within the private sector as a whole. (In fact, the growth rate for debt declined significantly after tax reform).[13] For upper-income taxpayers, the reduced incentive to invest in preferred assets extends to such items as vacation homes. In this case, many tax breaks remained—the imputed rental value remained nontaxable and capital gains tax on any increase in value remained deferred from taxation—but lower tax rates still increased the relative value of alternative taxable investments and reduced the value of the interest deduction.

In choosing among financial assets, taxpayers became more likely to invest directly in equities or savings accounts. Under pre-reform law, the large potential tax saving from various portfolio strategies subsidized and supported the use of additional agents and transactions. While there is no good estimate of the attrition of saving due to these additional transaction costs, the amount was probably substantial. For instance, many tax shelters ultimately spent on assets 80 percent or less of the dollars originally invested, with 20 percent or more going simply to brokers, salesmen, lawyers and accountants. As tax savings fell relative to transaction costs in the post reform world, taxpayers became more likely to avoid those additional costs by channeling saving more directly into investments requiring fewer of these additional intermediaries.

SOME SIMPLIFICATION

Although the 1986 Tax Reform Act did increase the complexity of many types of calculation, it also achieved simplification in a number of areas. Under pre-reform law, there were significant tax savings available to those who did elaborate tax planning involving the use of numerous agents. In many ways, the reduced influence of taxes on economic decision making made life simpler for the saver and investor, who could now concentrate more effort on economic issues and less on tax issues. For those who still invested in shelters subject to minimum tax, the complexity of filing may have increased, but there were many fewer individuals who diverted their investments in that direction. Similarly, the use of trusts for tax planning purposes was largely eliminated.

Among the major simplifications achieved by tax reform was the elimination of record keeping and tax calculations for those no longer eligible for certain deductions. The increase in the standard deduction meant that there was a significant decrease in the number of individuals who had to keep records by which to itemize their tax returns. In addition:

□ Fewer individuals needed to keep track of medical expenses;

□ Sales tax receipts no longer had to be kept, nor did sales tax deduction calculations need to be made;

□ Fewer record-keeping requirements were required of those with employee business expenses, expenses of producing investment income, and other miscellaneous itemized deductions;

□ Calculations were no longer required for income averaging, second-earner expenses, political contribution credits, or dividend exclusions; and

□ Capital gains were made easier to calculate, and the game-playing induced by a capital gains preference was largely, if temporarily, eliminated. (Some this simplification would later be offset in the 1990 Act.)

OTHER GAINS

Tax reform also helped households with dependents by giving the largest increase in the standard deduction to single heads of household. This partly corrected for a situation in which single heads of household had borne the largest percentage tax increases in the postwar era (see appendix table A.2).[14]

The lowering of rates not only improved the efficiency of individual decision making; it reduced the inequity between those who could still make use of deductions and those who could not. For instance, those who receive nontaxable fringe benefits from employers became less favored relative to those who do not receive such benefits.

Equals were also treated much better relative to each other. In particular, those whose earnings came mainly in the form of cash income such as wages and salaries and interest, and had few or no tax deductions, received the largest tax reductions.

The law created limitations on losses for real estate and so-called passive activities; inclusion of intangible drilling costs, private activity state and local bond interest, and other preference items in a minimum tax; limits on the cash method of accounting; and elimination of many industry-specific exclusions and deductions.

Tax reform made more equal the prices paid for meals and entertainment for those who pay for this consumption directly and those who receive the benefits from businesses. The reform reduced slightly in the short-run, but more significantly over the long-run, the tax benefits to those owning residences and vacation homes relative to those with taxable income from wages. It reduced the size of the federal subsidy to state and local borrowing.[15] And it reduced somewhat the inequities between those who do and those who do not receive prizes and awards, in-kind assistance for services rendered to educational institutions, and a few other items of formerly non-taxable income.

SOME FURTHER IMPLICATIONS FOR MACROECONOMIC AND MONETARY POLICY

The economic experience of the late 1970s and early 1980s provided a major lesson for economic policymakers: when negative after-tax interest rates and/or negative tax rates for a significant portion of taxpayers are allowed to persist for extended periods of time, investment will be diverted toward less productive activities, the rate of growth of the economy will be slowed, and productivity increases will be moderated. Because these conditions are more likely to hold in an inflationary economy, sluggish growth can be seen as resulting from the interaction of the tax system with inflation.

Because the misallocation of investment is caused by both inflation and tax policy, the implications extend beyond tax policy itself. For instance, in the late 1970s high inflation and high tax rates essentially left monetary policy in a dilemma. If monetary authorities attempted to tackle the problem alone and raise interest rates to a level necessary to make after-tax rates of return positive for most taxpayers, those sectors for which cash flow was crucial were especially hard hit.

Potential new homeowners and new car purchasers were deterred by increases in nominal interest rates. New business formation was also discouraged by high inflation-induced interest rates, as cash flow from economically sound investments was far from sufficient to pay interest costs, and the tax system favored old over new business.

On the other hand, if the monetary authorities lowered interest rates, taxpayers were given added incentive to invest in unproductive capital. In some cases, borrowing to stockpile commodities even became profitable and price inflation was further encouraged. In addition, low and negative after-tax interest rates stimulated the private demand for loans.

Tax reform made the nation less likely to be confronted with the same set of problems in the near future. Changes in nominal interest rates would translate more readily into changes in real, after-tax interest rates, even for taxpayers in the top bracket.

Of course, it was not simply lower and more equal tax rates that brought about this result. Lower inflation helped greatly. The combined effect may be clarified by a simple example. At a 50 percent tax rate and a 7 percent inflation rate, it requires an 18 percent interest rate to reach an after-tax rate of return of 2 percent. At a 33 percent tax rate and an inflation rate of 3 percent, the same after-tax rate of return can be attained with a nominal interest rate of 7.5 percent (see figure 8.1). Thus, tax reform added significantly to the downward pressure on interest rates and would affect the extent to which changes in monetary policy and inflation would translate into changes in after-tax interest rates.

SUMMARIZING THE GAINS

Although this chapter has presented details on many of the gains from tax reform, it might be useful to summarize the success of tax reform in terms of its impact on tax expenditures. Remember that the basic thrust of tax reform was to eliminate or cut back on expenditures hidden in the Tax Code so as to provide significant rate reductions for individuals and corporations and increases in personal exemptions for individuals.

According to John Witte (1991b), "Of the 72 provisions which tightened tax expenditures, 14 tax expenditures were eventually repealed, a figure approximately equal to the total that had been repealed from 1913 to 1985." Of course, this can be contrasted to the original proposals put forward in Treasury I, which advocated repeal of 38 tax expenditures.[16]

Another detailed analysis of the effect on tax expenditures was prepared by Thomas Neubig and David Joulfaian of the Treasury staff. Figure 8.4 summarizes their estimates that tax reform produced

Figure 8.4 TOTAL TAX EXPENDITURES BEFORE AND AFTER TAX REFORM

(at 1988 Levels of Economic Activity)

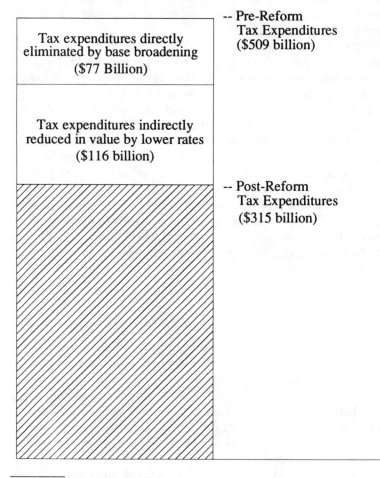

Source: Neubig and Joulfaian, 1988. See appendix table A.4.
Note: Details do not add to total due to rounding.

the equivalent of an annual net reduction of $193 billion in expenditures in the tax code for the year 1988.

Notes

1. After the release of the Treasury proposals, any of the following four individuals could easily have derailed reform: the president, Secretary of the Treasury James Baker (who exchanged positions with Donald Regan); Dan Rostenkowski, chairman of the House Ways and Means Committee; and Robert Packwood, chairman of the Senate Finance Committee. The eventual support and sometimes conversion of each is chronicled well in Birnbaum and Murray (1987), and Conlan et al. (1990).

2. An earlier warning about this tendency was given by Dan Throop Smith, another former Treasury Department tax official. "We now have embarked on an experiment in fiscal policy in which the deficit or surplus is made a third element for separate consideration. Some of us are fearful that the new policy will lead to excessive deficits and consequent inflationary pressures. But we must recognize that the deficit is now not necessarily regarded as a limiting factor holding expenditures down and taxes up. It is an end in itself which may permit increases in expenditures or reduction in taxes even when a deficit already exists" (Smith 1965, p. 16). Smith was reacting to the use of the deficits and tax cuts as a Keynesian policy tool, but the macroeconomic emphasis of supply-siders on tax rates also tended to move away from the immediate connection of taxes with the expenditures that they financed.

3. Estimating changes in progressivity is a difficult business, especially when issues of incidence or shifting of taxes are pursued. Except for certain capital income taxes, most models assume that those who pay the tax bear the tax burden. The Congressional Budget Office's estimates of distributional changes over the decade are discussed in chapter 12; they also tended to show that tax changes between 1980 and 1986 were regressive, but those between 1986 and 1990 were progressive. Joseph Pechman of The Brookings Institutions ran separate estimates that showed the tax reform was progressive.

4. For further discussion of issues surrounding the EITC, see Steuerle and Wilson (1987); Steuerle (1990c); and Hoffman and Seidman (1990). The EITC also has income effects: increases in income that could lead to decreases in labor supply for those receiving the credit. In any comprehensive bill one also needs to examine the income (and substitution) effects throughout the income distribution. Thus, increases in income for EITC recipients are paid for by decreases in income for other taxpayers in a revenue-neutral bill.

5. Increases in the standard deduction offset only a part of the decline in the personal exemption, mainly for smaller households that did not make use of many exemptions.

6. The marginal rates used are effectively averaged across individuals by weighting each taxpayer relative to the amount of interest, dividends or capital gains received. Different "marginal" rates are used for capital gains, interest, dividends, and so forth. A constant debt/equity ratio for corporate investments is also assumed. For further details, see Gravelle (1984 and 1986).

7. Charles R. Hulten and James W. Robertson (1984) make essentially the same argument in their finding that high-technology industries within manufacturing experienced higher average effective tax rate during the 1970s than other manufacturing industries.

8. In some cases, this limitation could be offset through carryback of current-year tax losses and credits to offset income and taxes in previous years.

9. In a pure capital market where assets can be sold short (so that in effect, lending can take place at the rate of return for that asset), problems are caused not only when tax rates are negative but when they are greater than 100 percent. Thus, in the case of interest payments, a tax rate of more than 100 percent can convert a positive before-tax rate into a negative after-tax rate.

10. While it is true that investors should still invest in those assets with the highest rates of return, different assets have different amounts of risk. With a negative after-tax interest rate, investment in assets with little perceived or actual risk may become competitive on a risk-adjusted basis. For instance, if commodities are expected without much risk to increase in price with inflation, some saving may be diverted to the wasteful storage of commodities. The corporate manager may also be induced to invest in riskless assets that almost surely would not have been purchased if the after-tax interest rate were positive.

11. If n = the inflation rate, i = the nominal interest rate and t = the tax rate, then the after-tax interest rate is negative whenever i-ti-n is less than zero, or i is less than $n/(1-t)$.

12. An investment is "passive" if the taxpayer does not materially participate in the conduct of the activity. Limited partnerships are presumed to be passive, as are most rental activities. Most activities in which the taxpayer provides substantial services are not defined as passive.

13. Tax reform was only one of many factors affecting the growth of debt aggregates. For more detail, see Steuerle (1990b). Total domestic nonfinancial debt grew at 12.3 percent in 1986, then at 9 percent, 9.1 percent, and 7.4 percent in the succeeding years. Nonfederal debt showed a drop of nearly the same magnitude. See *Federal Reserve Statistical Release* Z.7, September 20, 1990, p. 1.

14. This proposal was based partly on my earlier research showing how different family groups had been affected over time (see figure 2.2). Nonetheless, the change itself involves increases in marriage penalties that might be avoided by adjusting the standard deduction for number of children. This differs from the current method, which takes away some of the standard deduction of two adults who marry, especially if one or both separately file as head of household.

15. "Changes in the 1980s, and especially in the Tax Reform Act of 1986, have reduced the size of the federal subsidy to state and local borrowing but improved the relative allocation of benefits to those governments rather than to high-income investors" (Break 1991, p. 527).

16. See Witte (1991b). Also, according to Witte (1989, p.11), "Treasury I called for the outright elimination of 38 of the approximately 105 tax expenditures on which we have long-term data. To put this in context, in the prior history of the income tax we had only eliminated 13 tax expenditures, once permanently enacted."

Chapter Nine

FAILURES OF THE 1986 TAX REFORM EFFORT

The amount of change introduced by tax reform was significant by almost any standard. Hundreds of billions of dollars of tax liability were switched, not so much from one group of taxpayers to another, as away from promotion of certain types of investment and consumption toward fewer tax disincentives to work, save, and invest. For many, the drop in the top tax rates—from 46 percent to 34 percent for corporations and from 50 percent to 33 or 28 percent for individuals—symbolized the extent of these changes.

Despite the successes, a number of reform items did not make it through the process. Many inefficient and inequitable differentials in taxation remained. New problems were also created. These sources of neglect and failure would come to haunt tax policy deliberations not long after the passage of the major overhaul of 1986.

NEGLECTED ISSUES

Among the most important issues neglected by 1986 tax reform were the limited amount of base broadening for individuals, and the failure to index the measure of income to account for inflation.

Limited Base Broadening for Individuals

Certainly one of the major failures of tax reform was that the amount of base broadening for individuals, while significant, was still fairly limited. Failure to expand the tax base meant higher remaining tax rates and greater losses of economic welfare arising from tax-created distinctions among types of activities.

Individual base broadening was restricted because of undue attention to the top rate of tax rather than to the marginal rates faced by all taxpayers. This focus meant that for low- and middle-income groups there was always considerable political flexibility as to which provisions could be accepted and which could be dropped. Even the original Treasury proposal did not tackle the problem of taxing most transfer payments. The taxation of fringe benefits was largely rejected by the time of Treasury II. Finally, from the beginning, most itemized deductions were deemed to be justifiable on the basis of equity or other policy principles or were too politically sensitive to be changed more than modestly.[1]

The most significant revisions in the individual tax base were the full taxation of capital gains, the elimination of a special deduction created in 1981 for two-earner couples, the repeal of income averaging, the elimination of the sales tax deduction, and the reduction in the availability of Individual Retirement Accounts for taxpayers at upper income levels who already had employer-provided qualified pensions. Other lesser but important changes included an extension to all income levels of the taxation of unemployment insurance, a floor on miscellaneous deductions, an increase in the floor on medical contributions, and elimination of the small dividend exclusion and the political contributions credit. Many of these latter items were desirable for simplification reasons.

Outside of the capital gains exclusion, however, this list does not include most of the major preferences granted to individuals. These were left untouched or touched only slightly. Nontaxable compensation provided in the form of health and life insurance remained available to employees, while other temporary fringe benefit exclusions for educational assistance, legal service plans, and dependent care assistance were extended. Employer-provided pensions were affected in only modest ways.

Except for the small change in the taxation of unemployment compensation, most transfer payments—workers' compensation, most Social Security retirement and disability benefits, and veterans' compensation—remained largely untaxed, often without regard to the needs or income of the recipient.[2] State and local deductions of income taxes and of real estate and personal property taxes were still allowed.[3] Most interest payments by individuals are in the form of payments on residential mortgages and these, too, remained generally deductible. In fact, returns from homeownership remained greatly favored relative to other returns from capital.[4]

Because nontaxable fringe benefits, nontaxable transfer payments, deductions of state and local taxes, and mortgage interest payments comprise such a large portion of the total tax benefits granted to individuals, the amount of individual base broadening—and the amount of rate reduction that it could have made possible—remained limited. Figure 9.1 shows the importance of various individual provisions to the tax expenditures that remained after tax reform.

Whether to treat the full taxation of capital gains as a broadening of the base is not clear. In many cases, the failure to account for inflation brought into the tax base more than complete taxation of the real income. Of more relevance here, the discretionary nature of the capital gains tax meant that any increase in tax rates was significantly offset by a lower rate of realization of such gains. By some estimates, net taxes on capital gains go down when rates increase in certain ranges. Other estimates predict a modest increase, but all conclude that a higher rate means fewer realizations.[5] Thus, even though these estimates are subject to much debate, it is clear that the extent of any capital gains base broadening is limited because the tax is discretionary and can be avoided.

At the same time, the elimination of a differential tax rate for realized capital gains helps to deter the most common form of tax arbitrage—borrowing to purchase appreciating capital assets and profiting from the tax differential. Legal experts also argue that the capital gains exclusion has caused much of the complexity in taxation. The exclusion requires taxpayers to distinguish between capital income and ordinary income and between capital assets and ordinary assets. It also forces Congress and the Treasury to formulate and enforce recapture rules to prevent the benefits of the exclusion from going to taxpayers who already take advantage of accelerated depreciation or other tax deferrals.[6] In effect, all of these rules try to prevent situations in which the taxpayer deducts $100 of "ordinary" expense while excluding from tax some portion of $100 of "capital" income.

Some elements of tax reform should not be put in the category of base broadening. The so-called phase outs of "the benefits of the bottom brackets" and of the personal exemption, later called the "bubble effect," were simply disguised rate increases. These phase outs created a tax rate schedule in which marginal rates were 15-28-33-28, in that order (the bubble is demonstrated in Figure 8.2). In addition, elimination of income averaging implied some increase in rates and no expansion of the tax base, although this change was justified partly on grounds of simplification and partly because the old law did not target well those persons deemed most deserving of averaging provisions.

Figure 9.1 TAX EXPENDITURES AFTER TAX REFORM

(at 1988 Levels of Economic Activity)

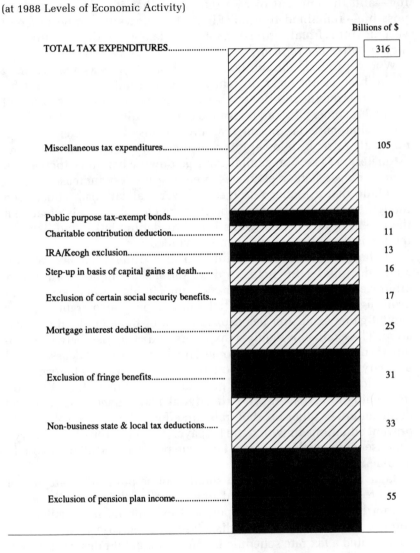

Source: Neubig and Joulfaian (1988). See appendix table A.5.

Indexing to Account for Inflation

Congress also declined to deal with the problems of inflation and of indexing the measure of income to account for that inflation. Accordingly, future changes in the inflation rate will continue to play havoc with the effective tax rate that applies to different forms of investment income.

In the case of depreciation allowances, the failure to index the basis of the assets means that less than 100 percent of the real value of an investment is allowed to be depreciated. To compensate for this deficiency, depreciation allowances continue to be accelerated, in many cases almost as fast as under old tax law. The overstatement of the depreciation in the early years then compensates, at least on a present value basis, for most of the understatement in the later years of the investment.

At least three major difficulties are caused by the failure to index depreciation allowances. First, the effective value of the depreciation allowances varies widely with the rate of inflation. A decline in inflation can lead to increased incentives to invest, while a rise can significantly decrease the value of the depreciation allowances. Second, in using acceleration to compensate for the failure to index, the new Tax Code continues to favor old business over new enterprise, albeit not as much as under previous law. Many start-up firms will still not be able to make full use of the up-front tax incentive, and the competitiveness of established domestic business can still be expected to suffer. Third, because financial accounting and tax accounting fail to index, many decision makers—investors, union negotiators, and firm managers—may continue to be misled by inappropriate calculations of income. The tendency to overstate income in the later years of an investment, for instance, can easily lead to such miscalculations as excess demands for wage increases in declining or older industries, and understatements of the true cost of providing energy by utilities in those years when reliance on older plant and equipment is heavy.[7] For retirees who lend, interest income is overstated, sometimes leading to excess consumption in early years of retirement. For those who borrow, cash flow problems can be created when the inflationary as well as the real component of the interest rate must be paid each year.

Failure to index for capital gains implies that the tax base will in many cases be more than capital income. The expansion of the tax base beyond economic income (or the double taxation of certain types of income) causes the same problems as does limitation of the tax base through exclusions or special preferences. That is, many if not most of the economic, legal, and accounting problems associated with income taxation are caused by the differential taxation of different types of income. The capital gains tax change moved too far in one direction rather than trying to strike a balance.

Because of the discretionary nature of capital gains taxation, however, the net impact of this change on the cost of capital or on effective tax rates is minimal. Taxpayers offset much of the increase simply by realizing fewer gains. Deferral of tax reduces tax rates significantly and, of course, exclusion of gains at death continues to leave a large portion of capital gains untaxed. Overtaxation occurs mainly for those taxpayers who sell assets after short holding periods.

Even if the capital gains revisions involve no increase in effective tax rates on capital income and do not change aggregate saving in the economy, they are still distortionary. First, there is a reduction in the relative amount of capital invested in shorter term, risky projects. Second, individuals become "locked" into their existing portfolios. The economy suffers to the extent that markets are made less liquid and saving is deterred from moving to the highest and best use.

Finally, the failure to index implies that the rates of return on different types of investment continue to differ, as inflation has differential impacts according to type of investment and form of financing. John Makin and Michael Allison, for instance, estimate that with inflation indexing, the present value of welfare in the economy could be improved by several hundred billion dollars. Of course, the higher the rate of inflation, the more the gains from indexing increase. (The present value estimates include not only gains in the current year, but the discounted value of gains in future years as well.) These gains derive from the reduced disparities in the taxation of different sources of income, as well as from the tendency of a fully indexed system to avoid increases in taxes on capital at higher inflation rates.[8]

Although the failure to index creates significant economic problems, the implementation of indexing would not be easy. The calculations, for instance, could become quite complex unless financial institutions are able to make the calculations on computers (Halperin and Steuerle 1988). The complexity of indexing was perhaps the major reason for its rejection in tax reform.

Other Neglected Issues

Despite the comprehensiveness of the Tax Reform Act of 1986, it failed to deal with a large number of other relevant tax issues. Although it contained some pension changes, notably with respect to Individual Retirement Accounts, rules regarding "401 (k)" plans, and the ways in which private pension plans must be integrated with Social Security, pension policy was never examined in a comprehensive way. There was never a thorough examination, for instance, of whether existing policy was optimally designed to encourage saving. Estate taxation and capital gains at death were also never studied in depth. In the latter case, the post-1986 combination of the minimum tax on gifts of appreciated property and the complete exclusion from taxation of gains at death unnecessarily encouraged the retention of capital gain property rather than its donation to charity.

Although many scattered international tax issues were raised in the tax reform process, the provisions finally enacted for the most part were not based upon a comprehensive notion of how international tax issues should be treated over the long run. Congressional action in the international area was driven partly by a desire for a predetermined revenue goal.

In order to maintain a number of existing preferences, significant integration of corporate and individual income taxes was quickly abandoned after the original Treasury proposal.[9] Remaining in the new tax system, therefore, were many of the problems associated with taxing corporate income twice, both at the corporate and individual level: the encouragement of debt rather than equity financing; legal problems associated with distinguishing between dividends and interest; and the discouragement of corporate as opposed to noncorporate ownership. Similarly, problems remained in measuring the tax base of partners in noncorporate business where rights of ownership, as well as types and timing of income payments, were difficult to value and separate among the various partners. Especially anomalous are limited partnerships where some partners are allowed to be "limited" in the extent of their liability—the primary benefit usually associated with corporate ownership. Nonetheless, tax reform retained taxation of owners of corporate capital at a higher rate than most noncorporate owners with equal or higher incomes.

Finally, the corporate and top individual tax rates were not made the same. Under the old law, individual rates were often higher than corporate rates, thus encouraging the taking of deductions (e.g., tax shelter expenses) in the individual sector. Once top individual rates became lower than corporate rates, even without taking into account the double taxation of dividends, incentives were reversed. Deductions now became more valuable in the corporate sector. For instance, the after-tax interest rate will be lower for the corporate investor facing a 34 percent interest rate than for the noncorporate investor facing a 28 percent rate (or the 31 percent rate that was established in 1990). On the other hand, equity investments were given greater incentive than ever to be held in the individual sector, as taxable receipts from equity investments are always most valuable when taxed at the lowest rate. Not long after tax reform, some corporations began to disincorporate, only this time the corporations involved in reorganization were those with fixed investments with generous yields. When the corporate rate was much lower than the individual rate in the pre-reform days, disincorporation mainly took place among corporations holding preferential assets or assets that could be highly leveraged to produce large deductions and negative statements of taxable income.

NEWLY CREATED PROBLEMS

So far our discussion has focused on the neglected issues of tax reform. A number of new problems were also created. These include an increase in the effective tax rate on returns for capital investment, the expansion of the tax base to items other than income, and the introduction of "backdoor" complications to raise the revenues necessary to finance rate reduction.

An Increase in the Cost of Capital

As tax reform worked its way through the political process, the effective tax rate on returns from capital investment—the rate that results from the combination of individual and corporate rates and rules applying to different types of investments and institutions—was increased. Both table 8.2 and table 9.1, derived under slightly different estimating assumptions, show the 1986 law with a higher effective tax rate on capital than was present under old law. The original Treasury proposal and the Administration proposal (sometimes referred to as Treasury II) were criticized by some for their changes in effective tax rates and cost of capital. Under the estimating procedure in the two tables, however, the administration proposal lowered the effective tax rate, except at a zero inflation rate in table 9.1. The original Treasury proposal also lowered effective tax rates in table 8.2.

Perhaps the principal technical difference in the estimating pro-

Table 9.1 TOTAL EFFECTIVE TAX RATES ON CORPORATE INVESTMENT, BY
BROAD ASSET TYPE AT DIFFERENT RATES OF INFLATION[a]
(percent)

	Old law	Treasury[b]	Administration[b]	House	Senate	New law
			0% Inflation			
Total	35	43	37	40	38	39
By Asset Type						
Equipment	− 15	41	28	33	26	29
Structures	36	46	40	37	39	39
Public utilities	26	44	31	39	35	39
Inventories	50	43	42	44	43	44
Land	52	45	44	46	45	46
Addendum: residential						
structure plus land	21	25	25	22	21	21
			4% Inflation			
Total	37	44	36	42	41	42
By Asset Type						
Equipment	5	41	27	41	33	37
Structures	42	46	38	41	44	44
Public utilities	33	44	30	43	40	44
Inventories	48	43	41	42	43	43
Land	50	46	43	45	45	46
Addendum: residential						
structure plus land	19	21	24	20	20	20
			8% Inflation			
Total	38	44	34	43	43	44
By Asset Type						
Equipment	17	41	24	44	38	43
Structures	44	47	36	42	47	47
Public utilities	36	44	28	44	43	47
Inventories	45	43	38	41	43	43
Land	47	46	41	43	45	46
Addendum: residential						
structure plus land	17	16	23	19	19	19

Source: Henderson (1986), plus unpublished data.

a. Calculations assume separate marginal rates of tax for corporations, interest income, dividend income, and capital gains. Corporations finance 33.7 percent by debt. Only effective tax rates on corporate investments are shown here, but the effective tax rates include both personal and corporate taxes. Addendum item is not part of total.

b. Dividend relief in Treasury and administration proposals is here treated as influencing effective tax rates only through issuance of new shares. Under the "old view" that taxation of dividends on existing shares matters, at 4 percent inflation the effective tax rate falls in moving from current law to the Treasury proposal.

cedures in the two tables is the assumption with regard to the importance of dividends. Table 9.1 essentially assumes that a lowering of the tax rate on dividends has no effect on total tax rates on capital income, while table 8.2 assumes that reduced taxes on dividends do lower these rates. The new view that dividends don't matter is that once income has already been taxed in the firm, paying the tax on dividends is a toll charge that ultimately must be paid. The choice to invest retained earnings, therefore, is not affected by this unavoidable tax. If one replaces this "new" view of dividend taxation with the "old" or traditional view that dividend taxes do matter, table 9.1 would also show a reduction in effective tax rates under the original Treasury proposal.[10]

There is a common perception that business was successful in negotiating with Congress to lower effective tax rates on capital, at least relative to the proposals first put forward by the Treasury Department. The perception is wrong. Certainly, some compromises helped certain types of investment. For instance, equipment does fare better under the Senate bill than under the House bill. To achieve this gain, however, negotiators implicitly accepted an increase in the effective tax rate on many types of structures, inventories, and on the returns to invention and "ideas."

In addition, among the important compromises made along the way to a final tax act were abandonment of a number of means of lowering the cost of capital, including dividend relief (if one takes the old view that dividend taxes do matter), and indexing of depreciation allowances. The revenue pick up from these changes allowed some acceleration of depreciation allowances for equipment, and retention of some early write-offs for intangible drilling costs and expenses of long-term contracts. While these trade-offs were supposedly designed to improve the overall cost of capital, they actually did the opposite.

One way to explain this surprising outcome would be as follows: through retention of some up-front deductions and slight acceleration of depreciation allowances, certain types of capital expenditure, especially equipment purchases, were given slightly better treatment than they otherwise might have obtained. The acceleration of deductions and depreciation allowances, however, is equivalent to an increase in loans from the government (a tax deferral), albeit at a zero interest rate. Those loans are repaid through a reduction in deductions or depreciation allowed in later years. In terms of current budget costs and the accounting system for tax reform—revenue estimates are made for only 5 years—loans are much less valuable than direct grants, direct rate decreases, dividend relief (if counted in the cost of capital), or other forms of relief that do not later get "recaptured" or repaid. Thus, when revenue-neutral exchanges were made in the corporate and business sector, they tended to be of the type that exchanged direct tax decreases for loans.

As a result of these compromises, the costs of capital and effective tax rates were raised over old law (again, see tables 8.2 and 9.1). If indexing of depreciation allowances and dividend relief had been retained, the revenues so used would have been much more valuable in terms of lowering the cost of capital than were the slight accelerations of deductions that were put in as substitutes. Even if one takes the "new view" that dividend taxes don't matter, the same case can be made, except that revenues spent on dividend relief should instead have been spent on rate reduction. In either case, the preferences given or retained were among the most inefficient means of reducing the cost of capital.

THE EXTENT OF THE SHIFT

From old law to new law, table 8.2 shows an increase in total effective tax rates on all capital from 38 percent to 41 percent, while table 9.1 shows the increase from 35 percent to 39 percent. Yet, there was a much larger percentage increase in tax burdens of corporations over the estimating period. A corresponding fear at the time was that this change in revenues would reduce capital investment. Economic analysis, however, emphasizes that it is the total tax burden on investment over time, not the corporate tax burden at a point in time, that is most important for long-term investment policy. Therefore, the shift in timing of payments may be relatively unimportant if the cost of capital is little changed. Similarly, total taxation of capital income includes both corporate and individual taxation. To the extent that individual tax reductions compensate for corporate tax increases, the shift in which sector withholds the payments for the government should make little difference.

To be sure, any shift does contain some elements of disruption and, therefore, some transition cost. Traditional macroeconomic analysis, however, has tended to associate little effect to revenue-neutral acts. Some econometric models do predict that money in different sectors will be treated differently, that is, that individuals will have a greater propensity to consume additional money than will corporations and that, somehow, the increased consumption will not lead to increased investment. This conclusion is certainly debatable. Even if true, the amount of the shift in tax burdens from corporations to individuals is on the order of about half of 1 percent of GNP. Sensitivity analyses tend to show that typical changes in other variables—exchange rates, growth of the money supply, or total taxes relative to expenditures—dominate even over the short run the effects of this type of revenue-neutral tax change.

In summary, there were bound to be some transition costs associated with any shift in incentives and tax burdens. Moreover, there was a slight increase in the cost of capital and, according to some estimates, a higher cost of capital will eventually lead to a smaller capital stock. Nonetheless, the amount of change in cost of capital was small and there was almost no change in broader macro variables such as total tax collections.

Tax reform, therefore, was never likely to have a large impact on demand, investment, or consumption *in the aggregate.* This result was later confirmed in a conference of economists examining the effect of the 1986 Tax Reform Act (Slemrod 1990). At this conference, the principal behavioral changes that could be noted as significant were confined to financial behavior, such as the dramatic decline in use of tax shelters. Investment and domestic saving both increased after tax reform, while economic growth accelerated, despite the occurrence of tax reform in the late years of a long economic expansion. That tax reform did not decrease investment in physical capital—the fear voiced most often by reform's opponents—should not be surprising for a process that was mainly designed to deal with the composition rather than the aggregate size of tax burdens.

Inclusion of More than Income in the Tax Base

Many of the problems in the tax system are caused by the differential taxation of income. These differentials not only result in inefficient portfolio shifts, but can lead to further difficulties such as investment in unproductive capital. Tax differentials, however, can be caused not just by granting preferential treatment to some types of income, but by penalizing or overtaxing certain sources of income relative to others.

As the tax reform process evolved, the desire to keep down the top rate for both individuals and corporations generated pressure not only to expand the tax base to include all income, but to go beyond that tax base to add items that would not, under most theories, be considered items or flows that should be taxed.

First, as noted above, the failure to index depreciation and capital gains in some cases means that more than 100 percent of the returns from some depreciable and capital assets are to be taxed.

Second, one of the largest revenue raisers in the corporate minimum tax was the taxation of alternative measures of income when they were in excess of income normally reported for tax purposes.[11] These alternative accounting measures of income tended to overstate income because of the failure to adjust for inflation. Moreover, one of the alternative measures of income initially used—book income as reported for financial purposes—was especially arbitrary because accountants could choose among accounting methods. Not surprisingly, later evidence suggested that they chose their tax base in a way that would reduce taxes (Boynton, Robbins, and Plesko 1991). Although some modest simplification was made to the corporate minimum tax in 1989, it remained a source of great complexity not simply in filing, but in corporate planning.

Third, unlike Treasury I, the final tax bill eliminated income averaging. Although the former averaging provision was poorly targeted and might justifiably be pared for certain groups, there nonetheless remain some taxpayers who still bear higher-than-average tax burdens because the period used for income tax accounting is annual.

Fourth, almost entirely for revenue reasons, Congress took no action or inappropriate action with respect to a number of small provisions. Moving expenses typically exceeded the amount that was deductible, but no adjustment was made. Reasonable costs of childcare, treated conceptually as a cost of working, were still not allowed to be fully deducted for many middle- and upper-income taxpayers (a credit, rather than a deduction is allowed). Miscellaneous expenses of work and asset management became deductible only if in excess of 2 percent of AGI. This proposal was initially put forward as a 1 percent floor and as a simplification measure—eliminating filing and record keeping for those with small amounts of expenses. In the later process, however, it became recognized as a source of revenues, and the floor was raised to 2 percent, thus hitting unnecessarily hard those who have much higher-than-normal expenses of this type.[12]

Backdoor Complications and Complexity

Political constraints on direct means of base broadening meant that more and more of the revenues necessary to finance rate reduction would come in through the backdoor. Make no mistake about it: "backdoor" increases in taxes are purposely designed to be complicated—the complications being a way of befuddling opponents, making costs difficult to calculate, and otherwise hiding what is taking place. While backdoor approaches are often attempted to achieve certain distributional, equity, or appearance goals, such approaches are used without defining a single tax base correctly. Because of the additional effort necessary to come in through the backdoor, the tax code was almost inevitably made more complex.

Many of these backdoor approaches involved expansion of the tax base beyond a realistic measure of income or ability to pay. Already mentioned have been some of the ways in which the tax base included more than simply income and in which appropriate deductions were disallowed.

The Alternative Minimum Tax

One of the more significant of the backdoor proposals was the new alternative minimum tax. Among the additions to the minimum tax base were "excess" depreciation (the difference between the amount of depreciation that would be taken under two different sets of calculations), certain benefits from accelerations of deductions under long-term contracts, certain mining and development costs expensed for purposes of the regular tax, the excess of bad debt deductions over deductions taken on the basis of experience, some amount of book income, untaxed appreciation on charitable contributions, and deductions for passive losses.

The minimum tax presented a number of examples of needless complexity. For instance, the small amount of additional revenues gained by the additional calculation of depreciation allowances under the minimum tax could easily have been obtained by a tiny adjustment to normal depreciation allowances. Moreover, the new minimum tax depreciation schedule was quite unfair, as it allowed less than economic depreciation for many assets. In addition, many taxpayers were forced to go through the calculations just to find out that they owed no minimum tax after all, while many of those who technically should have been paying minimum tax probably remained in noncompliance with the law.

It is difficult to assess the full impact of such a minimum tax. First, there are ways to avoid the tax. Since the minimum tax is only assessed when it is higher than the regular tax, a corporation with many preferences can avoid a minimum tax by merging with a corporation with significant regular tax liability and few preferences. Second, many who owe minimum tax probably fail to pay the tax. It would be too burdensome to require all taxpayers to report both a regular tax base and a minimum tax base. Error rates have been quite high even in the more simple minimum taxes of the past.[13]

PASSIVE ACTIVITIES

The new tax code also made crucial the definition of "passive activities." Such activities included "trade or business activities in which the taxpayer does not materially participate [for example, a limited partnership interest in an activity] and rental activities" (Joint Committee on Taxation 1986, p. 17). Deductions from passive activities, to the extent that they exceeded income from such activities, generally had to be deferred until receipts exceeded deductions or the assets were sold. The definition of a passive activity becomes critical, as material participation can convert passive losses into active ones. In effect, the limitation on passive losses did not prevent the sheltering of income within a given business, but reduced the marketing of such shelters to wage earners and salaried professionals.

INTEREST PAYMENTS

Also facing different types of limits are various forms of interest payments. Much interest is paid by active businesses and remains deductible. Other interest is paid by passive businesses, where the amount of current deduction depends upon the net amount of income declared. Personal interest payments on automobile loans and credit card balances (for personal expenditures, somehow separated) are not deductible. Mortgage interest is deductible, but only for a taxpayer's first and second residences. Mortgage interest on these homes, however, is not deductible to the extent that the mortgage debt exceeded the original purchase price of the residences, plus the cost of major improvements. An exception to the exception was initially provided if the excess mortgage debt was incurred for educational or medical purposes.

INTERNATIONAL INCOME

The taxation of international income was made extraordinarily complex and represented one of the major sources of complaint by tax practitioners. Some complexity was caused by the drive to achieve a revenue target, rather than a target based upon some set of principles. On the other hand, some complexity was inevitable, as the attribution of cost and income among various affiliates and subsidiaries operating in multiple jurisdictions at different exchange rates is necessarily complicated. Another source of difficulty was the simple lack of a consensus on how to tax and measure income of multinational companies and their owners. The common practice—where corporate income was taxed on the basis of the source while interest, dividends and other payments were taxed on the basis of residence of the recipient—has a long history that is embodied in both law and tax treaties, although it results in inconsistent treatment of income from equity versus income from debt.

TIME VALUE OF MONEY

Additional complexities were also caused by a broad set of changes falling under the rubric of "time value of money" issues. Many of these complexities, however, were required for an accurate income accounting system. Still, many of these changes were made complex by political bargaining. Calculating taxable income under multiple methods for installment sales, for instance, was made needlessly complex and violated both equity and simplification goals.

COMPLEXITY: A CASE IN POINT

How increased complexity was to occur can perhaps best be demonstrated through an anecdotal story that in many ways typifies the tax reform process and the gradual downgrading of the goal of simplification. The treatment of the income of minors provides a classic case of how tax reform increased equity and decreased the complexity of tax planning, while unnecessarily increasing the complexity of filing.

The genesis of the change in the tax treatment of minors can be traced to the early period in Treasury I when I sought out ideas from every member of the tax policy staff. In attempting to expand beyond the more narrow confines of previous tax reform, it was important to deal with issues as peripheral as simplification of the taxation of trusts. Significant tax planning came from making transfers to children through trust instruments.[14] At Treasury we concluded that much tax planning could be eliminated if these incentives were reduced and those children who had received sizable financial transfers were required to pay tax on the income from those assets at the tax rate of the parent, rather than at their own lower rates.

What we also proposed—and this was vitally important—was that minors be allowed to retain their own personal exemption. In typical cases, then, capital income would only be taxed for amounts in excess of the new personal exemption of $2,000. At an interest rate of 10 percent, for instance, this would require $20,000 in assets or more—an amount likely to be achieved only when there were transfers from parents, guardians, or other taxpayers. As the reform process wound through Congress, however, various give-aways in other parts of the tax code resulted in a shortfall of revenues. Some participants then noted that on pure equity grounds there was little justification for allowing personal exemptions for dependents twice: once to the head of household or parent, and once to the dependent himself. They then proposed to eliminate this second personal exemption and leave only a small standard deduction.

What they really created was a significant increase in complexity. The additional personal exemption for minors was not required on equity grounds, but was absolutely essential on grounds of simplicity. The amended rules meant that hundreds of thousands of children with only modest amounts of assets were now required to file tax forms. (To add to the complexity, some income was to be taxed at the child's rate and some at the parent's rate, while those with only moderate amounts of nontaxable wage income needed to file to report a few dollars of interest from a small checking or saving account.) There is little doubt that after 1986 a significant portion of children and their parents violated this section of the tax code, often without knowing it. Here then was a classic case of the political system simply giving too little weight to the issue of administration and simplification.

ECONOMIC EFFECTS OF COMPLEXITY

It is easy to assess various backdoor approaches as costly relative to a better designed tax system. Relative to past law, it is also clear that many needless complications were added to the tax code. Countless disputes have arisen and will continue to arise, especially for businesses and individuals with significant income from business activity subject to possible minimum taxes and passive loss rules.

In the years after tax reform, efforts were made to simplify some of these provisions, although revenue constraints limited how much could be done. Some simplification of interest deductions, corporate AMT, and passive loss rules, for instance, had been achieved by the end of 1990, yet each of these provisions remained important parts of the law.

Despite the problems created by this increased complexity, the costs in terms of total economic activity are less clear, especially when compared to former law. Where the minimum tax base included more than economic income, as in the case of depreciation under the minimum tax, efficient behavior was certainly deterred. The rules that separate out various types of interest and try to trace them from one asset to another also somewhat reduced the liquidity of financial markets and raised administrative costs. Competitive problems can be expected to arise when some persons borrow at substantially different after-tax rates than do others engaged in the same economic activity.

On the other hand, much of the deterred activity was likely to fall in those categories of unproductive investments in the economy. For instance, in the case of the passive loss rules, the greatest impact was on tax shelters that were generating large statements of negative taxable income. To avoid some of the added complications, taxpayers became more liable to channel saving directly to corporations or through financial intermediaries. Moreover, it has never been possible for corporate shareholders to set up corporations that would generate losses and negative taxes. Within the corporation, losses could only be used to offset other capital income within the corporation. If the individual investors sold their shares, loss deductions were also limited. "Passive" individual investors were merely put on a footing similar to corporate investors.

SUMMARY

For tax practitioners, of course, whether the economic effect was minor was not the issue at hand. For them the major cost imposed by tax reform was the additional complexity required for the calculation of business income and certain sources of capital income for individuals. Many of these additional complexities could easily have been removed without large revenue cost in the years after tax reform, if only there was some political will to do so. As it turned out, the next three years were to witness a return to a government that acted mainly in response to crisis and for which the budgetary stalemate was often the excuse for inaction.

Notes

1. Additional taxation of transfer payments such as Security Security was excluded from consideration in the Treasury proposals because of a political decision that some Social Security payments had just been made subject to tax in the 1983 Social Security compromise. Another Social Security compromise would also have involved many more agencies and committees of Congress in the decision making process, and might appear to go against the 1983 agreement. Unemployment compensation was made subject to taxation, while workers' compensation and certain veterans' transfers were dropped from consideration after Treasury I. Fringe benefit preferences were retained

as the price that Senator Packwood required for cooperating with any effort at reform. Although Treasury I was to conclude that itemized deductions such as charitable contributions and medical expenses were legitimate, it was unable to deal adequately with interest deductions because of a presidential statement sanctifying the mortgage deduction. Here see McLure 1986. Restoring state and local tax deductions was a requirement insisted upon by representatives of high tax states, such as New York.

2. Up to one-half of Social Security benefits are taxable for higher income recipients. Still, the bulk of Social Security payments remains nontaxable.

3. Some would hold that such deductions are appropriate adjustments to measuring ability to pay federal tax. The Treasury Department originally argued that the deduction favored the provision of state and local services over private services. In either case, the net rate reduction brought about by elimination of the income tax deduction would be spurious if the decrease in effective federal tax rate was offset by an increase in the state income tax rate.

4. The real preference for owner-occupied housing is that rent paid to others is taxable, whereas rent paid to oneself is tax-free. In other words, ownership of a house provides nontaxable income equal in value to the rent that would otherwise have to be paid.

5. The debate on the relationship between tax rates and capital gains realizations has not been settled. See Feldstein, Slemrod, and Yitzhaki (1980); Auten and Clotfelter (1982); Minarik (1984); Office of Tax Analysis (1985); and Lindsey (1988). The debate is explained well and in perhaps the most unbiased fashion in Auten and Cordes (1991).

6. Rules attempt to "recapture" the difference between "accelerated and normal" depreciation so that this excess is not taxed at preferential capital gains tax rates.

7. Some economists believe or at least assume that financial accounting is irrelevant, and that economic actors either see through all "veils" or at least act accordingly. The argument in the text, on the other hand, assumes that information is costly to gather and that inaccurate information does indeed lead to inefficient decision making.

8. See Makin and Allison (1986). Their estimates actually compare the new tax law with the original Treasury Department proposal, but relate much of the gain in welfare to the indexing provisions of the former proposal. At 4 percent inflation, the present value of welfare gains in 1973 dollars are $131 billion for the new tax law and $393 billion for the Treasury proposal. At 7 percent inflation, the corresponding numbers are $63 billion and $505 billion. As inflation increases from 4 percent to 7 percent most of the relative gains are due to inflation indexing under the Treasury proposal.

9. A corporate deduction, rising eventually to 50 percent of dividends paid out of previously taxed earnings, was proposed in Treasury I. Treasury II (the president's proposal) lowered the proposed deduction to 10 percent. The Ways and Means Committee phased in this lower 10 percent deduction over 10 years, and the Senate Finance Committee abandoned integration completely.

10. See Fullerton and Henderson (1987). Using basically the same model as shown in table 9.1, but assuming the old view of dividend taxes, the authors find a decrease in effective tax rates.

11. More precisely, initially one-half the excess of book income or earnings and profits over a measure of alternative minimum taxable income was added to the latter tax base. For years after 1989, 75 percent of the excess of adjusted current earnings—a measure similar to E & P—over AMTI was added.

12. I initially designed the 1 percent floor not only to eliminate recordkeeping for taxpayers with few expenses, but also to deal with the large amount of miscellaneous expense that was claimed, but was not really deductible. The IRS has never been able to audit but a small percentage of returns. In addition, I had gone through the tax

forms and saw an opportunity to combine together lines that were both on the front of the 1040 (the basic income filing statement) and Schedule A (the forms filed by those itemizing deductions).

13. Even the much simpler alternative minimum tax in prior law resulted in understatement of tax on at least 32.6 percent of returns. See IRS (1985, Table 10).

14. Victor Thuronyi, one of the most important contributors to the early tax reform work of the Treasury, led much of the effort to reform the taxation of minors as a way to reduce tax planning through trusts.

Chapter Ten

THE AFTERMATH TO TAX REFORM, 1987–1989

Tax reform was possible because it accommodated the realities of the new era. Whatever its failings and neglects, it recognized the nature of the broad trade offs that were required to make significant headway in public policy. It was also based upon a set of principles against which it could be assessed.

In many periods, the politics of governing seldom extend beyond efforts to survive and, when necessary, confront the crisis of the moment. Even many of those who eventually involve themselves in reform efforts often react to a process that has already been started in motion without ever realizing how such motion is initiated. From 1987 to 1989, legislative activity was notably muted and reactive. There were several major reasons for this development.

WHY SO LITTLE ACTIVITY?

First, the amount of tax legislation in previous years had been extraordinary. For many persons, particularly tax practitioners who had had no chance to absorb all of the developments, there was a feeling that the tax code should be left alone. Some of those who had advocated tax reform, such as Secretary of the Treasury Baker, also feared a rear-guard action against reform and did not want to open up tax reform issues that had just been settled.

Second, the economy performed remarkably well during the years after tax reform. Initially, predictions of a near-term recession were common since the economy had already benefited from several years of growth following the 1981–1982 recession. Opponents of reform, moreover, had predicted cataclysmic results, while even proponents recognized that there were some short-term transition costs as resources shifted from one function to another. All the predictions of a downturn, however, turned out to be false. Instead, the economy jumped from a growth rate of 2.7 percent in 1986 to 3.4 percent in 1987 and 4.5 percent in 1988 (U.S. Department of Commerce 1990, Tables 2 and 8.1).

This growth occurred even while the budget deficit was declining significantly. Tax reform, while approximately revenue neutral, raised about $20 billion in the first year, although this was offset by reductions of between $5 billion and $17 billion in each of the following several years. When combined with the strong economic performance of the economy in 1987, as well as the peaking of the Defense Department build up in 1986, the deficit declined substantially from $221 billion in FY 1986 to $150 billion in FY 1987.[1] This remarkable drop provided temporary political relief from tackling the ever nagging issue of a debt and deficit policy that was still unsustainable. Other fiscal crises, such as the long-term insolvency of Medicare, were still in the future, while inadequate accounting systems left hidden the real costs to the government of the failure of many savings and loan and banking institutions.

The lack of a crisis, a strong economic performance, and the desire to "leave the tax code alone" reinforced perhaps the strongest political tendency of all in 1987 and 1988: to delay any major decision making until past the election of 1988. Within the administration there existed the same vacuum that had been around since the end of 1981—a tendency to react to events rather than act to determine the future direction of policy.

Even in this environment, it was not possible to avoid tax legislation. As indicated throughout this book, when almost all revenues and a significant fraction of expenditures fall in the tax code, it is not surprising that shifts in budget, tax, and expenditure policy require changes in the tax code. While the legislation that occurred was modest, it remained consistent with all legislation passed in the post-1981 period in one important respect: no important bill lost revenues. For the 1987–1989 period, legislation can be divided conveniently into two categories: modest attempts to reduce the size of the deficit, and deficit-neutral attempts to change some aspect of social policy.

THE DEFICIT REDUCTION ACTS OF 1987 AND 1989

In 1987 especially, there was little desire to consider enacting any major tax legislation after the three years of intense battle leading up to tax reform. Nonetheless, budget legislation (under the so-called Gramm-Rudman-Hollings rules) required some action, or else the president would be required to sequester or cut back substantially the size of various programs. These cutbacks were so arbitrary in nature and excluded so many choices that they generally were viewed as impossible to implement. At a minimum they were not politically palatable either for the administration or the Congress. Of course, as in the past, any dire budget requirements could easily have been waived simply by passing legislation to that effect. Either way, some legislation was required to reduce the deficit or change deficit targets.

Recognizing that the deficit would not simply go away, the tax policy staff at the Treasury Department put together a modest deficit reduction package for consideration by the secretary. The package would have allowed for some tax increases along with expenditure decreases.[2] As in the case of tax reform, this proposal was immediately opposed by the top officials of the Treasury's Office of Economic Policy, arguing that all tax increases were harmful and led to expenditure increases. Of more consequence, the proposal was left in limbo by those who felt that no tax increases would be acceptable to the president.

The notion that no tax increases were acceptable to the president, of course, fit the rhetoric but not the history of budget proposals and tax bills in almost every year of the Reagan administration. Bureaucratically and organizationally, however, the inability to take early leadership on the budget issue meant that the administration once again would react to events, not act to develop a set of tax and expenditure policies that might meet some set of goals and principles.

By late 1987, the economy itself was to seize the initiative through a nosedive in the stock market. On October 19, 1987, the Dow Jones average dropped 508 points in one day to a level of 1738.74—a drop that followed a decline the previous week of 235 points. On a percentage basis, the one-day drop of 22.6 percent far exceeded the 12.8 percent drop of October 28, 1929.[3] Reaction was swift. There was a fear that inaction in 1929 had contributed to the depression. Swift corrective action, therefore, had to be taken to avoid all appearances of inattention to the problem at hand. The monetary authorities responded by providing liquidity to financial markets, while the White House and the Treasury Department moved quickly to insure that some deficit reduction package would be passed.

"Reconciliation" in 1987

The resulting Omnibus Reconciliation Act of 1987 was achieved largely through a chaotic bargaining session involving numerous members of the congressional leadership, heads of committees, and members of the administration. (This pattern would repeat itself in future years.) Despite the early 1987 bias toward doing very little, the 1987 Act ended up as a modest piece of tax legislation—in fact, measured by the amount of revenues involved, it was the largest of those enacted and sustained in the 1987–1989 period. Still, its total revenue impact was small relative to every other year of the decade except 1985, when Congress was in the midst of the tax reform debate.

The main goal of the conferees was to minimize political damage by finding tax changes that would be little noticed by individual taxpayers. With respect to individual income taxation, therefore, the only significant items finally passed were simplification of the mortgage interest limits passed in the 1986 Act and an increase from 80 to 90 percent in the amount of current year's tax liability that must be paid by individuals in order to avoid penalties. The latter item, like many items adopted in attempt to reduce the deficit for a short-run period, had almost no long-run effect on revenues. It simply speeded up payments slightly.

Under the 1987 Act, businesses were to bear increased burdens, both financial and transactional. In a few cases, such as installment sales and methods of calculating income before a contract was completed, there was actually some modest reform. A number of attempts were made to tax various types of corporate transactions, such as conversions of corporations to a special, lower tax status (conversion from "C" to "S" corporations), special limits on the extent to which losses could be carried over when there was an ownership change, and cutbacks in the use of deductions received by corporations for dividends paid by other corporations. Some changes had questionable revenue effect in the long run, as alternative forms of organization and transactions could be used to avoid these taxes. Employment taxes—expansion of the wage base for Social Security and an increase in tax rates for unemployment compensation—provided modest revenues. Closing some unanticipated loopholes created in the 1986 Act also provided significant revenues.[4]

All in all, the 1987 Act raised between $14 billion and $16 billion in each of the fiscal years, 1989–1992, or about 0.3 percent of GNP in years with deficits of 3 to 3.4 percent of GNP. On net, the 1987 Act could probably be considered pro-reform.[5]

The 1987 Act followed the tradition of previous attempts at deficit reduction during the decade. The amount of deficit decrease achieved legislatively through tax increases was significantly in excess of the amount achieved through expenditure decrease. The tax committees could deliver; the expenditure committees could not.

The Election Year of 1988

There is little that can be said about 1988 in terms of action on the deficit. Without a stock market crash to spur them on, Congress and the executive branch made little attempt to cut back the deficit. The presidential campaign was a strong deterrent, with neither political party willing to suggest any pain that might have to be borne. In fact, because of the relatively good performance of the economy, there were even some modest, last-minute expenditure increases made possible under the Gramm-Rudman-Hollings budget rules.

The year did see the enactment of the Technical and Miscellaneous Revenue Act of 1988, which provided technical corrections to the 1986 reform, some minor simplifications (mainly with respect to complications created in the 1986 tax reform), extensions of provisions that would otherwise expire, some special interest exceptions, some restrictions on the use of life insurance sold mainly for deferral of tax on investment income (single premium life insurance), and the adoption of a special tax break for those purchasing U.S. Savings Bonds spent for educational purposes (advocated by then Vice President George Bush). Even "minor" tax bills in the 1980s were not so minor by the time all the bells and whistles were added.

As for major changes in taxes, the year did see some significant attempts at social legislation, as will be discussed below.

The Honeymoon Year of 1989

The first year under a new president is often considered to be a honeymoon year in which the president can ask for and achieve major legislative change. In 1989, however, once again the prevailing sentiment was for inaction. President Bush, after campaigning on a pledge of no new taxes, made no major push for deficit reduction during this year. The Congress, in turn, was in no mood to attempt much by itself. In the Omnibus Budget Reconciliation Act of 1989, both branches of government essentially agreed to defer decision making. On the tax side, there were modest increases of about $3 billion to $5 billion per year (or less than one-tenth of 1 percent of GNP), mainly through corporate transaction changes and some small excise and social insurance tax increases.[6] Completed contract reform was again extended, some speed-up in corporate payments was enacted, and there was a cutback in a generous give-away for employee stock ownership plans (ESOPs) that had been put into the 1986 Tax Reform Act as the price for obtaining Senator Russell Long's (D-La.) vote. Some simplification was achieved in the corporate minimum tax calculation.

The year ended on a note of great skepticism. Many believed that most of the changes on both the tax and expenditure side of that deficit agreement were "smoke and mirrors" or, at best, temporary speed-ups in revenues or slowdowns in expenditures. The games played in the budget process left a sour taste in almost everyone's mouth, with even those playing the games feeling that they had been pushed into a situation that was out of control.

SOCIAL POLICY CHANGES

More telling for the future of tax policy were the social policy changes that were attempted in the 1987–1989 period. Traditionally, throughout the postwar years social policy had been treated almost as if it were separate from tax policy. In some cases, expenditure increases were enacted without attention to the source of financing. In other cases, such as Social Security, the principal focus had been on the benefit side of the equation, with much less time and debate spent on the employment taxes raised to pay for the benefit expansions.

The year 1988, on the other hand, witnessed attempts to expand a number of social programs in a pay-as-you-go, or deficit-neutral manner. One of these changes, the Family Support Act of 1988, raised a small amount of revenues for expansion of welfare programs by eliminating the availability of a dependent care deduction for children aged 13 to 15 and by providing taxpayer identification numbers for dependents.[7] Cutbacks in some welfare benefits paid for much of the rest of the change, as did mandates that states meet certain criteria for percentage of welfare recipients who worked and for coverage of the poor. The Family Support Act of 1988 can be contrasted with the attempt at welfare reform of the late 1970s. President Carter had then been rejected even by his own party in his attempts to provide some reform in a deficit-neutral fashion.

Catastrophic Health Insurance for the Elderly

A much more elaborate attempt to extend social policy was made through the Medicare Catastrophic Coverage Act. A modest expansion of Medicare benefits was proposed by the president at the beginning of 1987.[8] Congress quickly decided to take advantage of this foot in the door and moved toward enactment of a major expansion of Medicare benefits. The final act, initially passed in 1988, expanded catastrophic and drug health benefits for the elderly by approximately $7 billion in the first year or two, but by large multiples of that amount as time progressed. The cost was to be covered in large part by a surtax on the income of the elderly, with rates rising over time from 15 to 40 percent or more of income tax liability.

By the next year, 1989, the Act was repealed, largely because it had been designed with a failed concept of tax policy. Its history provides a number of important lessons for the future use of the tax code in deficit-neutral attempts to change social policy. In enacting catastrophic health care legislation for the elderly and disabled, Congress attempted to achieve a number of worthwhile objectives without devoting adequate attention to the financing, or cost side of the issue.

Two errors were fatal. First, there was inadequate recognition of what had become "ordinary" in the way of medical expenses. Second, collecting an additional premium or surtax for the Medicare system through use of the income tax system would have tied both systems into knots and created fundamental problems of tax administration. The first error led to the second.

Average or ordinary medical expenses at the time of the 1988 legislation were around $2,000 per person. Congress decided that it did not want the nonelderly to pay for expanded Medicare benefits, as most economic measures showed the elderly on average to be as well off as—by some measures, better off than—the rest of the population (U.S. Treasury Department 1990, pp. 21–35). But it didn't want most of the elderly to pay for these costs either. Even a few hundred dollars—which was much less than the $2,000 cost to the average person and the much higher cost to the average elderly person—seemed too high a charge to impose on most of the elderly.

As can already be seen, Congress was in a bind: average costs were considered too high to impose on the average person in a group that had above-average wealth and average incomes. Despite these cost problems, Congress proceeded to engage in a bidding war to see just how much medical coverage could be put under the catastrophic umbrella without worrying about long-run costs or taxes. For a while, it even appeared that decisions would be made without any long-run estimates of the cost of benefits and of taxes that would be paid.[9]

As the amount of new insurance benefits grew, it was decided that the elderly majority were even less capable of paying for the additional coverage. These various constraints imposed a dilemma. Someone had to pay, but Congress had already decided that the nonelderly and the average-income elderly should not pay. The solution was to impose a progressive income tax surcharge on a minority of the elderly, a surcharge that for many would well exceed the value of new benefits provided.[10]

Progressivity may have been a laudable goal, but even an equal flat premium would have achieved progressivity by redistributing benefits to those with the most medical needs. Moreover, changes in the Social Security benefits schedule (for example, a higher minimum benefit) could have been used to provide greater progressivity or to cover additional premium costs for the low-income elderly.

Consider, however, what a catastrophic surtax would have done to the Medicare system and the income tax system. First, unlike ordinary medical premiums, Medicare recipients would not have known the cost of their catastrophic insurance until they knew their regular tax liability at the end of the year. That is, any surtax or additional medical premium was based on year-end tax liability.

Second, unnecessary and difficult audit and collection responsibilities would have been placed on the IRS. Goodwill toward the IRS would hardly have been enhanced by sending letters and agents to nursing homes to collect additional premiums from those who underpaid their estimated taxes during the year.

Third, no income tax change could have been made without having an additional impact on the Medicare trust funds. An increase in the personal exemption, for instance, would have reduced trust fund income as well.

Finally, the elderly and disabled would have been required to file complex schedules to pay the surtax. In many cases, more filing requirements would be imposed for a small surtax than for regular tax liability.

There was certain opposition to the surtax from those who would have had to pay—the higher-income elderly—just as some of them opposed the partial taxation of benefits in 1983. In this case, however, the match of benefits and taxes was confusing, and the surtax often treated equals unequally. For instance, many opponents were those who already received catastrophic benefits from private and government employers, and who believed that their additional payment would mainly benefit their former employers.[11] The real lesson from the 1988 experience is that there is no substitute for doing things right. In the case of catastrophic care, it meant that the financing side of the issue should have been given weight at least equal to the benefit side. Congress cannot continually impose new administrative complexities on taxpayers and the IRS simply to achieve a relatively minor goal of redistribution. Grafting a monthly benefit system onto an annual collection (income tax) system made little sense from the beginning.

Notes

1. See *Budget of the U.S. Government, Fiscal Year 1991.* Washington, D.C.: Superintendent of Documents, 1990, p. A-281.

2. As the instigator and principal designer of this package, I attempted to sell the deficit reduction on the grounds that the debt to GNP ratio should be stabilized, if not reduced. That is, debt could not always increase relative to income in the economy, and the economy was already several years into a recovery period.

3. See *The Wall Street Journal*, October 20, 1987, p. 1.

4. These included estate tax deductions for sales of employer stock to an employee stock ownership plan (ESOP), a requirement that certain publicly traded partnerships be treated like corporations, and limitations on the use of net operating loss carryforwards (NOLs) following ownership change of a loss corporation.

5. See *Budget of the U.S. Government, Fiscal Year 1990.* Washington, D.C.: Superintendent of Documents, 1989, p. 4-4.

6. See *Budget of the U.S. Government, Fiscal Year 1991.* Washington, D.C.: Superintendent of Documents, 1990, pp. A-50 to A-51.

7. See *Budget of the U.S. Government, Fiscal Year 1990.* Washington, D.C.: Superintendent of Documents, 1989, pp. 4-6 to 4-7.

8. According to some participants, the proposed expansion was partly a response to "Irangate." The administration was seeking some proposal to move attention away from the selling of arms to Iran and the misallocation of those funds to the Nicaraguan rebels. An expansion of benefits, proposed by then-Secretary of Health and Human Services Otis Bowen, was suddenly chosen to provide the necessary vehicle. Whether true or not, the proposal was to fill a vacuum in domestic policy suggestions coming out of the White House.

9. Having returned to Treasury as Deputy Assistant Secretary for Tax Analysis after this debate had already started, my own contribution was to get some focus on the ways in which catastrophic limits would grow over time, and to get the Treasury and Health and Human Services Departments to present the long-run projections of what would happen to the taxes and trust funds. By sending some sample tax forms under proposed legislation to Congress, I was also able to get some attention paid to the

complexity of the tax calculations that would be required. These initiatives, however, could not adequately constrain a process that, at least in my mind, had gotten out of control.

10. This surcharge had a "cap" or maximum amount so that the total additional premium would not exceed the calculated value of both the additional benefits and other subsidized benefits under Medicare.

11. The agreement required employers to return any saving on their retiree health plans to the retirees in the form of additional benefits for the first couple of years, but the enforcability of that requirement was open to question.

Chapter Eleven

THE BUDGET COMPROMISE OF 1990

By foregoing opportunities to deal with the deficit situation in 1988 and 1989, and by responding weakly to the opportunity presented in 1987, policymakers greatly exacerbated the problems they faced by 1990. The deficit had fallen from a peak of 6.3 percent of GNP in fiscal year 1983 to a little more than 5 percent in fiscal years 1984 to 1986, to between 3 and 3.4 percent in fiscal years 1987 to 1989. Since tax cuts from 1981 were still being implemented in 1984, this progress was significant. A further reduction to 2 percent of GNP would have been about the level required to prevent debt from growing faster than income in the economy. The gradual success in reducing the deficit, however, was thrown off track by the failure to enact further deficit reduction during the prosperous years of the late 1980s.

By early 1990, it became apparent that the deficit was beginning to increase once again relative to the size of the economy (the final figure for fiscal year 1990 was 4.1 percent of GNP, while for fiscal year 1991, which started in the last quarter of 1990, the deficit was estimated to rise to closer to 5 percent of GNP). These increases would be affected by the rising levels of payments necessary to cover guaranteed deposits in failed savings and loans institutions. In addition, what goes up must come down: the higher-than-normal growth rates for the economy in 1987 and 1988 were to be succeeded by lower-than-normal growth rates as the country moved into 1990. A recession, in fact, was to hit by mid-1990. Lower growth rates, in turn, translated into decreased revenues and increased outlays for safety net programs.

To the credit of both the president and the Congress, an agreement was reached in mid-year to seek to reduce the deficit by $500 billion over a five-year period. Work toward compromise began not long after President Bush abandoned his "no new taxes" pledge of the

1988 campaign. He quickly received the support of the Democratic leadership and of Dan Rostenkowski, chairman of the Ways and Means Committee, who had earlier put forward an initiative for deficit reduction. President Bush also intimated that he would accept further sizable cuts in defense expenditures.

In achieving a large portion of the deficit reduction goal, the budget summit between the executive branch and the Congress must be labeled as a success. The debt of the United States could not have been allowed to rise continually relative to national income. The summit succeeded in reducing the size of the annual deficit by between 1 percent and 2 percent of GNP, depending upon the year being measured and how one treats uncertainties with respect to out-year promises of reductions. Both Congressional Budget Office and Office of Management and Budget figures initially projected that deficits would decline relative to the size of the economy—although not for the first couple of years.[1]

Of course, the initial projections were quite optimistic, because they only held if the country faced no new emergencies. In fact, by mid-year of 1991, OMB would raise five-year deficit estimates by over $200 billion (OMB 1991, p. 1). The initial projections had quickly become outdated by the need for an unknown amount of additional payments to cover guarantees of bank and savings and loan deposits, and by the greater certainty of the recession. Even if intermediate-term deficits eventually would be improved, moreover, a number of longer term problems were held in abeyance: Medicare and Social Security remained incapable of covering promised benefits in future decades under the current law.[2] In effect, the day of reckoning for many budgetary problems was simply delayed. Despite these important caveats, most of the deficit reduction was real and the package was one of the largest in peacetime history.

A LACK OF GUIDING PRINCIPLES

Although the budget agreement was the most important tax or budget enactment since the Tax Reform Act of 1986, it differed greatly in the way it was organized and arranged. Perhaps the most common item—and the one most important to achieving passage—was that the onus of failure could be placed upon specific individuals once the president became committed and OMB director Richard Darman took the leadership position within the administration. Failure would have reflected badly upon them, as well as upon a Democratic leadership that had pushed hard for deficit reduction. Beyond reducing the deficit by a target of almost $500 billion over five years, however, there was no guiding set of principles or goals established at the beginning. There was a call to bargain, but the administration never put forward a blueprint to try to guide action. Even the $500 billion target was set without regard to any desired level of government long-term debt or future interest payments. Without any guidelines for program changes, much effort was made to put forward the least politically offensive changes possible. The president separately pushed hard for a capital gains tax cut, but that provided little help in deciding which taxpayers or expenditure recipients should bear the costs of deficit reduction. If anything, it set the process on the opposite track of debating who would get special treatment.

In contrast, the 1986 tax reform had proceeded from a set of principles—in particular, equal treatment of equals and efficiency. These principles helped lay out which tax expenditure programs could be reduced in size or eliminated, while at the same time limiting the extent to which other changes could be pushed onto the system. Distributional constraints had been established early on to maintain focus on the real targets of the legislation and, indeed, they did help keep the process on track.

In tax reform, ideas had also been collected from many different sources, with most political choices delayed until these ideas had been examined. Proposals that were accepted were collated together in ways that would enhance the overall appeal of the package. Substantial work proceeded on preparing data files to show the distributional effect of the package.

During the 1990 budget process almost none of this organizational work was done. The result was a continual series of surprises. The Bush administration, for instance, was taken aback when late in the process the Joint Committee on Taxation began to prepare tables of distributional effects of parts of the package. These tables showed the original agreement between the president and the congressional leaders to be regressive in nature, that is, to require a greater percentage reduction in after-tax income from lower-income than from higher-income households. As a result, the tables helped to mobilize opposition, especially among Democrats who, together with Republicans who opposed the tax increases, defeated the initial agreement.

The lack of organizational work meant that the choices among tax and expenditure programs were more arbitrary than necessary. The amount of an increase in consumption or income taxes normally had little relation to energy and health policies, government incentives and disincentives, or principles of tax policy. And with some exceptions, expenditure program cuts were not based on policy criteria such as administrability, progressivity, or efficiency.

SOURCES OF DEFICIT REDUCTION

In the end, the administration's failure to provide a set of guiding principles made certain that the tax-writing committees would maintain their powerful position relative to the expenditure committees. Outside of defense cuts, the final agreement concentrated on increases in taxes, fees, and premiums as the principal means of deficit reduction. To a great extent, then, the 1990 bill followed the pattern of the deficit reduction bills of 1982, 1984, and 1987 in its emphasis on taxation relative to cutbacks in domestic expenditures. If one excludes interest savings and promises (deficit cuts yet to be enacted) for the fourth and fifth years, table 11.1 shows that almost 50 percent of total deficit reduction from the legislation came from taxes, fees, and premiums—that is, higher charges rather than lower outlays.

Cutbacks in gross domestic expenditures, on the other hand, add up only to about 7 to 17 percent of the total package. (The principal difference between these calculations and those presented in official budget documents are that fees and premiums are treated here as part of taxes, fees, and premiums, while in the Budget of the U.S. Government, they are often treated as negative outlays.) There were also some increases in expenditures, as well as decreases. If one also excludes hoped-for reductions due to regulations and attempts at price controls, the reductions in expenditures amount to only 7 percent of the total deficit reduction. Another 10 percent of the total deficit reduction comes from attempts to regulate prices and levels of payments made to providers of services, in particular, those paid through Medicare and Medicaid.

Even if the regulatory efforts are successful—and the evidence is weak—cutbacks in gross domestic expenditures may still not add up to 17 percent of the total deficit reduction. Many of the increases in user-related taxes and user fees are thrown directly into trust funds instead of being placed in general revenues. This accounting treatment was deliberately designed by Congress to provide pressures to increase the spending of those funds in the succeeding years.

Table 11.1 THE BUDGET AGREEMENT: SLICING THE PIE
(in billions of dollars)

	Total	Percentage
TAXES, FEES, AND PREMIUMS	**181.0**	48.9%
Net Change, Income Tax Base Provisions −15.4		
Income Tax Base Erosion (− 27.4)[a]		
Income Tax Base Expansion (12.0)		
Income Tax Rate Increases[b] 40.2		
Employment Payroll Tax Increases 41.5		
IRS Enforcement and Penalties 11.2		
Excise Tax Increases, not user-related[c] 42.1		
User-related Taxes and Fees[d] 61.4		
User-related Excise Taxes[e] (27.0)		
User Fees (19.4)		
Other Premiums/Contributions for Pension/Health/		
Housing Programs (15.0)		
NET CUTBACKS IN GROSS DOMESTIC EXPENDITURES	**27.2**	7.3
ATTEMPTS TO REGULATE PRICES OR EXPENDITURES	**37.4**	10.1
DEFENSE CUTS − FIRST 3 YEARS + ESTIMATED	**124.8**	33.7
CARRYOVER TO 4TH–5TH YEARS[f]		
TOTAL, CURRENT LEGISLATION	**370.4**	100.0
OTHER		
(Promises[f] mainly 4th & 5th Year Defense/Domestic Cuts)	**57.6**	
Interest Savings	**68.5**	
TOTAL	**496.5**	

Source: Author's calculations based on Congressional Budget Office preliminary estimates of the Deficit Reduction Reconciliation Conference Agreement, October 1990.
a. Includes $18.2 billion progressivity offset and $9.1 billion in miscellaneous tax incentives.
b. Includes $11.2 billion personal income tax rate increase, $10.8 billion personal exemption phaseout, and $18.2 billion limit on itemized deductions.
c. Assumes no increase in transportation spending because of new motor fuels taxes.
d. Ignores increases in user-related activities (e.g., new air traffic control) because of new user-related taxes and fees.
e. Assumes that half of motor fuel taxes are put in trust funds, half are treated as general revenues.
f. Example assumes that defense cuts in first 3 years yield half of saving committed for 4th and 5th years (i.e., half of $115.2 billion), even without major changes and that the other half represents new "promises" under revised budget procedures.

Despite its similarities to earlier budget agreements, the 1990 Budget Act also differed in a number of ways that may serve as a harbinger of the 1990s. First, there was almost nothing in the way of reform of the income tax and expansion of the corporate or individual income tax base. Having gone that route throughout the 1980s, the Congress sought revenues from elsewhere. In fact, excluding "progressivity enhancements" for low-income individuals, the bill created a number of new special preferences for oil and gas and other activities that just about offset the revenues picked up from yet another reform of the taxation of insurance companies, plus a few other minor attempts to broaden the tax base. Although the tax reform dam still held, new holes and leaks were created.

Second, a significant amount of attention was paid to revenues and fees within pay-as-you-go programs and programs with trust funds. Employment payroll taxes were increased by maintaining a higher fee to cover unemployment insurance, by increasing the amount of wages subject to Hospital Insurance (HI) tax in Social Security to $125,000, and by expanding Social Security and Medicare tax coverage of state and local employees. User fees within expenditure programs were increased by over $19 billion; user-related excise taxes such as those designated for trust funds for highways and airports were increased by $27 billion; and higher premiums for Medicare, pension guarantees in the Pension Benefit Guarantee Corporation, and various financial programs were raised by $15 billion.

Closely related to the movement toward pay-as-you-go programs was the enactment of significant reform of governmental credit systems. In many cases, the reform was to charge the private sector for the value of the government insurance provided. In addition, budget accounting rules were to require greater up-front recognition of the real cost of these guarantees down the road.

Charging taxpayers directly for services and for the value of government guarantees had already achieved some momentum in the earlier years of the tax decade, but this was the first budget bill to give these efforts such prominence relative to changes in the income tax.

THE PROGRESSIVITY REVIVAL

While little attention was paid to base broadening within the income tax, significant attention was paid to its overall progressivity. The final bill modestly increased the progressivity of the overall tax system, but this was only partly a response to the political debate over the budget package and the presentation of distributional tables by the Joint Committee on Taxation. During the 1988 presidential campaign, then-candidate George Bush pledged to try to enact a "child credit."[3] His credit was to apply only to workers with children.[4] Eventually this proposal was translated into a large addition to the existing Earned Income Tax Credit (EITC) available to low-income households with children, a supplement for young children (demanded by President Bush), a requirement that the supplement would not be made available to those with credits for work-related child care expenses (also demanded by President Bush), and a supplement for low-income workers with children who pay money out-of-pocket for health insurance (added by Senator Lloyd Bentsen).

These changes succeeded in making the overall bill much more progressive, but at a cost. All of the alternatives were to make the tax schedule for low-income individuals extraordinarily complex. Moreover, conferees had not provided means of dealing with the cheating that would be encouraged by a subsidy rate for earnings that would make it worthwhile for individuals to claim earnings from work even when they had none. Further reform and simplification was made inevitable.

When put into the budget document, the EITC change, along with a few others, were labeled "progressivity offsets" against some of the increases in excise taxes on low- and moderate-income individuals. Or one could state it in reverse. Some of the increases in taxes in the budget compromise were used to provide the revenues necessary for additional child-related expenditures. Of course, even here, games were played to enhance the appearance of progressivity. At the last minute, it was discovered that adjustments in the EITC for household size would provide most benefits at income levels just above the bottom. That is, larger sized households, partly as a result of their size, were measured in income distribution tables as being at slightly higher income levels than smaller households. Therefore, to make the income distribution table look more progressive, a last minute change eliminated most of the adjustments for family size and simply increased the basic credit equally for all families, regardless of size.

Bubbles, Bangles, and Beads

Meanwhile, at the top of the income distribution, President Bush's effort to decrease the capital gains tax not only was rejected, but was probably responsible for raising the tax rates for high-income individuals.

Recall that in the 1986 tax reform, Congress created what eventually came to be called a "bubble" in the tax rate schedule. Taxpayers in succeedingly higher income levels would pay a tax rate on their last dollar earned of 15, 28, 33, and, then, 28 percent again (see figure 8.2). The 33 percent bubble between the two 28 percent brackets was always a bit suspicious and was the result, as noted earlier, of an attempt to proclaim a top marginal rate of 28 percent, while actually imposing a higher rate through "phase out of the personal exemption and of the benefits of the 15 percent bracket."

At one point the conferees for the 1990 budget agreement agreed to get rid of the bubble. Rather than raise the last rate to 33 percent, however, they combined the 33 and the latter 28 percent rates into a single top rate of 31 percent. Because of the amount of income in the 28 percent bracket, the change actually raised revenues, but not enough for a majority of the conferees. Accordingly, two other proposals were retained or added. First, a bangle: itemized deductions would be limited by 3 percent of the extent to which adjusted gross income exceeded $100,000, with some exceptions. For almost all affected taxpayers, this translated into nothing more than an increase in the marginal tax rate of 0.93 percent.[5]

Next, a bead: the value of the personal exemption would again be phased out at higher income levels. The conferees decided to add further complication by making the rate of phase out depend upon the number of personal exemptions. For a family of four, this translated into an increase in marginal tax rates of 2.13 percent, while for a family of two the increase in rates would be 1.06 percent.[6]

Despite this unnecessary complexity, legislators prided themselves on their handiwork. Believing they had met some arbitrary standard to which the public had acquiesced (e.g., a maximum statutory tax rate of some amount), they delighted in finding ways to circumvent that standard while still declaring it. In certain high-income ranges, the maximum tax rate was now 31 percent + 0.93 percent through reduction in itemized deductions + some additional amount for phase out of the personal exemption (2.13 percent for families of four).

The bottom line was that this part of the package succeeded in raising taxes on higher income individuals by about $40 billion over five years. Thus, the ultimate goal of the majority of conferees—to increase overall progressivity—was reached. These changes implied that the debate over progressivity was to continue into the future.

WHAT WAS NEW AND WHAT WAS NOT

In many of their actions, the 1990 Budget Act conferees attempted to return to the same sources of funds that they had relied upon in previous years. The Act contained yet one more attempt to increase revenues through IRS enforcement, although the amounts claimed were unrealistic. One more attempt was made to rely upon Social Security taxes, but the revenues raised were small relative to those provided by tax increases of the past. In many ways, the defense cuts in the bill represented the last spending of the post-World War II peace dividend—a dividend that has been spent in gradual stages with the exception of build ups in Korea, Vietnam, and the early 1980s. Even a delaying of indexing of tax brackets in the individual income tax had been included in a House bill, but later dropped.

The 1990 budget agreement offered a temporary reprieve from major tax legislation. Certainly it was designed to forestall major tax or expenditure legislation for a couple of years. If there was to be legislation, however, the 1990 agreement almost insured that it would again take place in the tax-writing committees.

Here is why. For the near term, different programs have been placed in different "baskets" or piles for which future changes must be enacted on a "pay-as-you-go" basis. All "discretionary" spending has been divided into three baskets: defense, international, and domestic. Each of these is subject to a spending cap. Any increases in spending above what was allocated to programs in a given basket must be balanced by at least an equal spending decrease somewhere in the same basket. If the spending cap for a given basket is exceeded, then all programs within that basket will be cut back through a presidential "sequester." Trade offs cannot be made with anything outside the basket; increased spending in one discretionary basket cannot be paid for through decreases in spending in a different basket. The trade offs that can be made by the expenditure committees, therefore, are small. Although these baskets are combined together in later years, the expenditure committees will still be unable to finance changes through increases in revenues.

Revenues, tax expenditures, and "mandatory" entitlement programs such as Social Security and Medicare—that is, programs that are mainly under the jurisdiction of the tax-writing committees— are lumped together in one huge basket that is also subject to a cap. A variety of trade offs may be made within and/or between revenues and mandatory programs so long as the net effect on the deficit is zero. Under the new budget rules, therefore, broad expenditure or tax reform remains achievable only by going through the tax-writing committees.

The turn toward pay-as-you-go financing is also likely to lead to higher fees and payments by beneficiaries of government programs. In practice, the easiest way for many expenditure committees to follow the new rules is for individual programs to adopt internal fee and collection mechanisms. The Act thereby placed extraordinary additional pressure on federal programs to raise fees and premiums on beneficiaries, for example, user fees for parks, roads, bridges, and medical care. More broadly, the Act entrenched pay-as-you-go financing within the entire congressional budgetary process, so that most program expansions could not even be brought up on the floors of Congress without some payment mechanism attached.

One important change in the bill is a de-emphasis of deficit targets per se. The focus is switched to changes in the deficit due to changes in the current law. As long as the law doesn't change, therefore, no recession or crisis necessarily requires deficit reduction, as was the case under the rules applying through the second half of the 1980s. By the same token, further straightjackets have been placed around existing law, making changes from the status quo more difficult.

Unfinished Business

So much attention had been paid to the deficit in the 1980s that it became a good excuse for not dealing with other issues of concern to society. Although the 1990 Act was successful in reducing the deficit and in achieving some financing reform, it dealt with few of the problems within the thousands of expenditure and tax expenditure programs on the books. Some of these programs worked and some did not. Some needed to be expanded and some, contracted. Some responded to the needs of yesterday, but many were no longer adaptable to the needs of tomorrow.

It is the combination of expenditure and tax programs that makes the federal government effective or ineffective. The cost of the expenditure programs, less the revenues collected through the tax programs, equals the budget deficit—the dissaving of the U.S. government. One can think of the bond financing of this dissaving as simply one more governmental program. Fixing up this program could hardly be considered a panacea for the other ailments of society: it could not clean up the environment, make our educational system work, increase our inventiveness, reduce our crime rate, improve health coverage, or adapt our defense policy to the 21st century. Enactment of the deficit reduction package did have one important effect on future policy and on the country's perception of what had to be done: it dispelled the myth that enactment of the long-awaited deficit reduction package would solve all problems. How this change in perception will play itself out in the future remains to be seen at the time of this writing.

Notes

1. Assuming compliance with the discretionary spending caps in the 1990 Budget Enforcement Act, federal debt as a percentage of GNP would rise from 44.6 percent of GNP in 1990 to 49.7 percent by fiscal year 1993, then fall to 45 percent by fiscal year 1996. See Congressional Budget Office (1991, p. 98).

2. The conferees had available information showing that under typical assumptions, the Old Age and Survivors and Disability Insurance (OASDI) program in Social Security is expected to continue accumulation in the Trust Fund until it reaches a peak in 2014. After that, it will draw down a large accumulated trust fund, which at the time was projected to last until 2043. After 2043, OASDI would have to increase payroll taxes, cut benefits, or be subsidized by general revenues to avoid bankruptcy. Medicare Hospital Insurance (Part A) was expected to exhaust its trust fund as soon as 2003. See *1990 Annual Report of the Federal Old-Age and Survivors Insurance and Disability Insurance Trust Funds* and *1990 Annual Report of the Federal Hospital Insurance Trust Fund*, Washington, D.C.: Superintendent of Documents, 1990. There were modest changes in Social Security in 1990—mainly in the tax base for Hospital Insurance—but these were to affect the calculations only slightly, with bankruptcy for Hospital Insurance to come later in the same decade. The 1991 Trustees Reports would also move up to 2041 the date of exhaustion of the OASDI trust fund. See *1991 Annual Report of the Federal Old-Age and Survivors Insurance and Disability Insurance Trust Funds* and *1991 Annual Report of the Federal Hospital Insurance Trust Fund*, Washington, D.C.: Superintendent of Documents, 1991.

3. The campaign promise was partly an attempt to offer an alternative to Candidate Dukakis's support of bills to provide monies directly to states to establish day care programs for young children.

4. The credit was to be made available only to workers, but "worker" was not defined in the campaign. Still at the Treasury Department in early 1989, I deliberately interpreted the "work" requirement to imply a phase-in schedule identical to the one in the earned income tax credit, in the hope that for administrative simplicity the two might be combined. As the process evolved, that is exactly what happened.

5. The calculation is as follows: an additional dollar of income reduces itemized deductions by 3 cents. At a tax rate of 31 percent, this increases taxes by 0.93 cents for each additional dollar of income. The tax rate, however, applies to adjusted gross income rather than taxable income—that is, income after deductions.

6. For a joint return with income between $150,000 and $272,500, personal exemptions were phased out at a rate of 2 percent for each $2,500 by which the taxpayers' income exceeded the threshold amount. In effect, assuming a personal exemption of $2,150 in 1991, additional income produces an increase in taxable income of (.02 × $2,150)/$2,500 for each exemption. For 4 exemptions and a taxpayer in the 31 percent tax bracket, net tax burden increases by: 4 × [(.02 × $2,150)/$2,500] × .3, or .0213.

Chapter Twelve

IMPLICATIONS FOR THE FUTURE

The 1981 to 1990 decade began with one of the largest tax cuts in the history of the United States. The rest of the decade was to witness the enactment of a continual series of tax changes, five of which each increased tax receipts by over $10 billion annually, and three of which raised tax receipts by over $30 billion annually. In addition, the year 1986 was to herald a tax reform so detailed and comprehensive that the new tax code itself was to be named the Internal Revenue Code of 1986.

TAXES—UP OR DOWN?

Despite this extraordinary outpouring of legislation, by the time the tax decade was over and the smoke had cleared, total tax receipts at all governmental levels, as a percentage of gross national product, were not far from where they they had been at the beginning of the decade. Actually, state and local taxes were slightly higher, while federal taxes by themselves were to comprise almost exactly the same percentage of gross national product or income (see figure 2.1).

This result may not be surprising in light of the fact that a similar constancy (or slight upward trend) prevailed throughout much of the postwar era. In 1956, federal tax receipts represented 17.3 percent of GNP; in 1966, 17.4 percent; in 1976, 17.4; and in 1986, 18 percent. Since 1959, total receipts at all governmental levels have never been less than 24 percent or more than 28 percent of GNP—although the 1990 Budget Act and and a continuation of recent trends toward higher state and local taxes could push beyond the upper end of that range in the early 1990s.

Table 12.1 summarizes the changes in receipts due to the many legislative enactments of the tax decade. While the Economic

Table 12.1 CHANGES IN RECEIPTS IN THE TAX DECADE
(in billions of dollars)

		Estimated receipts in FY 1990
Receipts under tax rates and structure in effect January 1, 1981[a]		1,167.3
Administrative action		0.6
Enacted legislative changes:		
Economic Recovery Tax Act of 1981		−322.8
Individual Indexing after 1984	−57.4	
General Rate Reductions	−164.3	
Accelerated Cost Recovery	−53.2	
Other	−47.9	
Tax Equity and Fiscal Responsibility Act of 1982		57.2
Highway Revenue Act of 1982		5.1
Social Security Amendments of 1983[b]		14.5
Interest and Dividends Tax Compliance Act of 1983		−2.5
Railroad Retirement Revenue Act of 1983		1.1
Deficit Reduction Act of 1984		31.0
Consolidated Omnibus Budget Reconciliation Act of 1985		3.0
Federal Employees' Retirement System Act of 1986		−0.3
Omnibus Budget Reconciliation Act of 1986[c]		1.0
Superfund Amendments and Reauthorization Act of 1986		0.8
Continuing Resolution for 1987		2.6
Tax Reform Act of 1986		−20.3
Omnibus Budget Reconciliation Act of 1987		16.1
Continuing Resolution for 1988		2.6
Medicare Catastrophic Coverage Act of 1988[d]		7.0
Family Support Act of 1988		0.2
Technical and Miscellaneous Revenue Act of 1988		−0.5
Social Security taxable earnings base increases[e], 1982–90		42.6
Social Security (OASDHI) tax rate increases[e,f], 1982–90		48.0
Financial Institutions Reform, Recovery and Enforcement Act		0.5
Treasury, Postal Service, and General Government Appropriations Act for 1990		0.2
Medicare Catastrophic Coverage Repeal Act		−7.5
Omnibus Budget Reconciliation Act of 1989		5.7

Table 12.1 CHANGES IN RECEIPTS IN THE TAX DECADE (continued)
(in billions of dollars)

	Estimated Receipts in FY 1990
Total receipts before 1990 budget legislation	1,053.2
Tax reduction	−114.1
Increase in receipts in 1995, when 1990 budget legislation is more fully implemented, discounted to 1990 income levels	+28.5
Total receipts after 1990 budget legislation	1,081.7
Tax reduction	−85.6

Sources: *Budget of the U.S. Government, Fiscal Year 1990,* Washington, D.C.: U.S. Government Printing Office, 1989, pp. 4–18; and Office of Tax Analysis, U.S. Department of the Treasury.
a. These estimates assume a Social Security taxable earnings base of $29,700 through 1992.
b. Excludes the effect of increases in the old age and survivors, disability, and hospital insurance (OASDHI) tax rate that are shown below.
c. Excludes the effect of increases in the Social Security taxable earnings base that are shown below.
d. Includes the effect on income taxes of the substitution of cash benefits for a portion of employer medigap insurance that would have been otherwise provided.
e. When the tax rate and the taxable earnings base increase at the same time, dividing up the total effect on receipts is arbitrary to some extent because of an interaction effect. The increase in receipts due to this interaction effect is attributed to the rate and base changes in proportion to the increases in receipts that would occur if the rate and base were each changed separately.
f. The combined employer-employee OASDHI tax rate.

Recovery Tax Act of 1981 reduced receipts by over $300 billion by fiscal year 1990, later tax increases were to offset most of this reduction. The net tax decrease, in fact, was only slightly in excess of the cost of individual indexing of tax brackets for inflation (but not real growth) after 1984.

Why didn't the tax cuts of 1981 hold up? One answer is that demand for government services remained high throughout the 1980s, and eventually the taxpayer had to pay for these services. This answer would be true by definition if one concluded that what was furnished by the government equaled what was demanded by the public, but false if one believed that the government was consistently providing less or more than demanded. Public preferences, of course, are not easy to interpret. Often the public demands both lower taxes and higher services. Does this reveal an inconsistent set of preferences or a rational desire for more efficiency in government? Probably both.

Another answer is that the tax cuts of 1981 did not last because the budget numbers accompanying them never added up. They never forced a decision on the expenditures that would have to be foregone to justify the drop in taxes. There was no concerted effort in the 1980s, for instance, to deal with the pressure of rapidly rising health costs. Moreover, by pushing effective tax rates for certain types of capital and some profitable businesses toward zero, the 1981 changes led to a political reaction. This reaction was based upon the simple but fundamental democratic notions that the government must run equitable tax and expenditure systems and that those with wealth receive many of the benefits of the society and, therefore, have a societal obligation to pay a fair share of the tax burden on a current basis.

Whether the relative constancy or slight growth in taxation observed in the 1980s will last into the future will depend upon economic forces just as large and unexpected as those of the past. Recent worldwide reaction against government inefficiency and the movement toward greater reliance upon the market tend to support fewer government programs and lower taxes. On the other hand, the United States also has among the lowest taxes in the developed world, and the longer our debt continues to increase relative to income, the higher the level of taxes necessary to support the interest payments on that debt. Built-in expenditure growth in a number of programs also adds to the pressure for tax increases.

For most of the 20th century, crises such as war and depression have been the major source of tax increases. Relying solely on this past reckoning, future crises would lead to future, permanent tax increases. One wonders, however, if that long, historical trend is not coming to an end.

The simple question of whether taxes go up or down has often received an improper degree of attention. The 1981–1990 tax decade started with this debate, but by its end tax rates and tax expenditures were cut significantly even while measures of total revenues changed hardly at all. Perhaps the decade signals the beginning of a period when attention will turn more to the trade-offs among various tax and expenditure programs than to the simple and sometimes misleading question of how big government is or should be. The overall levels of taxation and expenditures tell us little about government's good or bad effects on the economy. Tax expenditures, for instance, reduce the level of total revenues even as they increase government interference. On the other hand, in many formerly communist countries now converting to market economies, higher taxes are being used to replace more cumbersome government involvement through command and control systems. In established market economies, direct environmental taxes would often interfere less in the economy than existing regulations.

THE LASTING IMPACT OF TAX CHANGES

Regardless of the overall level of taxation, many of the changes of the 1981–1990 tax decade will most likely have a lasting impact. To some extent, the permanency of the tax changes is a consequence of permanent changes in the economy itself. Take the case of investment incentives. Just like the leaders of socialist economies, the Congress and the executive branch had never shown any great ability to decide which industries and businesses to support and which to ignore. As years went by and past investment incentives showed little or no evidence of working, they became harder and harder to maintain. By promoting the more visible inefficiencies of the tax shelter market, the 1981 incentives only served to highlight the weakness of the arguments in favor of implementing industrial policy through the tax code.

The paring of investment subsidies, however, was made possible only by other unabated trends in society: the movement of jobs to the service rather than the goods sector of the economy; a downsizing of the idealized invention from the large machine with cogs, wheels, nuts, and bolts to the mini-machine whose principal components were tiny microchips; and, more generally, a continuing movement from an industrial age to a technological age to an age of information. Both politicians' and economists' fixation on physical capital, therefore, was bound to relax as the new focus turned toward human capital, ability, and education. While Congress is never likely to abandon altogether its attempts to manipulate the economy, it is doubtful that it will turn toward the growth industries of the past to achieve this objective. It is more likely to expand upon grants and tax credits for research and technology than to add to investment incentives for plant and equipment.

Ronald Reagan had been elected in part because of an outcry against the problems of a highly inflationary economy. Here, too, the political reaction led to a change in the tax laws that is likely to retain some degree of permanence. Even if there had been no tax cuts in 1981, the time was ripe for some indexing of tax brackets—and the prevention of automatic increases in tax rates due to inflation. Over time this change proved to be the most permanent, as well as the most quantitatively important of all the 1981 changes. And it wasn't even part of the original package proposed by the president! As long as monetary policy maintains its orientation toward an economy with at least some inflation—an orientation now sustained for over half a century—indexing is likely to last. Even if tax brackets temporarily become unindexed in the future, a permanent retreat back to a non-indexed system seems unlikely.

Other lasting changes in tax policy can also be related directly to the end of the "Easy Financing Era" following World War II. Not only were inflationary increases in tax rates eliminated through indexing, but the half-century trend of increasing Social Security tax rates by 3 percentage points per decade could not continue forever. By 1990, Social Security tax rates had peaked; even if there are some adjustments in the future, their historic growth rate will not be repeated.

Although cutbacks in defense did provide financing for other budgetary changes between 1986 and the early 1990s, these reductions were smaller than those available in previous cutback periods. Sometime in the 1990s, therefore, declines in the defense budget relative to GNP will also become a source of financing that has been depleted. Certainly, the early 1980s give us a foretaste of how institutions might react when this source of financing is foregone or there is an increase in the percentage of society's income devoted to defense.

In moving to a new era of policymaking, different sources of financing had to be found. In the 1980s, base broadening in the income tax turned out to be the most important of these sources. Base broadening was often more palatable than other alternatives, especially when those alternatives involved reducing the deficit by either raising tax rates or cutting expenditures. Base broadening was also a logical and appealing source of revenues for reducing tax rates. Even without the deficit increases of 1981, it is likely that base broadening would have been tapped.

By 1990, however, even base broadening had declined in importance as a source of funds. The easier political choices had already been made, the list of potential base broadeners had been reduced in size, and the tax expenditure budget had been cut by almost 40 percent by tax reform and even more by other enactments during the decade.

Will Tax Reform Survive?

Will all elements of tax reform survive? No. Like a child's room, one has little expectation that when it is cleaned up, it will stay tidy forever. By the same token, however, permanent improvements can often be made along the way.

Some saw the beginning of tax reform's dissolution in the enactment of higher tax rates on higher income individuals in 1990. Many supporters of the Tax Reform Act of 1986, however, made little claim about the ideal amount of progressivity. Many wanted higher rates at the top, and many wanted lower rates. One tax reform ideal holds that for a given amount of revenues it is better to tax income equally at a lower rate than to tax only a portion of income at a higher rate. Another ideal holds that tax reform is concerned with the inefficiency aspects (including tax shelters) of higher rates. In any event, it is likely that tax rates will vary over time, especially in the case of war or some major emergency. Then, again, they *should* vary with the needs of the nation.

The most serious threat to tax reform comes from the quickly rediscovered tendency to add new special preferences to the tax code. In truth, that tendency had never been abandoned. As long as the tax code remains a major source of expenditures, it is unrealistic to expect that these expenditures will not be tinkered with in ways similar to direct expenditures. In effect, whether the tax code will move toward deform or more reform will depend upon the combined net impact of all provisions and will vary cyclically over time.

The requirement for budgetary balance in the new era provides the greatest constraint on abandoning tax reform. Without easy sources of financing to pay for deform, major increases in tax expenditures will be difficult to enact. If tax expenditures are increased, then tax rates must be raised or other expenditures must be reduced to pay for the initial changes.

The Spread of Tax Reform

One reflection of the power of tax reform was in its extension beyond U.S. federal taxes. Table 12.2 shows the dramatic reduction in tax rates around the world as many countries followed the U.S. tax reform effort with efforts of their own. The worldwide drop was remarkable both in size and extent.

One difference is worth noting. Except for the United States, almost none of these countries used distributional tables to show the results of the tax changes that were proposed. (Recall the power of the distributional and revenue constraints on the U.S. process.) As a result, base broadening was often insufficient to pay for the drop in the top rates, and these countries' income taxes often became less

Table 12.2 TOP AND FIRST POSITIVE RATES OF THE CENTRAL GOVERNMENT[1] PERSONAL INCOME TAX: 1986 AND LATEST ANNOUNCED DATE[2]
(to nearest percentage point of taxable income)

	TOP RATES				FIRST POSITIVE RATES		
COUNTRY	1986 Top tax rate	Tax rate in latest announced year[3]	Difference	COUNTRY	1986 First positive rate	Tax rate in latest announced year[3]	Difference
Sweden	50	20[d]	−30	Netherlands	19	7[c]	−12
New Zealand	57	33[b]	−24	Austria	21	10[b]	−11
United States[1,4]	50	28[b]	−22	Ireland	35	30[c]	−5
United Kingdom	60	40[b]	−20	United Kingdom	29	25[b]	−4
Japan[1]	70	50[b]	−20	Australia	24	21[b]	−3
Norway[1,4]	40	20[b]	−20	Germany	22	19[c]	−3
Belgium[1]	72	55[c]	−17	Italy	12	10[b]	−2
Greece	63	50[c]	−13	Luxembourg	12	10[a]	−2
Austria	62	50[b]	−12	Japan	10.5	10[b]	−0.5
Italy	62	50[c]	−12	Switzerland	1	1[a]	0
Netherlands[5]	72	60[c]	−12	France	5	5[b]	0
Australia	57	47[c]	−10	Turkey	25	25[b]	0

Spain	66	56[b]	−10
France	65	57[b]	−8
Finland[1]	51	43[c]	−8
Iceland	38.5	33[c]	−5.5
Denmark[1,4]	45	40[b]	−5
Canada[1,4]	34	29[a]	−5
Ireland	58	53[c]	−5
Germany	56	53[c]	−3
Luxembourg	57	56[a]	−1
Turkey	50	50[b]	0
Switzerland	13	13[a]	0
Belgium	24	25[b]	+1
Denmark	20	22[b]	+2
Finland	6	9[c]	+3
United States	11	15[b]	+4
New Zealand	17.5	24[c]	+6.5
Norway	3	10[b]	+7
Greece	10	18[c]	+8
Canada	6	17[a]	+11
Iceland	18.5	33[c]	+14.5
Sweden	4	20[d]	+16
Spain	8	25[b]	+17

Source: Organisation for Economic Development and Co-operation, unpublished material furnished to author.

1. Countries with important taxes at subordinate levels of government, typical rates for 1988 being *flat*: Belgium 7, Canada 17, Denmark 30, Finland 16, Iceland 7, Norway 25, Sweden 31; progressive: Japan 5 to 16, Switzerland 5 to 31 (cantonal and communal), United States 2 to 14.

2. Comparison not possible for Portugal.

3. (a) = 1988, (b) = 1989, (c) = 1990, (d) = 1991.

4. Countries with separate alternative minimum or additional income taxes on a wider tax base. In Norway the latter were increased from 6 to 8.5 percent in 1989.

5. 1986 figures refer to the personal income tax only, whereas 1989 refer also to Social Security contributions, now levied on the same base as the income tax.

progressive. Without this base broadening, it was often necessary to expand other taxes such as the value-added tax. Hence, the United States achieved much more progressive reform than did many other countries.

Tax reform spread not only to other countries, but internally to various states within the United States. Enactment of federal tax reform was followed almost immediately by a variety of state tax reform efforts. Some of these efforts were mandated by practice. Many states piggyback their tax bases—in particular, business tax calculations—on to the federal tax base. In addition, federal attention to the taxation of the poor established momentum for state legislators to give attention to the same issue. States had been especially guilty of allowing bracket creep to move the poor onto the tax rolls throughout the 1960s, 1970s, and 1980s.[1]

PROGRESSIVITY AND EQUITY

The 1981 tax changes had been slightly regressive. The 1986 changes were slightly progressive, mainly because of the elimination of taxation of the poor, the expansion of the earned income tax credit, and the increase in corporate taxes relative to individual taxes. The 1990 changes were also slightly progressive because an expansion of the EITC and the modest increase in tax rates at the top tended to offset excise tax increases elsewhere.

What was the net impact of all of the tax changes of the tax decade? Figure 12.1 shows one estimate of the change in effective tax rates from 1980 to 1991 for different income classes within the population. The result: almost no change in the effective tax rates of almost all income groups. The effective tax rate for the bottom quintile (the poorest 20 percent of the population) goes from 8.4 to 8.5 percent, and for the richest 20 percent of the population, from 27.3 percent to 26.8 percent. No quintile in the figure witnesses tax changes of more than 1 percent of income. In fact, the differences are so small that they are easily within the margin of error that results from attempts to measure income and taxes correctly.[2]

Even for the top 20 percent, the tax reduction is concentrated at the top 1 percent of the population. The benefits of the drop in the top tax rate of 70 percent in 1980 to the low 30s in 1991 (taking into account the backdoor rate implicit in the way itemized deductions are treated) were essentially offset by base broadening for all but the very richest.

Figure 12.1 EFFECTIVE FEDERAL TAX RATES FOR ALL FAMILIES

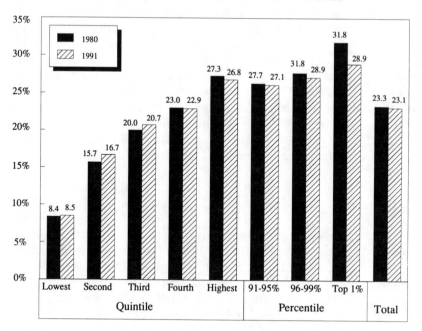

Sources: Committee on Ways and Means (1990, p. 1173); and unpublished
estimates from the Congressional Budget Office Tax Simulation Model.

For the middle-income groups, perhaps the only change worth noting
is that, even with all the increases in the earned income tax credit,
there continued the movement toward similar average or effective tax
rates at both the low and high ends of the classes or quintiles that
define "middle" income. Between 1981 and 1990, the second lowest
quintile bore tax increases of about 1 percent of income—moving it
ever closer to the rates paid by quintiles above it. This result is consistent with the congressional tendency to concentrate earned income
tax credits and other tax relief at the very bottom, while allowing Social
Security taxes to increase for all income groups but the top.

It is important to note also that most, but not all, of the estimates
shown in figure 12.1 are based mainly upon who is liable to pay the
tax. The incidence of a tax—who loses or wins in the long run—
depends upon a variety of factors. Higher taxes can lead to changes
in interest rates, work effort, distribution of investment among assets
and sectors, consumption patterns, relative prices, and other economic behavior. When these factors are taken into account, it is even

more difficult to assess whether the overall tax system has become more or less progressive over the decade.

Another weakness of tables showing who bears the tax burden is that especially at the very top of the income distribution, the income measures are inadequate.[3] When faced with lower tax rates, individuals may simply recognize more income, while with higher rates they recognize less. Capital gains is perhaps the most important of those items for which the tax is dependent upon the discretionary realization of income. Some would argue that the lower top rates were offset by increases in income realizations among high-income individuals—hence, even the top 1 percent had no real drop in tax rates.

Tax versus Income Shifts

The debate over whether the tax system had become more or less progressive was complicated by a shift in the percentage of tax paid by different income groups. Statistics prepared by the Statistics Division of the Internal Revenue Service, in fact, demonstrated that the percentage of the total income tax burden paid by the top income groups rose steadily throughout the 1980s.[4] For instance, the top five percent of all taxpayers paid 35.4 percent of the total income tax in 1981, but paid 45.6 percent in 1988. This increased skewing of the individual income tax burden toward higher incomes, however, was matched by an increased skewing of income toward these same classes. That is, there is some evidence that the rich have been getting richer and the poor poorer during the tax decade—a continuation of a trend since the mid-1970s (Gramlich et al. 1991).

Both the meaning and the extent of increased income inequality are still being debated. The increase in number of two-earner couples appeared to shift the share of income toward those households—who in turn tended to show up in higher income classes because of their additional sources of income. The cost of health care benefits increased dramatically throughout this period, but data usually do not show employer-provided health benefits as part of the wages of individuals. Many tables reporting transfer income fail to take into account benefits provided in the form of housing, medical services, and other in-kind rather than cash benefits. The break up or slower formation of households with married couples reduces average household size and makes many households show up in lower income classes even when total income in the economy does not go down. Finally, capital gains recognition is clearly a discretionary event, so that changes in patterns of capital gains realization may present a distorted picture of the changes in the real income being received.

Whatever the extent of redistribution of income during the decade, figure 12.1 makes clear that this redistribution can hardly be attributed to changes in taxes. These tax changes are almost negligible relative to total income of each income group.[5]

Workers and Children

Two issues of progressivity and equity are likely to carry forward beyond the tax decade. One has already been mentioned above—the tax rates paid by the very highest income individuals. Even if these rates are raised, however, they will have at best a modest impact on the overall budget. The number of individuals involved and the amount of tax change is simply not that large relative to the population and total tax collections.

An issue likely to have greater impact on future budgets is the tax treatment of workers and households with children—issues that are often considered simultaneously. The expansion of the earned income tax credit for low-income working households with children in 1986 and 1990 showed a clear and growing concern for this particular group in the population. This concern was also revealed in proposals in 1989 and 1990 to lower Social Security taxes.[6] In turn, children themselves had become a focus of attention in the late 1980s, through dissemination of information revealing them to be the poorest group in the population, the establishment of a National Commission on Children, and other high visibility efforts.[7]

For a family of four with fully taxable earnings from labor equal to one-half median income, Social Security taxes (counting both the employer and employee portion) and federal income taxes together accounted for 5 percent or less of income before 1960. By 1990 these taxes had risen to about 20.9 percent of income. Even the drop in income tax rates from 1986 to 1990 is only about -1 percent of income for this group, and that drop is offset by Social Security tax increases of 1 percent of income during the same period (Steuerle and Wilson 1986).

The status of low-income workers and children is clearly one of the major tax, as well as expenditure, issues remaining from the tax decade.

OTHER TAX ISSUES FOR THE 1990s AND BEYOND

The necessity of adjusting any tax system to the demands of the time, as well as the power of the tax-writing committees, insure that the tax system will not remain stagnant for the 1990s nor beyond. Following are some of the more likely candidates for change in the period after the tax decade. Note that while a number of income tax issues are listed, the most important changes are likely to occur with respect to the reform of other parts of government—reforms that cannot be achieved without attention to important tax issues.

Social Security Tax Reform

With respect to base broadening, the income tax itself may not be the principal focus of future attention. The income tax is no longer the most important tax on most workers. Now it is the Social Security tax that takes an ever-bigger chunk out of the paycheck of working people.

Fringe benefits have slowly eroded the Social Security tax base. Over the past 30 years, the Social Security tax base has declined by 10 percent because of such fringe benefits, while another 10-percent decline is projected over the next 40 years under assumptions used by Social Security actuaries. Each 10-percent decline translates to about $35 billion that does not accrue to the trust funds in a year such as 1990.

Finally, the long-term insolvency of the Old Age and Survivors Insurance trust fund, and the shorter term insolvency of the Hospital Insurance trust fund will add to the pressure for Social Security tax reform.

Health Reform

Just beneath the surface of the major budgetary debates of the tax decade was one nagging and politically sensitive fact: the continual rise in health and Medicare expenditures was the major source of pressure on the budget, as well as the most significant expenditure expansion of the period. From the beginning to the end of the decade, the real rate of growth of federal health expenditures continued to exceed the real rate of growth in the economy by several percentage points.

This trend is unsustainable, among other reasons because the Hospital Insurance trust fund (HI) remains insolvent over the long run. The system is also imbalanced because it favors acute medical needs over long-term care needs and because tax policy favors those with generous employer health plans over those with less generous plans or no plans at all.

Tax policy will be intimately involved in resolving these issues. A 1990 Treasury report demonstrates ways that tax rules can be changed and fringe benefits limited to encourage health insurance and distribute tax benefits more equitably and efficiently.[8] Other rules—such as providing tax benefits for children in middle- and upper-income families only when they are insured for health—are likely to be debated and perhaps adopted.

Transfer Payments and Welfare Reform

Major efforts to restructure transfer and welfare systems are likely in the future, and tax issues again will probably come to the fore in the process.

Taxation of benefits, as mentioned above, was an item neglected in tax reform. As part of a package of expenditure and tax reform, however, expanded taxation of Social Security benefits is likely to be passed as a means of dealing with the medium-term insolvency of Medicare or the long-term insolvency of Social Security. Taxation of welfare benefits would be a means of recouping some benefits when overlapping layers of eligibility result in combined benefit levels that exceed tax-free levels of income. The revenues could then be used to pay for other welfare changes.

Taxing transfer payments would represent another major step toward structuring programs in a more integrated fashion. Taxation would centralize—in the Internal Revenue Service—the data necessary to examine the interaction of all the various tax and transfer systems, which are currently designed in isolation from one another.

Traditional Tax Reform Issues

A number of more traditional tax issues remain unaddressed or inadequately dealt with after all the reforms of the tax decade.

Simplification. A major need remaining from tax reform was to simplify the tax code. Whenever there is major governmental reform, it is often followed by a period in which a strong focus is placed on simplifying the new system and making it administrable. By 1990, this effort had not yet occurred although some modest, revenue neutral, bipartisan efforts were under consideration in 1991.

Simplification will not eliminate all of the complexity of income accounting—a complexity that many firms face for financial reasons, as well as tax ones. As a simple guess, however, I would conjecture that it is possible to reduce the time that taxpayers spend on their tax returns by about 25 percent, a saving roughly equal to about $25 billion per year.

Integrating Corporate and Individual Income Taxes. The double taxation of corporate income continues to create disparities in taxation between corporate and noncorporate capital and between debt and equity. Corporate integration was discussed by the Carter administration and proposed by the Reagan administration. Despite the difficulty of passing legislation implementing even partial integration in the United States, the issue will not go away. Several events or considerations are likely to reawaken interest among policymakers in the integration of corporate and individual income taxes: future increases in the debt of the corporate sector; indirect integration achieved by the formation of new businesses in partnership form; and the prejudice in the current tax system against new, risky ventures that must be formed as corporations.

The United States remains among the few developed countries of the world without some form of corporate individual tax integration. The push toward greater uniformity in taxation—as witnessed by the copying of tax reform throughout the world—will continue to create a push toward corporate integration (and perhaps even a value-added tax) in this country.

International Tax Issues. For several reasons, international tax issues will become one of the more active areas in tax policy for a considerable period of time. First, some of the changes enacted in 1986 were so complex that few practitioners understood what was required. At a minimum, there will be some attempts to make the rules workable. Second, the growing interdependence of different economies and the ease with which financial capital can be transferred across boundaries force renewed consideration of how taxes on international businesses should be assessed. Finally, the old consensus that real corporate capital should be taxed at the source, while individual receipts of interest and dividends should be taxed at place of recipient's residence, has resulted in the uneven taxation of different sources of capital income.

In the tax reform effort, it had proven impossible to develop a consensus on either what could be done or how to do it. What is fair by one country's standard becomes unfair by another's. Meanwhile, the very existence of different tax rates among countries forces inefficient decision making and tax shopping, just as do differences in taxes among jurisdictions within the United States. Moreover, exchange of records among countries is often difficult, and the use of such records when obtained by tax authorities is in its infancy. A consensus is likely to remain elusive. Some simplification and greater exchange of information through tax treaties seem to be the surest routes for positive improvement, but many will find these incremental efforts inadequate.

Inflation and the Taxation of Capital Income. One failing of the current tax system continually forces capital income issues back on the table. The U.S. tax system fails to index for inflation, with several important consequences. First, owners of farmland and real estate, as well as corporate stock, can be subject to significant amounts of taxation on their assets even when no real income has been earned. This factor makes it especially difficult to avoid some form of change in the treatment of capital gains. Second, in times of high inflation, equity ownership of depreciable capital can be heavily taxed. Finally, interest income and expense become among the worst measured of all items of income. A person paying 10 percent interest in a world of 5 percent inflation is deducting twice the real amount of interest expense. Because borrowers and lenders are in different tax brackets, this last factor encourages shifts of hundreds of billions, if not trillions, of dollars of assets among owners.

My own guess is that this problem will not be solved until accounting systems are able to measure real income correctly. Absent this change—which may be some time down the road—the tax system could continue to go back and forth between attempts to cut back on tax arbitrage by taxing all nominal income equally, and the recognization that the full taxation of all nominal income in periods of inflation can lead to tax rates that are almost confiscatory (Steuerle and Halperin 1988).

BROADER IMPLICATIONS FOR BUDGET POLICY

The power to tax and the power to spend have usually been separated jurisdictionally. Tax committees typically are separated from expenditure committees, while Finance and Treasury departments are separated from Housing and Welfare and Transportation departments. The legal separation is mirrored by a separation in theory. As Richard Musgrave points out, John Stuart Mill "separated the analysis of tax equity from the expenditure side of the budget, a separation which for better or for worse (and mostly worse) has dominated tax analysis ever since" (Musgrave 1990, p. 115). The separation, however, is often arbitrary and awkward, as evidenced by the presence of tax expenditures in the tax code and fees and taxes in expenditure programs.

The Problems Created by Jurisdictional Separation

That this separation has profound implications for budget, tax, and expenditure policy can been seen from the budget and tax bills of the tax decade. In almost every deficit reduction package of the decade, tax policy was dominant. Several reasons have been offered in this book. The tax-writing committees control most of the revenue side of the budget, over 40 percent of direct expenditures, and all of the expenditures in the tax expenditure budget. They can make trade offs and deliver a comprehensive bill when no other committee or leadership group in Congress can do so. Indeed, as the decade shows, they can deliver both tax expenditure increases and decreases, and both rate increases and decreases, and both deficit increases and decreases.

At the same time, this jurisdictional separation in both Congress and the administration often precludes other trade offs from being made. Early in the tax reform process, it became clear that the traditional argument against tax expenditures could not be used. The Treasury Department has long maintained that most subsidies and incentives should be made on the direct expenditure side of the budget, and not be hidden in the tax code. Tax expenditures, of course, have the advantage of appearing to lower the cost of government. Increasing tax expenditures reduces measures of both taxes collected; if tax expenditures replace direct expenditures, the measure of total expenditures goes down. Average tax rates hide the true tax rate, which must be measured before deducting the expenditure that is floated through the tax code.

The tax reform process, however, allowed only a trade off of base broadening for rate reduction. Except in a couple of minor cases, no tax expenditure could be replaced with a more efficient or more controllable budgetary program. Many departments of the executive branch and many committees of Congress worked against the Treasury and the tax-writing committees by trying to maintain both their direct expenditures and tax expenditures. Only in the area of tax expenditures could the tax authorities claim clear jurisdiction. These jurisdictional constraints still prevent such trade offs from being made among the departments of the executive branch or among the committees of Congress.

Attempts at budget reform face a complementary set of constraints. In recent decades especially, expenditure decreases have not been traded directly for tax rate decreases. The former are used primarily or exclusively to reduce the government deficit or increase the government surplus. Direct expenditure programs are seldom, if ever, merged or combined with tax expenditure programs to prevent duplicate administration or provide a better overall targeting of benefits.

These jurisdictional problems present a barrier to leaner government (a conservative principle) and to a more progressive government (a liberal principle). They explain a great deal of the tax policy themes of the 1980s—the importance of the tax expenditure budget, the dominance of the tax-writing committees in deficit reduction action, and the painfully slow and inadequate attempt of government policymakers to tackle both the tax and expenditure side of many important social issues.

TOWARD THE FUTURE

A common notion throughout the tax decade was that once the deficit was eliminated, choices of policy would become easier. I believe this is incorrect. The debate over the deficit is mainly a debate over how to provide sources of expenditure reduction or tax increase to pay for an increase in national saving. Once that national saving is achieved—only one of many possible new priorities—the same dispute remains. Any other change in priorities also requires expenditure reduction or tax increases, and cannot be financed in the same way as changes were financed throughout most of the postwar era. The deficit debate, therefore, masks the more basic question that confronts any republic: How can the people through their elected representatives and their institutions shift public policy priorities over time? No matter how many budget compromises meet some agreed-upon deficit level, the same process issues remain.

Some argue that the many impasses in the tax decade over how to achieve shifts in priorities are a permanent feature of government. While there is some logic to this scenario over the short run, it is also destined to be wrong. Why? The demands of the U.S. population for all types of goods and services and its sense of priorities continue to change in a rapid manner. Part of this change is due to an expanding economy and a changing technology. We do not find it surprising, for instance, that private demands change annually by several percentage points of total income or by several hundred billion dollars as needs shift and income rises. It should not then be surprising that the public's demand for government goods and services should change at an equally rapid rate.

If new trade offs are to be made, the next question is: How will they be achieved? The answer is that institutions and institutional processes will—indeed, must—change to accommodate new demands. How those institutions will evolve is highly speculative and will depend in no small part upon both presidential and congressional leadership. My own guess is that the budget process in Congress will be strengthened significantly by vesting more authority in the congressional leadership or in the budget or appropriations committees, while the executive branch could strengthen the budget process by concentrating greater power in those parts of government with broad oversight over many or most tax and expenditure functions (i.e., the OMB and the Treasury Department).

A more adaptable process also requires that a broad range of programs be redesigned so that future growth is left to future decision makers, rather than determined so far in advance that no slack is left in the budget. This requires taking some of the built-in growth and permanent features out of entitlement and tax expenditure programs. In the meantime, our government will muddle through, reacting well at times to current crises, but doing less well at deterring or avoiding future crises that need not occur at all.

Stalemate in government is primarily a procedural problem. It is not, as some would argue, simply a political problem that derives from a president's unwillingness to increase taxes or from the populace's inability to deal with any type of reduction in perceived benefits. This stalemate will probably not be solved until the day that the power of the leadership, appropriations, or budget committees is enhanced or Congress develops some true decision making mechanism by which to make trade offs among expenditure programs. Until that day, most major decisions will continue to be made by the tax-writing committees, the only ones who normally have to deal in a more comprehensive manner with the balance sheet and trade-off facets of the multiple issues that fall within their jurisdiction.

Future Sources of Funds for Changing Priorities

Throughout this book, I have stressed that the events of the tax decade are consistent with the movement to a new era. The ready availability of funds from defense cutbacks, Social Security tax rate increases, and bracket creep in the income tax are gone or almost gone. The tax decade saw a significant turning to two alternatives: base broadening in the income tax, and the use of fees and premiums within expenditure programs. Partly because easier options had already been taken during the decade, by 1990 base broadening was pretty much ignored in the search for deficit reduction.

This implies that future, significant changes in priorities are likely to be funded from one of four sources. First, there will be continuation of the trend toward *increased fees and premiums*, many of which are treated as negative outlays for budget purposes. Fees and premiums also represent the only mechanisms by which expenditure committees can expand programs without cutting back on gross outlays or turning to the tax-writing committee. Because so many are set in fixed or nominal terms, and decline in importance as inflation and real growth in the economy proceed, governments may also begin to toy with ways to index fees and premiums to grow more steadily over time.

Second, there will be an important debate over the adoption of a *value-added* tax (VAT) or other major alternative revenue source. Traditionally, the United States has adopted a major new tax only in times of crisis or as a replacement for other taxes. It is hard to anticipate future crises, although some would argue that the rise in health care costs requires the adoption of a national health care system financed by a VAT. Replacement of the corporate tax with a VAT has never sold well in this country, but increased disenchantment with the Social Security tax could present an opportunity for the introduction of a VAT. In addition, the United States remains one of the few countries in the world without such a tax.

Third, increased examination will be made of existing excise taxes, as well as *new excises related to energy and the environment.* Environmental taxes are often proposed by both conservatives and liberals as alternatives to command and control or regulation. New ways of indexing these taxes are also likely to be considered.

Finally, Congress can no longer ignore the need to turn to *cutbacks in gross domestic expenditures* to pay for expansion of other expenditure programs. Adding new taxes or increasing existing ones can only delay the inevitable day of reckoning.

The Comprehensive Package

A model for achieving trade offs was presented in 1986. In the new era, comprehensive reforms must be considered. Government officials now have thousands of programs to administer. Many of them are directed in uncoordinated fashion at the same needs. No one president, member of Congress, policy analyst, or educated citizen can possibly understand more than a tiny portion of the system or how it works. Comprehensive approaches to issues are the only way to get a handle on what is and is not possible, what needs to be replaced and what retained, how all the many pieces fit together, and whether financing is adequate for all needs.

The type of organization and reorientation necessary to achieve major governmental reform has been applied all too infrequently in the recent past, leaving our nation with governmental policies and institutions that are more outdated than pernicious, more inflexible than inconsiderate. The years succeeding the tax decade will witness sporadic attempts by the nation to attain the will, the leadership, and the institutions that can organize and, more importantly, deliver, such comprehensive reform.

CONCLUSION

During the tax decade, tax issues were to dominate the political agenda in a manner seldom, if ever, seen in the nation's history. This dominance was due not to the magnitude of the tax changes, but to their volume and frequency, to the relative power of the tax-writing committees in Congress, to the need to make comprehensive trade offs after decades of expansion in often uncoordinated government programs, and to a budgetary stalemate during which many major social reforms or expenditure changes were forestalled.

A number of myths were created during the decade. By its end, the share of the nation's income paid in taxes was neither greatly increased nor decreased, nor was the tax burden spread much differently among income classes. Nor were the tax changes enacted in 1981 the sole, nor even the major, cause of the budgetary stalemate present throughout the rest of the decade. Instead, the nation was moving to a new era in which new sources of financing—including cutbacks in expenditures and tax expenditures—were becoming more and more necessary to move on to other priorities, both conservative and liberal.

In the midst of this period, some success—large by historical standards—was attained in improving the equity and efficiency of the tax system by broadening the income tax base, lowering marginal tax rates, reducing the incentive to invest in tax shelters and other less productive assets, and reversing the trend of higher taxes on low-income workers, the poor, and households with children. This success offers a telling example, and perhaps a model, of what the future may hold for reforms of other governmental systems.

Notes

1. See Gold (1988 and 1987). In fact, Steve Gold did more than report on these events. He served as a major catalyst for states to reform their income taxes, in particular, with respect to taxation of the poor.

2. Source: Congressional Budget Office and Ways and Means Committee. This estimate was prepared by comparing tables presented after the 1990 budget agreement with similarly derived tables used to estimate changes in tax burdens over time. See Committee on Ways and Means (1990a, p. 1173; and 1990b, unpublished). In both cases, the source of data is the Congressional Budget Office Simulation Model, with analyses performed by Rick Kasten and Frank Sammartino of that office. Note that some sources of tax change are not modeled. These same data sources were used separately by the Democratic Party to argue about the regressivity of changes during the Reagan era and, then again, in opposing an initial budget agreement for 1990 that was voted down. Hence, the numbers can hardly be considered to be biased toward showing greater progressivity.

3. Wage and salary income is the most accurately reported item of income and is the prevalent source of income in the middle-income groups. At the bottom of the income distribution, there are also additional measurement difficulties, such as the failure to measure in-kind transfers and inaccuracies in the measure of capital income.

4. See U.S. Treasury (1990a).

5. Economists would assert that it is the marginal, not average, tax rate that changes behavior. For most taxpayers, these marginal rates did not change dramatically either, as Social Security tax rate increases offset much of the individual income tax rate reduction in low- and middle-income groups.

6. These proposals attempted, if somewhat awkwardly, to deal with both the financing of the non-Social Security deficit through Social Security surpluses and the impact of Social Security taxes on low-income workers. Proposals by Senator Moynihan, for instance, would put Social Security on a pay-as-you-go basis. They would increase the deficit dramatically in the short-run, while over the long-run require significant increases in the rate of Social Security taxation.

7. Along with Jason Juffras, I have proposed a $1,000 tax credit as a means to help reform the tax and welfare systems. See Steuerle and Juffras (1991).

8. See U.S. Treasury (1990b). This report was prepared under my direction as Deputy Assistant Secretary of the Treasury from 1987 to 1989.

APPENDIX

Table A.1 TOTAL FEDERAL, STATE, AND LOCAL TAX RECEIPTS
(Amounts in Billions of Dollars)

Year	Gross national product	Federal individual income tax		Social security and railroad retirement taxes		Federal corporate profits tax		Other federal taxes (a)		State and local taxes (b)		Total tax receipts		State and local income tax receipts		Total individual income tax receipts	
		Amount	% of GNP	Amount	% of GNP	Amount	% of GNP	Amount	% of GNP	Amount	% of GNP	Amount	% of GNP	Amount	% of GNP	Amount	% of GNP
1929	103.9	1.2	1.15	0.0	0.00	1.2	1.15	1.3	1.25	5.8	5.58	9.5	9.14	0.1	0.10	1.3	1.25
1930	91.1	1.0	1.10	0.0	0.00	0.7	0.77	1.1	1.21	6.1	6.70	8.9	9.77	0.1	0.11	1.1	1.21
1931	76.4	0.5	0.65	0.0	0.00	0.4	0.52	1.0	1.31	5.9	7.72	7.8	10.21	0.1	0.13	0.6	0.79
1932	58.5	0.3	0.51	0.0	0.00	0.3	0.51	0.8	1.37	5.7	9.74	7.1	12.14	0.1	0.17	0.4	0.68
1933	56.0	0.4	0.71	0.0	0.00	0.5	0.89	1.6	2.86	5.4	9.64	7.9	14.11	0.1	0.18	0.5	0.89
1934	65.6	0.4	0.61	0.0	0.00	0.6	0.91	2.2	3.35	5.6	8.54	8.8	13.41	0.1	0.15	0.5	0.76
1935	72.8	0.6	0.82	0.0	0.00	0.8	1.10	2.3	3.16	5.8	7.97	9.5	13.05	0.1	0.14	0.7	0.96
1936	83.1	0.7	0.84	0.0	0.00	1.3	1.56	2.6	3.13	6.3	7.58	10.9	13.12	0.2	0.24	0.9	1.08
1937	91.3	1.3	1.42	0.8	0.88	1.3	1.42	2.8	3.07	6.6	7.23	12.8	14.02	0.2	0.22	1.5	1.64
1938	85.4	1.2	1.41	0.8	0.94	0.9	1.05	2.5	2.93	6.8	7.96	12.2	14.29	0.2	0.23	1.4	1.64
1939	91.3	0.9	0.99	0.8	0.88	1.3	1.42	2.6	2.85	7.0	7.67	12.6	13.80	0.2	0.22	1.1	1.20
1940	100.4	1.0	1.00	0.8	0.80	2.6	2.59	2.9	2.89	7.2	7.17	14.5	14.44	0.2	0.20	1.2	1.20
1941	125.5	1.6	1.27	1.0	0.80	7.3	5.82	3.8	3.03	7.8	6.22	21.5	17.13	0.3	0.24	1.9	1.51
1942	159.0	4.0	2.52	1.2	0.75	11.1	6.98	4.5	2.83	7.7	4.84	28.5	17.92	0.3	0.19	4.3	2.70
1943	192.7	15.9	8.25	1.4	0.73	13.6	7.06	5.3	2.75	7.7	4.00	43.9	22.78	0.3	0.16	16.2	8.41
1944	211.4	16.8	7.95	1.4	0.66	12.5	5.91	6.5	3.07	8.0	3.78	45.2	21.38	0.4	0.19	17.2	8.14
1945	213.4	18.5	8.67	1.4	0.66	10.2	4.78	7.6	3.56	8.4	3.94	46.1	21.60	0.4	0.19	18.9	8.86
1946	212.4	16.3	7.67	1.8	0.85	8.6	4.05	8.7	4.10	9.2	4.33	44.6	21.00	0.4	0.19	16.7	7.86
1947	235.2	18.8	7.99	2.2	0.94	10.7	4.55	8.9	3.78	10.7	4.55	51.3	21.81	0.5	0.21	19.3	8.21
1948	261.6	18.1	6.92	2.2	0.84	11.8	4.51	9.0	3.44	12.2	4.66	53.3	20.37	0.6	0.23	18.7	7.15
1949	260.4	15.4	5.91	2.2	0.84	9.6	3.69	8.9	3.42	15.0	5.76	51.1	19.62	0.7	0.27	16.1	6.18
1950	288.3	17.4	6.04	3.2	1.11	17.2	5.97	9.7	3.36	16.4	5.69	63.9	22.16	0.8	0.28	18.2	6.31
1951	333.4	25.4	7.62	4.0	1.20	21.7	6.51	10.3	3.09	18.1	5.43	79.5	23.85	0.9	0.27	26.3	7.89
1952	351.6	30.1	8.56	4.2	1.19	18.6	5.29	11.3	3.21	19.6	5.57	83.8	23.83	1.0	0.28	31.1	8.85
1953	371.6	31.3	8.42	4.6	1.24	19.5	5.25	12.0	3.23	21.1	5.68	88.5	23.82	1.0	0.27	32.3	8.69
1954	372.5	28.0	7.52	5.8	1.56	16.9	4.54	10.8	2.90	22.2	5.96	83.7	22.47	1.1	0.30	29.1	7.81
1955	405.9	30.4	7.49	6.5	1.60	21.1	5.20	11.8	2.91	24.3	5.99	94.1	23.18	1.3	0.32	31.7	7.81
1956	428.2	33.8	7.89	7.1	1.66	20.9	4.88	12.7	2.97	27.0	6.31	101.5	23.70	1.6	0.37	35.4	8.27

Continued

Table A.1 TOTAL FEDERAL, STATE, AND LOCAL TAX RECEIPTS (Amounts in Billions of Dollars) (continued)

Year	Gross national product	Federal individual income tax		Social security and railroad retirement taxes		Federal corporate profits tax		Other federal taxes (a)		State and local taxes (b)		Total tax receipts		State and local income tax receipts		Total individual income tax receipts	
		Amount	% of GNP	Amount	% of GNP	Amount	% of GNP	Amount	% of GNP	Amount	% of GNP	Amount	% of GNP	Amount	% of GNP	Amount	% of GNP
1957	451.0	35.9	7.96	8.5	1.88	20.4	4.52	13.4	2.97	29.0	6.43	107.2	23.77	1.7	0.38	37.6	8.34
1958	456.8	35.4	7.75	8.5	1.86	18.0	3.94	13.0	2.85	30.5	6.68	105.4	23.07	1.8	0.39	37.2	8.14
1959	495.8	38.5	7.77	10.3	2.08	22.5	4.54	14.2	2.86	33.9	6.84	119.4	24.08	2.2	0.44	40.7	8.21
1960	515.3	41.8	8.11	12.5	2.43	21.4	4.15	15.4	2.99	37.1	7.20	128.2	24.88	2.5	0.49	44.3	8.60
1961	533.8	42.7	8.00	12.8	2.40	21.5	4.03	15.8	2.96	39.8	7.46	132.6	24.84	2.8	0.52	45.5	8.52
1962	574.6	46.5	8.09	13.9	2.42	22.5	3.92	17.4	3.03	43.0	7.48	143.3	24.94	3.2	0.56	49.7	8.65
1963	606.9	49.2	8.11	16.4	2.70	24.6	4.05	18.0	2.97	46.0	7.58	154.2	25.41	3.4	0.56	52.6	8.67
1964	649.8	46.0	7.08	17.3	2.66	26.1	4.02	18.9	2.91	50.0	7.69	158.3	24.36	4.0	0.62	50.0	7.69
1965	705.1	51.1	7.25	18.3	2.60	28.9	4.10	19.1	2.71	54.1	7.67	171.5	24.32	4.4	0.62	55.5	7.87
1966	772.0	58.6	7.59	26.0	3.37	31.4	4.07	18.4	2.38	59.1	7.66	193.5	25.06	5.4	0.70	64.0	8.29
1967	816.4	64.4	7.89	29.4	3.60	30.0	3.67	19.1	2.34	64.5	7.90	207.4	25.40	6.1	0.75	70.5	8.64
1968	892.7	76.5	8.57	32.9	3.69	36.1	4.04	21.0	2.35	73.9	8.28	240.4	26.93	7.8	0.87	84.3	9.44
1969	963.9	91.5	9.49	38.5	3.99	36.1	3.75	22.4	2.32	83.0	8.61	271.5	28.17	9.8	1.02	101.3	10.51
1970	1,015.5	88.8	8.74	39.8	3.92	30.6	3.01	23.0	2.26	91.8	9.04	274.0	26.98	10.9	1.07	99.7	9.82
1971	1,102.7	85.7	7.77	44.1	4.00	33.5	3.04	24.8	2.25	102.3	9.28	290.4	26.34	12.4	1.12	98.1	8.90

1972	1,212.8	102.7	8.47	49.9	4.11	36.6	3.02	25.5	2.10	116.3	9.59	331.0	27.29	17.2	1.42	119.9	9.89
1973	1,359.3	109.5	8.06	64.7	4.76	43.3	3.19	26.9	1.98	127.0	9.34	371.4	27.32	18.9	1.39	128.4	9.45
1974	1,472.8	126.4	8.58	73.8	5.01	45.1	3.06	26.7	1.81	136.8	9.29	408.8	27.76	20.4	1.39	146.8	9.97
1975	1,598.4	120.8	7.56	77.1	4.82	43.6	2.73	28.9	1.81	140.2	8.77	410.6	25.69	22.5	1.41	143.3	8.97
1976	1,782.8	141.5	7.94	85.4	4.79	54.6	3.06	29.4	1.65	166.6	9.34	477.5	26.78	26.3	1.48	167.8	9.41
1977	1,990.5	162.5	8.16	94.5	4.75	61.6	3.09	33.1	1.66	185.3	9.31	537.0	26.98	30.4	1.53	192.9	9.69
1978	2,249.7	189.5	8.42	109.3	4.86	71.4	3.17	34.6	1.54	199.2	8.85	604.0	26.85	35.0	1.56	224.5	9.98
1979	2,508.2	225.2	8.98	129.1	5.15	74.4	2.97	35.4	1.41	212.2	8.46	676.3	26.96	38.2	1.52	263.4	10.50
1980	2,732.0	251.1	9.19	142.4	5.21	70.3	2.57	44.9	1.64	217.4	7.96	726.1	26.58	42.6	1.56	293.7	10.75
1981	3,052.6	291.7	9.56	170.4	5.58	65.7	2.15	64.1	2.10	240.2	7.87	832.1	27.26	47.9	1.57	339.6	11.12
1982	3,166.0	296.5	9.37	179.8	5.68	49.0	1.55	56.0	1.77	257.2	8.12	838.5	26.48	51.9	1.64	348.4	11.00
1983	3,405.7	288.1	8.46	194.3	5.71	61.3	1.80	56.8	1.67	283.2	8.32	883.7	25.95	58.3	1.71	346.4	10.17
1984	3,772.2	303.7	8.05	219.9	5.83	75.2	1.99	60.8	1.61	317.6	8.42	977.2	25.91	67.6	1.79	371.3	9.84
1985	4,014.9	339.3	8.45	242.7	6.04	76.3	1.90	60.1	1.50	342.3	8.53	1,060.7	26.42	72.2	1.80	411.5	10.25
1986	4,231.6	353.6	8.36	264.5	6.25	83.9	1.98	58.3	1.38	366.7	8.67	1,127.0	26.63	76.8	1.81	430.4	10.17
1987	4,515.6	397.2	8.80	281.2	6.23	105.8	2.34	61.2	1.36	398.4	8.82	1,243.8	27.54	86.1	1.91	483.3	10.70
1988	4,873.7	405.7	8.32	315.2	6.47	110.5	2.27	65.4	1.34	419.1	8.60	1,315.9	27.00	90.1	1.85	495.8	10.17
1989	5,200.8	453.1	8.71	340.7	6.55	110.4	2.12	67.3	1.29	452.8	8.71	1,424.3	27.39	101.7	1.96	554.8	10.67
1990	5,465.1	479.1	8.77	371.9	6.80	108.5	1.99	73.2	1.34	477.9	8.74	1,510.6	27.64	106.2	1.94	585.3	10.71

Sources: U.S. Department of Commerce (1986); and U.S. Department of Commerce, *Survey of Current Business*, various years (Tables 1.1, 3.2, 3.3, and 3.6).

(a) Includes Federal estate taxes, gift taxes, excise taxes, and customs duties, plus employer contributions for Federal unemployment tax, railroad unemployment insurance, and Federal worker's compensation. Excludes Federal nontaxes.

(b) Includes all State and local receipts from taxes and licenses. Excludes nontaxes, receipts from contributions to social insurance and receipts from federal grants-in-aid.

Table A.2 TAX EXEMPT LEVELS OF INCOME BY FILING STATUS AND NUMBER OF DEPENDENTS, 1948–1990

Year	Per capita personal income	Single	Joint			Head of household	
		0 Dependents	0 Dependents	2 Dependents	4 Dependents	2 Dependents	4 Dependents
1948	$1,427	$667	$1,333	$2,667	$4,000	$2,000	$3,333
1954	1,797	667	1,333	2,667	4,000	2,000	3,333
1960	2,266	667	1,333	2,667	4,000	2,000	3,333
1966	3,057	990	1,600	3,000	4,000	2,300	3,700
1972	4,677	2,050	2,800	4,300	5,800	3,550	5,050
1978	8,143	3,200	5,200	7,200	9,200	5,200	7,200
1981	10,954	3,300	5,400	7,400	9,400	5,300	7,300
1984	13,117	3,300	5,400	7,400	9,400	5,300	7,300
1986	14,594	3,560	5,820	7,980	10,140	5,720	7,880
1988	16,527	4,950	8,900	12,800	16,700	10,250	14,150
1990	18,479	5,300	9,550	13,650	17,750	10,900	15,000
% Change							
1948–1990	1195%	695%	616%	412%	344%	445%	350%
1948–1981	668	395	305	177	135	165	119
1981–1986	33	8	8	8	8	8	8
1986–1990	27	49	64	71	75	91	90

Sources: Author's calculations, based on data from U.S. Department of Commerce (1986, 1990); and the Internal Revenue Service, *Individual Income Tax Returns*, various years.

Note: These figures assume no use of the Earned Income Tax Credit. Note the change in the Consumer Price Index was 442% between 1948 and 1990.

Table A.3 AVERAGE AND MARGINAL INCOME TAX RATES FOR FOUR-PERSON FAMILIES AT THE SAME RELATIVE POSITIONS IN THE INCOME DISTRIBUTION: 1955–1988

Year	One-half median income			Median income			Twice median income		
	Income ($)	Average income tax rate (%)	Marginal income tax rate (%)	Income ($)	Average income tax rate (%)	Marginal income tax rate (%)	Income ($)	Average income tax rate (%)	Marginal income tax rate (%)
1955	2,460	.00	.0	4,919	5.64	20.0	9,838	10.76	22.0
1956	2,660	.00	.0	5,319	6.38	20.0	10,638	11.22	22.0
1957	2,744	.00	.0	5,488	6.65	20.0	10,976	11.40	22.0
1958	2,843	.00	.0	5,685	6.96	20.0	11,370	11.59	22.0
1959	3,035	.00	.0	6,070	7.49	20.0	12,140	11.93	22.0
1960	3,148	.15	20.0	6,295	7.77	20.0	12,590	12.11	22.0
1961	3,219	.48	20.0	6,437	7.94	20.0	12,874	12.22	22.0
1962	3,378	1.19	20.0	6,756	8.30	20.0	13,512	12.44	26.0
1963	3,569	1.95	20.0	7,138	8.68	20.0	14,276	12.85	26.0
1964	3,744	2.06	16.0	7,488	7.56	18.0	14,976	11.66	23.5
1965	3,900	2.16	14.0	7,800	7.09	17.0	15,600	11.12	22.0
1966	4,171	2.72	14.0	8,341	7.48	19.0	16,682	11.50	22.0
1967	4,497	3.32	15.0	8,994	8.00	19.0	17,988	11.89	22.0
1968	4,917	4.03	15.0	9,834	9.21	20.4	19,668	13.37	26.9
1969	5,312	4.58	15.0	10,623	9.92	20.9	21,246	14.24	27.5
1970	5,583	4.65	15.0	11,165	9.35	19.5	22,330	13.47	25.6
1971	6,088	4.73	15.0	12,176	9.27	19.0	24,352	13.45	28.0
1972	6,404	4.37	15.0	12,808	9.09	19.0	25,616	13.52	28.0
1973	6,855	4.88	16.0	13,710	9.45	19.0	27,420	14.05	28.0
1974ʳ	7,485	4.17*	16.0	14,969	8.99*	22.0	29,938	14.35*	32.0
1975	7,924	4.22	17.0	15,848	9.62	22.0	31,696	14.86	32.0
1976	8,658	4.68	17.0	17,315	9.89	22.0	34,630	15.51	36.0

Continued

Table A.3   AVERAGE AND MARGINAL INCOME TAX RATES FOR FOUR-PERSON FAMILIES AT THE SAME RELATIVE POSITIONS IN THE INCOME DISTRIBUTION: 1955–1988 (continued)

Year	One-half median income			Median income			Twice median income		
	Income ($)	Average income tax rate (%)	Marginal income tax rate (%)	Income ($)	Average income tax rate (%)	Marginal income tax rate (%)	Income ($)	Average income tax rate (%)	Marginal income tax rate (%)
1977	9,362	2.84	16.0	18,723	9.81	22.0	37,446	15.51	36.0
1978	10,214	4.19	19.0	20,428	10.36	25.0	40,856	16.51	39.0
1979ʳ	11,256	5.11	16.0	22,512	10.84	24.0	45,024	17.20	37.0
1980	12,166	6.02	18.0	24,332	11.42	24.0	48,664	18.25	43.0
1981	13,137	6.82	17.8	26,274	11.79	23.7	52,548	19.11	42.5
1982	13,810	6.51	16.0	27,619	11.06	25.0	55,238	18.01	39.0
1983ʳ	14,591	6.53	15.0	29,181	10.38	23.0	58,362	16.83	35.0
1984	15,549	6.50	14.0	31,097	10.25	22.0	62,194	16.62	38.0
1985	16,389	6.56	14.0	32,777	10.34	22.0	65,554	16.78	38.0
1986	17,358	6.64	14.0	34,716	10.48	22.0	69,432	17.04	38.0
1987ʳ	18,543	5.16	15.0	37,086	8.90	15.0	74,172	15.80	35.0
1988	19,526	5.17	15.0	39,051	9.30	15.0	78,102	15.21	28.0
1989	20,382	5.29	15.0	40,763	9.36	15.0	81,526	15.28	28.0
1990	21,482ᴱ	5.47	15.0	42,964ᴱ	9.44	15.0	85,928ᴱ	15.38	28.0

Sources: U.S. Department of the Treasury Office of Tax Analysis (Allen Lerman); U.S. Bureau of the Census, Population Reports, Series P-60, various years; and author's calculations for 1986–1990.

* Adjusted to reflect rebates of 1974 tax liabilities provided by P.L. 94-12.

ʳ Median income based on revised methodology.

ᴱ Estimated from 1989 income as adjusted for price level (CPI-U) changes. Inflation is assumed to be 5.47 in 1990.

Note: Median income is for a four-person family. All income is earned by one spouse. Itemized deductions are assumed to equal 23 percent of income.

Table A.4 OUTLAY EQUIVALENT ESTIMATES FOR TAX EXPENDITURES UNDER CURRENT LAW AND PRE-TAX REFORM LAW BY TYPE OF TAX REFORM CHANGE
($ millions at 1988 levels)

Provisions repealed	Tax expenditures		Effect of tax reform		
	Pre-tax reform law	Current law	Total	Base broadening	Rate reduction
Investment credit other than ESOPs, rehabilitation of structures, energy, property, and reforestation expenditures	39,030	2,500	−36,530	−36,060	−470
Capital gains (other than agriculture, timber, iron ore, and coal)	27,730	—	−27,730	−27,730	0
Deduction for two earner married couples	8,495	—	−8,495	−8,495	0
Additional exemption for the elderly	4,025	—	−4,025	−4,025	0
Exclusion of untaxed unemployment insurance benefits	960	—	−960	−960	0
Capital gains treatment of certain agriculture income	935	—	−935	−935	0
Dividend exclusion	745	—	−745	−745	0
Capital gains treatment of certain timber income	665	—	−665	−665	0
Deductions for special percentage of taxable income for life insurance companies	610	—	−610	−610	0
Credit for political contributions	270	—	−270	−270	0
Capital gains treatment of royalties on coal	135	—	−135	−135	0
Additional exemption for the blind	35	—	−35	−35	0
Capital gains treatment of iron ore	25	—	−25	−25	0
Deduction for certain adoption expenses	*	—	*	*	0
Subtotal	83,660	2,500	−81,160	−80,690	−470

Continued

Table A.4 OUTLAY EQUIVALENT ESTIMATES FOR TAX EXPENDITURES UNDER CURRENT LAW AND PRE-TAX REFORM LAW BY TYPE OF TAX REFORM CHANGE (continued)
($ millions at 1988 levels)

	Tax expenditures		Effect of tax reform		
Provisions with rate effect only[1]	Pre-tax reform law	Current law	Total	Base broadening	Rate reduction
Exclusion of employer contributions for medical insurance premiums and medical care	40,990	31,005	−9,985	240	−10,225
Deductibility of mortgage interest on owner occupied-homes	34,295	25,015	−9,280	0	−9,280
Deductibility of State and local property taxes on owner-occupied homes	17,050	11,095	−5,955	0	−5,955
Exclusion of social security benefits:					
OASI benefits for retired workers	18,145	13,005	−5,140	0	−5,140
Reduced rates on the first $100,000 of corporate income	8,060	4,720	−3,340	0	−3,340
Exclusion of interest on public purpose S&L debt	13,310	9,975	−3,335	−265	−3,070
Deductibility of charitable contributions, other than education health	12,605	9,920	−2,685	0	−2,685
Net exclusion of pension contributions and earnings:					
Keogh Plans	4,040	1,475	−2,565	0	−2,565
Exclusion of interest on life insurance savings	9,230	7,000	−2,230	0	−2,230
Tax credit for corporations receiving income from doing business in U.S. possessions	4,570	2,455	−2,115	−245	−1,870
Deferral of income for foreign sales corporations (FSC)	2,445	780	−1,665	0	−1,665
Exclusion of social security benefits:					
Benefits for dependents and survivors	3,855	2,770	−1,085	0	−1,085
Exclusion of income earned abroad by U.S. citizens	2,705	1,710	−995	−45	−950
Exclusion of interest on State and local debt for private non-profit health facilities	3,060	2,270	−790	−60	−730

Exclusion of interest on small-issue IDBs.	3,400	2,650	−750	−70	−680
Excess of percentage over cost depletion:					
Oil and gas	1,390	660	−730	0	−730
Exclusion of workers' compensation benefits	3,210	2,570	−640	0	−640
Exclusion of interest on owner-occupied mortgage subsidy bonds	2,455	1,905	−550	−50	−500
Exclusion of benefits and allowances to Armed Forces	2,710	2,170	−540	0	−540
Credit for child care expenses	5,765	5,265	−500	0	−500
Deductibility of charitable contributions (education)	2,060	1,570	−490	0	−490
Exclusion of social security benefits:					
Disability insurance benefits	1,465	1,050	−415	0	−415
Exclusion of interest on IDBs for pollution control and sewage and waste disposal facilities	2,285	1,870	−415	−45	−370
Exclusion of other employee benefits:					
Premiums for group term life insurance	2,365	1,955	−410	0	−410
Deductibility of charitable contributions (health)	1,785	1,380	−405	0	−405
Exclusion of veterans disability compensation	1,780	1,420	−360	0	−360
Exclusion of public assistance benefits	690	345	−345	0	−345
Excess of percentage over cost depletion, nonfuel minerals	630	305	−325	0	−325
Exclusion of interest on State and local debt for rental housing	1,670	1,395	−275	−35	−240
Excess of percentage over cost depletion:					
Other fuels	415	185	−230	0	−230
Deferral of interest on savings bonds	1,080	890	−190	0	−190
Safe harbor leasing	850	660	−190	0	−190
Exclusion of interest on IDBs for airports, docks, etc.	835	675	−160	−15	−145
Exclusion of veterans pensions	195	75	−120	0	−120
Exemption of credit union income	285	175	−110	0	−110
Exclusion of interest on State and local debt for private nonprofit educational facilities	340	250	−90	−5	−85
Exclusion of interest on State and local student loan bonds	455	375	−80	−10	−70
Exclusion of interest on State and local debt for veterans housing	320	240	−80	−5	−75
Exclusion of railroad retirement system benefits	430	360	−70	0	−70

Continued

Table A.4 OUTLAY EQUIVALENT ESTIMATES FOR TAX EXPENDITURES UNDER CURRENT LAW AND PRE-TAX REFORM LAW BY TYPE OF TAX REFORM CHANGE (continued)
($ millions at 1988 levels)

Provisions with rate effect only[1]	Tax expenditures		Effect of tax reform		
	Pre-tax reform law	Current law	Total	Base broadening	Rate reduction
Amortization of start-up costs	300	240	-60	20	-80
Deductibility of casualty losses	320	265	-55	0	-55
Exclusion of interest on IDBs for certain energy facilities	215	175	-40	-5	-35
Exclusion of other employee benefits:					
Premiums on accident and disability insurance	155	120	-35	0	-35
Exclusion of special benefits for disabled coal miners	140	110	-30	0	-30
Investment credit and seven-year amortization for reforestation expenditures	240	210	-30	0	-30
Deferral of tax on shipping companies	115	85	-30	0	-30
Exclusion of military disability pensions	130	100	-30	0	-30
Exclusion of interest on mass commuting vehicle IDBs	85	60	-25	0	-25
Expensing of certain capital outlays	500	480	-20	0	-20
Exclusion of GI bill benefits	80	65	-15	0	-15
Special rules for mining reclamation reserves	55	45	-10	0	-10
Expensing of exploration and development costs, nonfuel minerals	40	35	-5	0	-5
Exclusion of employer provided child care	85	80	-5	0	-5
Income of trusts to finance supplementary unemployment benefits	30	25	-5	0	-5
Expensing of exploration and development costs:					
Other fuels	40	35	-5	0	-5
Oil and gas	-960	-435	525	0	525
Exception from source rules for sales of inventory	1,650	3,320	1,670	0	1,670
Subtotal	21,6445	15,8605	-57,840	-816	-57,024

Expanded provisions	Tax expenditures		Effect of tax reform		
	Pre-tax reform law	Current law	Total	Base broadening	Rate reduction
Parental personal exemption for students age 19 and older	915	430	-485	610	-1,095
Tax credit for orphan drug research	—	*	*	*	0
Five year amortization for housing rehabilitation	45	45	0	10	-10
Alternative, conservation, and new technology credits:					
Supply incentives	-70	5	75	65	10
Targeted jobs credit	35	305	270	270	0
Credit for increasing research activities	195	1,310	1,115	1,270	-155
Earned income credit	560	1,850	1,290	1,205	85
Exclusion of capital gains on home sales for persons age 55 and older	2,040	3,860	1,820	3,170	-1,350
Deferral of capital gains on home sales	2,560	4,605	2,045	5,115	-3,070
Carryover basis of capital gains at death	10,105	16,025	5,920	15,155	-9,235
Accelerated depreciation of machinery and equipment	15,600	24,860	9,260	17,440	-8,180
Subtotal	31,985	53,295	21,310	44,310	-23,000

Continued

Table A.4 OUTLAY EQUIVALENT ESTIMATES FOR TAX EXPENDITURES UNDER CURRENT LAW AND PRE-TAX REFORM LAW
BY TYPE OF TAX REFORM CHANGE (continued)
($ millions at 1988 levels)

New provisions	Tax expenditures			Effect of tax reform		
	Pre-tax reform law	Current law	Total	Base broadening	Rate reduction
Additional deduction for the elderly	—	1,275	1,275	1,660	−385
Exception from passive loss rules for $25,000 of rental losses	—	1,205	1,205	1,505	−300
Special ITC carryback rules for steel	—	565	565	565	0
Credit for low-income housing	—	425	425	610	−185
Expensing of multiperiod timber growing costs	—	265	265	360	−95
Special ITC carryback rules for farming	—	235	235	235	0
Exception from interest allocation rules for certain non-financial-institution operations	—	65	65	70	−5
Additional deduction for the blind	—	15	15	15	0
Treatment of loans for solvent farmers	—	*	*	*	0
Subtotal	—	4,050	4,050	5,020	−970

Provisions unchanged	Tax expenditures			Effect of tax reform		
	Pre-tax reform law	Current law	Total	Base broadening	Rate reduction	

Provisions unchanged	Pre-tax reform law	Current law	Total	Base broadening	Rate reduction
Alternative, conservation, and new technology credits:					
Conservation incentives	—*	—*	0	0	0
Alternative fuel production credit	15	15	0	0	0
Alcohol fuel credit	10	10	0	0	0
Energy credit for intercity bus	—*	—*	0	0	0
Tax credit for the elderly and disabled	240	240	0	0	0
Subtotal	265	265	0	0	0

Source: Neubig and Joulfaian (1988).

* Under $2.5 million. All estimates are rounded to the nearest $5 million.

[1] Includes provisions with predominant rate effects not included elsewhere.

Table A.5 SUMMARY OF MAJOR ENACTED TAX LEGISLATION FROM
1981–1990

Economic Recovery Tax Act of 1981

☐ Individual income tax rate reductions. Reduced marginal tax rates 23 percent
over three years; reduced maximum rate to 50 percent and maximum capital
gains rate to 20 percent; indexed income tax brackets, personal exemption and
standard deduction for inflation beginning in 1985; and provided new deduction
for two-earner married couples.

☐ Capital cost recovery provisions. Replaced facts and circumstances and the Asset
Depreciation Range guidelines with Accelerated Cost Recovery System. Faster
write-off of capital expenditures under simplified rules. Most equipment written
off over 5 years, structures over 15 years. Allowed liberalized "safe-harbor"
leasing rules.

☐ Savings incentives. Extended eligibility for IRA's to include active participants
in employer pension plans. Increased Keogh annual contribution limit to
$15,000.

☐ Estate and gift tax provisions. Permitted unlimited marital deduction; increased
estate credit to exempt from tax all estates of $600,000 or less; and reduced
maximum estate tax rate from 70 to 50 percent.

☐ Accelerated corporated estimated tax payments and tightened rules on tax
straddles with mark-to-market rule.

Tax Equity and Fiscal Responsibility Act of 1982

☐ Improvements in compliance and collection. Imposed withholding on interest
and dividends; further acceleration of corporate estimated tax payments;
expanded information reporting; and increased penalties on non-compliance.

☐ Reduction in unintended benefits and obsolete incentives. Strengthened
individual minimum tax; repealed future acceleration of depreciation
allowances; repealed safe-harbor leasing; and tightened completed contract
method of accounting rules.

☐ Increased excise taxes. Increased airport and airway trust fund taxes, cigarette
excise taxes, and telephone excise tax.

☐ Increased employment taxes. Increased FUTA tax rate and wage base, and
extended hospital insurance taxes to Federal employees.

Highway Revenue Act of 1982

☐ Increased excise tax on gasoline and diesel fuel from 4 to 9 cents per gallon for
5 years.

Social Security Amendments of 1983

☐ Accelerated scheduled increases in OASDI payroll tax rate.

☐ Taxed some Social Security benefits. At most 50 percent of Social Security
benefits subject to tax if income exceeds $25,000 for a single taxpayer or $32,000
for a joint return.

Continued

Table A.5 SUMMARY OF MAJOR ENACTED TAX LEGISLATION FROM
1981–1990 (continued)

Interest and Dividends Tax Compliance Act of 1983

☐ Repealed interest and dividend withholding and replaced with "backup withholding" and expanded information reporting.
☐ Enacted Caribbean Basin Initiative (CBI) tax benefits.

Railroad Retirement Revenue Act of 1983

☐ Increased railroad retirement payroll taxes and railroad unemployment insurance taxes.
☐ Taxed railroad retirement pension plan benefits.

Deficit Reduction Act of 1984

☐ Increased excise taxes. Increased distilled spirits excise tax and extended telephone excise tax.
☐ Restrictions on leasing. Reduced benefits from tax-exempt leasing and postponed effective data of liberalized finance leasing rules.
☐ Increased depreciable life of structures from 15 to 18 years.
☐ Placed state volume limitation on private purpose tax exempt bonds.
☐ Placed time value of money restrictions on accounting rules.
☐ Repealed net interest exclusion (ERTA provision) before its effective date.
☐ Reduced long-term capital gains holding period from one year to six months.

Consolidated Omnibus Budget Reconciliation Act of 1985 (COBRA)

☐ Permanently extended 16 cents per pack cigarette excise tax.
☐ Enacted new excise tax on smokeless tobacco.
☐ Increased excise tax on coal production.
☐ Extended hospital insurance coverage to new state and local government employees.
☐ Repealed income averaging for former students.

Tax Reform Act of 1986

☐ Individual income tax provisions. Lowered top marginal tax rate to 28 percent; increased standard deduction to $5,000 for married couples; increased personal exemption to $2,000; and increased earned income tax credit.
☐ Repealed two-earner deduction, long-term capital gains exclusion, state and local sales tax deduction, income averaging, and exclusion of unemployment benefits. Limited IRA eligibility, consumer interest deduction, deductibility of "passive" losses, medical expenses deductions, deduction for business meals and entertainment, pension contributions, and miscellaneous expense deduction.
☐ Reduced corporate marginal tax rate to 34 percent, and tightened corporate minimum tax.
☐ Repealed the investment tax credit and lengthened capital cost recovery periods.
☐ Further tightened state volume limitations for private purpose tax-exempt bonds.
☐ Extended research and experimentation credit; initiated new low-income housing tax credit and deductibility of health insurance costs of self-employed individuals.

Continued

Table A.5 SUMMARY OF MAJOR ENACTED TAX LEGISLATION FROM
1981–1990 (continued)

Omnibus Budget Reconciliation Act of 1986

☐ Accelerated state and local government deposits of Social Security payroll taxes.
☐ Accelerated collections of alcohol and tobacco excise taxes.
☐ Increased substantial underpayment penalty and penalty for failure to comply
with deposit requirements.
☐ Increased customs user fee on value of imported merchandise.

Superfund Amendments and Reauthorization Act of 1986

☐ Enacted excise tax of 8.2 cents per barrel on domestic crude oil and 11.7 cents
per barrel on imported petroleum products.
☐ Enacted new broad-based tax on all corporations equal to 0.12 percent of
alternative minimum taxable income in excess of $2 million.
☐ To finance cleanup of wastes from leaking underground petroleum storage tanks,
enacted a 0.1 cent per gallon excise tax on gasoline, diesel fuels and other
special motor fuels.

Continuing Resolution for Fiscal Year 1987

☐ Increased Internal Revenue Service funding for staffing and equipment.
☐ Established Immigration and Naturalization Service inspection fee.

Omnibus Budget Reconciliation Act of 1987

☐ Repealed installment sales method of accounting for dealers and vacation pay
reserve.
☐ Tightened completed contract method of accounting.
☐ Reduced inter-corporate dividends received deduction.
☐ Accelerated corporate estimated tax payments.
☐ Limited employer deductible contributions to defined benefit pension plans.
☐ Limited mortgage interest deduction to debt less than $1 million and home
equity loans of less than $100,000.
☐ Extended telephone excise tax, FUTA tax, 55 percent estate tax rate, and
employer Social Security to cover cash tips.
☐ Increased IRS and BATF fees.

Continuing Resolution for Fiscal Year 1988

☐ Increased IRS funding for more enforcement staff and equipment.

Airport and Airway Trust Fund Extension of 1987

☐ Extended airport and airway trust excise tax.

The Family Security Act of 1988

☐ Extended the debt refund offset provision.
☐ Tightened eligibility for the dependent care credit.
☐ Required taxpayer identification number for younger children.

Continued

Table A.5 SUMMARY OF MAJOR ENACTED TAX LEGISLATION FROM
1981–1990 (*continued*)

Medicare Catastrophic Coverage Act of 1988

□ Passed new supplemental premium tax on all persons eligible for Medicare.
Premium rate is 15 percent of individual income tax liability in excess of $150,
increasing to 28 percent in 1993. Premium limited to $800 in 1989, rising to
$1,050 in 1993, with future premium cap dependent on medical care costs after
1993.

Technical and Miscellaneous Revenue Act of 1988

□ Passed technical corrections for the Tax Reform Act of 1986.
□ Extended expiring provisions: research and experimentation tax credit and
allocation rules; targeted jobs credit; mortgage subsidy bonds; employer-provided
educational assistance and group legal services; FSLIC relief provisions, and
mutual fund expense exclusion.
□ Restricted single premium life insurance, Alaskan Native Corporations, and
completed contract accounting rules; and accelerated corporate estimated tax
payments.

Financial Institutions Reform, Recovery, and Enforcement Act of 1989

□ Repealed three provisions which had provided tax relief to financially troubled
thrift institutions.

Medicare Catastrophic Coverage Repeal Act of 1989

□ Eliminated supplemental premium tax for Medicare catastrophic coverage.

Omnibus Budget Reconciliation Act of 1989

□ Limited tax deductions and exclusions for employee stock ownership plans.
□ Increased fees and excise taxes on air travel, ozone-depleting chemicals, and oil
spill liability.
□ Repealed completed contract method of accounting.
□ Modified the corporate alternative minimum tax.
□ Extended expiring provisions: employer provided educational assistance;
research and experimentation tax credit and allocation rules; low income
housing credit.

Omnibus Budget Reconciliation Act of 1990

□ Increased excise taxes. Imposed a 10 percent luxury tax on the amount of price
over $30,000 for autos, $100,000 for boats, $250,000 for airplanes, and $10,000
for furs. Increased motor fuels taxes by 5 cents per gallon. Increased taxes on
tobacco and alcoholic beverages: by 8 cents per pack of cigarettes; by $1.00 per
"proof gallon" of liquor; by 16 cents per six-pack of beer; and by 18 cents per
bottle of table wine. Extended Airport and Airway trust fund taxes and increased
them by 25 percent. Extended 3 percent excise tax on telephone service.
□ Raised income tax rates. Increased top statutory tax rate from 28 to 31 percent,
and increased the individual alternative minimum tax rate from 21 to 24

Continued

Table A.5 SUMMARY OF MAJOR ENACTED TAX LEGISLATION FROM
1981–1990 (*continued*)

---

percent. Limited value of high income itemized deductions: reduced by 3
percent times the extent to which AGI exceeds $100,000. Modified the "bubble":
moved the personal exemption phase-out to the range of taxable income between
$150,000 and $275,000.
□ Increased payroll taxes. Raised the cap on wages taxable for Medicare to
$125,000. Extended social security taxes to state and local employees without
other pension coverage. Imposed a supplemental 0.2 percent unemployment
insurance surtax.
□ Expanded Earned Income Tax Credit, adjusted it for family size. Created a low-
income credit for the premium costs of health insurance that includes coverage
for children.
□ Corporate income tax reform. Required insurance companies to amortize a
portion of "policy acquisition costs."
□ Income tax base erosion. Extended expiring provisions: tax credits for research &
exploration, low-income housing, business energy, targeted jobs, and orphan
drugs; tax exemptions for mortgage revenue and small issue bonds; exclusions
for employer-provided legal and educational assistance; and 25 percent health
insurance deduction for the self-employed. Extended and created new energy
producer tax benefits: extended nonconventional fuels credit and tax incentives
for ethanol production; created a new credit for enhanced oil recovery costs;
amended percentage depletion; reduced alternative minimum tax preference
treatment of energy items. Created a small-business oriented credit for
accommodations for disabled persons. Modified estate "freeze" rules. Eliminated
appreciation of certain donated property as a minimum tax preference item.
□ Miscellaneous revenue-raisers: permitted transfers from "overfunded" pension
plans for retiree health; added chemicals subject to ozone-depleting chemicals
tax; reimposed Leaking Underground Storage Tank Trust Fund tax; reduced loss
deductions by property and casualty insurance companies; improved IRS ability
to obtain information from foreign corporations; increased harbor maintenance
tax; reduced business income tax loopholes.

Sources: U.S. Department of the Treasury, Office of Tax Analysis (November 1, 1988);
and Office of Management and Budget, *Budget of the United States Government*,
various fiscal years. Summary of 1990 OBRA abstracted from U.S. House of Representatives Budget Commitee, "Summary of Reconciliation Conference Report," October 1990.

REFERENCES

ACIR (Advisory Commission on Intergovernmental Relations). 1989. *Changing Public Attitudes on Governments and Taxes.* Washington, D.C.: ACIR.

Auten, Gerald E. and Charles T. Clotfelter. 1982. "Permanent Versus Transitory Tax Effects and the Realization of Capital Gains." *Quarterly Journal of Economics*, vol. 97, no. 4 (November):613–632.

Auten, Gerald E. and Joseph Cordes. 1991. "Capital Gains Realizations." *Journal of Economic Perspectives*, vol. 15, no. 1 (Winter):181–192.

Bacon, Kenneth H. 1981. "Taxes to Balance Budget Rejected by President." *The Wall Street Journal*, December 18:3.

Berry, John M. and Helen Dewar. 1981. "Deficit of $80 Billion Looms for 1982, Hill Told." *The Washington Post*, September 11:1.

Birnbaum, Jeffrey H. and Alan S. Murray. 1987. *Showdown at Gucci Gulch.* New York: Random House.

Blum, Walter J. and Harry Kalven. 1953. *The Uneasy Case for Progressive Taxation.* Chicago, Il.: University of Chicago Press.

Boynton, Charles, Paul Robbins, and George Plesko. 1991. "Earnings Management and the Corporate Minimum Tax." Unpublished manuscript.

Break, George F. 1991. "Major Fiscal Trends in the 1980s and Implications for the 1990s." *Tax Notes*, vol. 50, no. 5, February 4.

Break, George F. and Joseph A. Pechman. 1975. *Federal Tax Reform: The Impossible Dream?* Washington, D.C.: The Brookings Institution.

Brownlee, W. Elliot. 1989. "Taxation for a Strong and Virtuous Republic: a Bicentennial Retrospective," *Tax Notes*, vol. 45, no. 13, December 25:1620.

Chapoton, John E. 1982. "Statement of The Honorable John E. Chapoton, Assistant Secretary of the Treasury for Tax Policy, Before the Senate Finance Committee, September 28." Washington, D.C.: Department of the Treasury.

Cogan, John F. 1988. "The Evolution of Congressional Budget Decisionmaking and the Emergence of Federal Deficits." *Working Papers in*

Political Science P-88-6. Stanford, Ca.: The Hoover Institution, Stanford University, November.

Committee on Ways and Means, U.S. House of Representatives. 1990a. *Overview of Entitlement Programs, 1990 Green Book: Background Material and Data on Programs Within the Jurisdiction of the Committee on Ways and Means*. Washington, D.C.: Superintendent of Documents.

————. 1990b. *Distributional Effects of the Reconciliation Conference Report with Child Care*. October 26 (table distributed, but not published).

Congressional Budget Office. 1991. *The Economic and Budget Outlook: Fiscal Years 1992–1996*. Washington, D.C.: Superintendent of Documents, January.

Conlan, Timothy J., Margaret T. Wrightson, and David R. Beam. 1990. *Taxing Choices: The Politics of Tax Reform*. Washington, D.C.: The Congressional Quarterly, Inc.

Davenport, Charles, Michael D. Boehlje, and David B.H. Martin. 1982. "The Effects of Tax Policy on American Agriculture." U.S. Department of Agriculture, Agricultural Economic Report 480, USDA.

Derthick, Martha. 1979. *Policymaking for Social Security*. Washington, D.C.: The Brookings Institution.

Economic Report of the President, 1991. 1991. Washington, D.C.: Superintendent of Documents.

Economic Report of the President, 1990. 1990. Washington, D.C.: Superintendent of Documents.

Economic Report of the President, 1964. 1964. Washington, D.C.: Superintendent of Documents.

Edsall, Thomas B. 1981. "GOP Hunts $60 Billion," *The Washington Post*, October 31:1.

Feldstein, Martin S., Joel Slemrod, and Shlomo Yitzhaki. 1980. "The Effects of Taxation on the Selling of Corporate Stock and the Realization of Capital Gains." *Quarterly Journal of Economics*, vol. 97, no. 4 (June):777–791.

Friedman, Milton. 1962. *Capitalism and Freedom*. Chicago, Il.: The University of Chicago Press.

Fullerton, Don and Yolanda Henderson. 1987. "The Impact of Fundamental Tax Reform on the Allocation of Resources." In *Taxes and Capital Formation*, ed. Martin Feldstein. Chicago, Il.: University of Chicago Press.

Galper, Harvey and Eric Toder. 1983. "Owning or Leasing: Bennington College and the U.S. Tax System," *National Tax Journal*, 36, June:257–61.

Gold, Steven D. (ed.). 1988. *The Unfinished Agenda for State Tax Reform*. Denver, Co.: National Conference of State Legislators.

————. 1987. *State Tax Relief for the Poor*. Denver, Co.: National Conference of State Legislators.

Goode, Richard. 1976. *The Individual Income Tax*. Washington, D.C.: The Brookings Institution.

Gramlich, Edward M., Richard Kasten, and Frank Sammartino. 1991. "Growing Inequality in the 1980s: The Role of Federal Taxes and Cash Transfers." Madison, Wi.: University of Michigan. Draft.

Gravelle, Jane G. 1986. *Effective Tax Rates in the Major Tax Revision Plans: Updated Tables Including the Senate Finance Committee Proposal*. Report 86-691 E, May 16. Washington, D.C.: Congressional Research Service.

————. 1984. *A Comparative Analysis of Five Tax Proposals: Effects of Business Income Tax Provisions*. Report No. 84-832 E, December 27. Washington, D.C.: Congressional Research Service.

Hall, Robert E. and Alvin Rabushka. 1983. *Low Tax, Simple Tax, Flat Tax*. New York: McGraw Hill.

Halperin, Daniel and C. Eugene Steuerle. 1988. "Indexing the Tax System for Inflation." In *The Uneasy Compromise: Problems of a Hybrid Income-Consumption Tax*. Henry Aaron, Harvey Galper, and Joseph Pechman, eds. Washington, D.C.: The Brookings Institution.

Haskel, Barbara. 1987. "Paying for the Welfare State: Creating Political Durability." *Scandinavian Studies*, vol. 59:221–53.

Henderson, Yolanda K. 1986. "Lessons from Federal Reform of Business Taxes." *New England Economic Review* (November/December):9–26.

Hoffman, Saul D. and Laurence S. Seidman. 1990. *The Earned Income Tax Credit: Antipoverty Effectiveness and Labor Market Effects*. Kalamazoo, Mi.: W.E. Upjohn Institute for Employment Research.

Hulten, Charles R. and James W. Robertson. 1984. "The Taxation of High Technology Industries," *National Tax Journal*, vol. 37, no. 3, September:327–346.

IRS (Internal Revenue Service). 1988. *1988 Package X*, vol. 1. Washington, D.C.: Internal Revenue Service.

————. 1985. "Taxpayer Compliance Measurement Program for 1982 Returns." Unpublished data.

IRS, Statistics of Income Division. Various years. *Individual Income Tax Returns*. Washington, D.C.: Internal Revenue Service.

Joint Committee on Taxation. 1987. *General Explanation of the Tax Reform Act of 1986*. Washington, D.C.: Superintendent of Documents.

————. 1986. *Summary of the Conference Agreement on H.R. 3838 (Tax Reform Act of 1986)*. Washington, D.C.: U.S. Government Printing Office.

————. 1982. *General Explanation of the Revenue Provisions of the Tax Equity and Fiscal Responsibility Act of 1982*. Washington, D.C.: Superintendent of Documents.

Lindsey, Lawrence B. 1988. "Capital Gains Rates, Realizations and Revenues." In *The Effects of Taxation on Capital Formation*. Martin S. Feldstein, ed. Chicago, Il.: University of Chicago Press.

Makin, John H. and Michael T. Allison. 1986. "Tax Reform 1986: A Fragile Victory." *AEI Occasional Papers*, Studies in Fiscal Policy #10. Washington, D.C.: The American Enterprise Institute.

Mayer, Jane and Doyle McManus. 1988. "How the Reagan Myth Was Made." *The Washington Post*, September 18:C 1–2.

McLure, Charles E. Jr. 1988. "The 1986 Act: Tax Reform's Finest Hour or Death Throes of the Income Tax?" *National Tax Journal*, vol. 41 (September):303–15.

————. 1986. "The Tax Treatment of Owner-Occupied Housing: The Achilles Heel of Tax Reform?" In *Tax Reform and Real Estate*. James R. Follain, ed. Washington, D.C.: The Urban Institute.

Minarik, Joseph J. 1987. "How Tax Reform Came About." *Tax Notes* (December 26):1359–73

————. 1984. "The Effects of Taxation on the Selling of Corporate Stock and the Realization of Capital Gains: Comment." *Quarterly Journal of Economics*, vol. 99, no. 1 (February):93–110.

Moynihan, Daniel Patrick. 1986. *Family and Nation*. San Diego, Ca.: Harcourt Brace Jovanovich.

Musgrave, Richard A. 1990. "Horizontal Equity, Once More," *National Tax Journal*, vol. 43 (June):113–22.

————. 1959. *The Theory of Public Finance: A Study in Public Economy*, New York: McGraw-Hill.

Nelson, Susan. 1985. "Taxes Paid by High-Income Taxpayers and the Growth of Partnerships." *Statistics of Income Bulletin*, vol. 5 (Fall).

Neubig, Thomas and David Joulfaian. 1988. *The Tax Expenditure Budget Before and After the Tax Reform Act of 1986*. Office of Tax Analysis Paper 60. Washington, D.C.: U.S. Department of the Treasury.

Office of Tax Analysis, Department of the Treasury. 1985. *Capital Gains Tax Reductions of 1978*. Washington, D.C.: Superintendent of Documents.

Okun, Arthur. 1975. *Equality and Efficiency: The Big Tradeoff*. Washington, D.C.: The Brookings Institution.

OMB (Office of Management and Budget). 1991. "Midsession Review of the Budget." Washington, D.C.: OMB, July 15.

————. 1988. *The Budget of the United States Government, Fiscal Year 1989*. Washington, D.C.: Superintendent of Documents.

————. 1984. *The Budget of the United States Government, for Fiscal Year 1985*. Washington, D.C.: Superintendent of Documents.

————. Various years. *The Budget of the United States Government*. Washington, D.C.: Superintendent of Documents.

————. Various years. *Tax Expenditures, Special Analysis to the Budget of the U.S. Government*. Washington, D.C.: Superintendent of Documents.

OECD (Organisation for Economic Co-operation and Development). 1990. *OECD Statistics on the Member Countries in Figures*. Supplement to the *OECD Observer* no. 164. Paris, France: OECD, June/July.

Pechman, Joseph A. 1983. *Federal Tax Policy*. Washington, D.C.: The Brookings Institution.

Regan, Donald T. 1988a. *For the Record: From Wall Street to Washington*. San Diego: Harcourt Brace Jovanovich.

_____. 1988b. "For the Record: Guesswork Presidency." *Time*, May 16:38-40.

Ruggles, Patricia. 1990. *Drawing the Line: Alternative Poverty Measures and Their Implications for Public Policy*. Washington, D.C.: The Urban Institute Press.

Schick, Allen. 1990. *The Capacity to Budget*. Washington, D.C.: The Urban Institute Press.

Simons, Henry C. 1938. *Personal Income Taxation: The Definition of Income as a Problem of Fiscal Policy*. Chicago, Il.: The University of Chicago Press.

Slemrod, Joel, ed. 1990. *Do Taxes Matter: The Impact of the Tax Reform Act of 1986*. Cambridge, Ma.: MIT Press.

Smith, Dan Throop. 1965. "Changes in the Nation's Tax Structure." *Proceedings of the 58th Annual Conference of the National Tax Association, New Orleans, November 9, 1965*. Columbus, Oh.: National Tax Association, pp. 15–23.

Stein, Herbert. 1969. *The Fiscal Revolution in America*. Chicago, Il.: The University of Chicago Press.

Steuerle, C. Eugene 1991. "Effects of the Budget Process on Tax Legislation." In *Improving the Tax Legislative Process: A Critical Need*. Washington, D.C.: The American Tax Policy Institute, the ALI-ABA Committee on Continuing Education, and the National Tax Association.

_____. 1990a. "Tax Reform: Just How Sweet Was It?" In *The Impact of the Tax Reform Act of 1986: Did It Improve Fairness and Simplicity?* U.S. Treasury. IRS Research Conference Report. Washington, D.C.: Internal Revenue Service.

_____. 1990b. "Federal Policy and the Accumulation of Private Debt in the Postwar United States." In *Debt, Taxes, and Corporate Restructuring*. John B. Shoven and Joel Waldfogel, eds. Washington, D.C.: The Brookings Institution.

_____. 1990c. "Tax Credits for Low-Income Workers with Children," *Journal of Economic Perspectives*, vol. 4 (Summer):201–212

_____. 1988. "U.S. Tax Reform: Implications for Other Countries." In *World Tax Reform: A Progress Report*. Joseph A. Pechman, ed. Washington, D.C.: The Brookings Institution.

_____. 1987a. "Effects on Financial Decision-Making." In *Tax Reform and the U.S. Economy.* Joseph A. Pechman, ed. Washington, D.C.: The Brookings Institution.

_____. 1987b. "The New Tax Law." In *Deficits, Taxes, and Economic Adjustments.* Philip Cagan, ed. Washington, D.C.: American Enterprise Institute.

_____. 1986a. "The Federal Tax Reform Process: Issues and Implications," *National Tax Journal—Proceedings of the Seventy-Ninth Annual Conference, 1986.*

_____. 1986b. "Lessons from the Tax Reform Process," *Tax Notes,* July.

_____. 1985a. "The Prospects for Tax Reform," *National Tax Journal,* vol. 37 (September).

_____. 1985b. *Taxes, Loans, and Inflation.* Washington, D.C.: The Brookings Institution.

_____. 1983a. "The Tax Treatment of Households of Different Size." In *Taxing the Family.* Rudolph G. Penner, ed. Washington, D.C.: American Enterprise Institute.

_____. 1983b. "Building New Wealth by Preserving Old Wealth: Savings and Investment Tax Incentives in the Post War Era." *National Tax Journal,* vol. 36, no. 3 (September):307–319.

_____. Various years. "Economic Perspective," *Tax Notes* Magazine.

Steuerle, C. Eugene and Michael Hartzmark. 1981. "Individual Income Taxation, 1947–79," *National Tax Journal,* vol. 34, no. 2 (June).

Steuerle, C. Eugene and Jason Juffras. 1991. "A $1,000 Tax Credit for Every Child: A Base of Reform for the Nation's Tax, Welfare, and Health Systems." Washington, D.C.: Changing Domestic Priorities Policy Paper, The Urban Institute.

Steuerle, C. Eugene, Richard McHugh, and Emil Sunley. 1978. "Who Benefits from Income Averaging?" *National Tax Journal,* vol. 31 (March):19–32.

Steuerle, C. Eugene and Paul Wilson. 1987. "The Earned Income Tax Credit." *Focus* 10. Madison, Wi.: University of Wisconsin, Institute for Research on Poverty.

_____. 1986. "The Taxation of Poor and Lower-Income Workers." In *Ladders Out of Poverty: A Report of the Project on the Welfare of Families.* Jack A. Meyer, ed. Washington, D.C.: American Horizons Foundation. Reprinted and updated for *Tax Notes,* vol. 34, no. 7, February 16, 1987:695–711. Reprinted again in *Clearinghouse Review,* vol. 21, no. 9, February 1988.

Stockman, David A. 1986. *The Triumph of Politics: How the Reagan Revolution Failed.* New York: Harper and Row.

Surrey, Stanley S. and Paul McDaniel. 1985. *Tax Expenditures.* Cambridge, Ma.: Harvard University Press.

U.S. Bureau of the Census. Various years. *Money Income and Poverty Status in the U.S.* Washington, D.C.: Superintendent of Documents.

————. Various years. *Population Reports*, Series P-60. Washington, D.C.: Superintendent of Documents.

U.S. Department of Commerce, Bureau of the Census. 1990. *Statistical Abstract of the United States, 1990*. Washington, D.C.: Superintendent of Documents.

U.S. Department of Commerce, Bureau of Economic Analysis. 1990. *Survey of Current Business*. September.

————. 1986. *National Income and Product Accounts of the U.S. 1929–1982*. Washington, D.C.: Superintendent of Documents.

————. Various years. *Survey of Current Business*. Washington, D.C.: Superintendent of Documents.

U.S. Department of the Treasury. 1990a. "Higher Income Taxpayers Pay a Larger Share of Income Taxes," *Treasury News*, November 2. Washington, D.C.: U.S. Department of the Treasury.

————. 1990b. *Financing Health and Long-Term Care: Report to the President and the Congress*. Washington, D.C.: Superintendent of Documents.

————. 1984. *Tax Reform for Fairness, Simplicity, and Economic Growth*. Washington, D.C.: Department of the Treasury, November.

Verdier, James M. 1988. "The President, Congress and Tax Reform: Pattern over Three Decades." *Annals of the American Academy of Political and Social Science*, vol. 499 (September):114–23.

White House, The. 1981a. "Fact Sheet: Fall Budget Program." Washington, D.C.: September 24.

————. 1981b. "A Program for Economic Recovery." Released February 18.

Witte, John F. 1991a. "Congress and Tax Policy: Problems and Reforms in a Historical Context." *Improving the Tax Legislative Process—A Critical Need*. Washington, D.C.: American Tax Policy Institute, ALI-ABA Committee on Continuing Education, and the National Tax Association.

————. 1991b. "The 1986 Tax Reform: A New Era in Politics?" *American Politics Quarterly*. October, forthcoming.

————. 1985. *The Politics and Development of the Federal Income Tax*. Madison, Wi.: University of Wisconsin Press.

INDEX

ABOUT THE AUTHOR

Eugene Steuerle is a senior fellow at The Urban Institute, the author of "Economic Perspective"—a weekly column in *Tax Notes* magazine—and the president of the National Economists Club Educational Foundation. From 1987 to 1989 he served as the nation's highest tax economic official in his capacity as Deputy Assistant Secretary of the Treasury for Tax Analysis. From 1984 to 1986 he served as economic coordinator and original organizer of the Treasury's tax reform effort. Other positions in which he served during the "tax decade" include director of Finance and Taxation Projects and resident fellow at the American Enterprise Institute, and federal executive fellow at the Brookings Institution. He has written over 75 published articles, books, and reports.